BERT SUGAR'S
BASEBALL HALL *of* FAME

A LIVING HISTORY OF
AMERICA'S GREATEST GAME

LOUISVILLE SLUGGER
HIT 3000 8-4-85
FRANK VIOLA - TWINS
ANGELS STADIUM
Powerized
GENUINE
LOUISVILLE SLUGGER
600
Powerized
LOUISVILLE SLUGGER
125
HILLERICH & BRADSBY Co
MADE IN U.S.A.
LOUISVILLE, KY.
GENUINE
LOUISVILLE SLUGGER
Powerized
LOUISVILLE SLUGGER
125
HILLERICH & BRADSBY Co
MADE IN U.S.A.
LOUISVILLE, KY.
Presented
TRADE MARK
Powerized
LOUISVILLE SLUGGER
125
HILLERICH & BRADSBY Co
MADE IN U.S.A.
LOUISVILLE, KY.
GENUINE
LOUISVILLE SLUGGER
Powerized
LOUISVILLE SLUGGER
125
HILLERICH & BRADSBY Co

DEDICATED TO BASEBALL
FANS EVERYWHERE AND TO
THE KEEPERS OF BASEBALL'S
EVERLASTING FLAME.

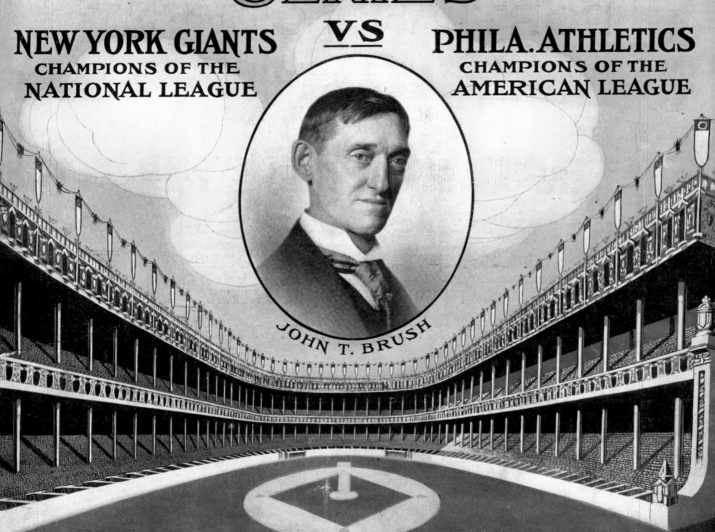

OFFICIAL SCORE CARD
WORLD'S CHAMPIONSHIP SERIES

NEW YORK GIANTS
CHAMPIONS OF THE NATIONAL LEAGUE

VS

PHILA. ATHLETICS
CHAMPIONS OF THE AMERICAN LEAGUE

JOHN T. BRUSH

BRUSH STADIUM
1·9·1·1
PRICE 10 CENTS

HARRY M. STEVENS
Publisher

The program for the 1911 World Series between the National League champion New York Giants and the American League champion Philadelphia Athletics, won by the Athletics in six games as Frank Baker of the A's earned his nickname "Home Run" by hitting home runs in two consecutive games against Giants aces Rube Marquard and Christy Mathewson.

BERT SUGAR'S
BASEBALL HALL *of* FAME

A LIVING HISTORY OF AMERICA'S GREATEST GAME

BERT RANDOLPH SUGAR

Photography by
BRUCE CURTIS

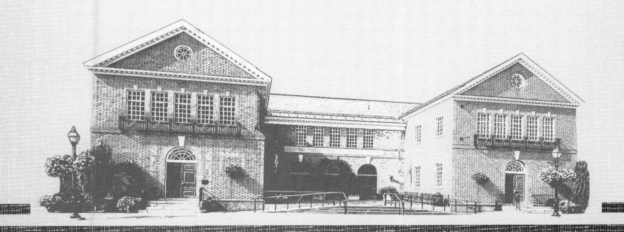

RUNNING PRESS
PHILADELPHIA · LONDON

9   8   7   6   5   4   3   2   1

Digit on the right indicates the number of this printing

Library of Congress Control Number: 2008926938

ISBN 978-0-7624-3024-6

Cover and interior design by Joshua McDonnell

Edited by Greg Jones

Typography: Avenir, Bembo, and Jocelyn

Running Press Book Publishers

2300 Chestnut Street

Philadelphia, PA 19103-4371

Visit us on the web!

www.runningpress.com

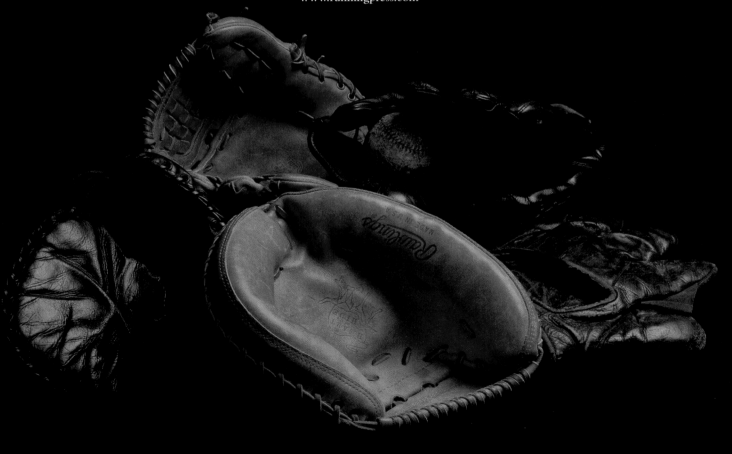

CONTENTS

INTRODUCTION

Standing proudly along Main Street in the quaint and attractive village of Cooperstown, New York, is an imposing red brick Colonial-era structure that is as American as the game of baseball. The building, however, is more than just a landmark. For this is the National Baseball Hall of Fame and Museum. To the millions who have visited, it is a source of enchantment and sentiment; the history and memories it houses are as permanent as its bricks and mortar.

The doors to the Hall of Fame were officially opened on Monday, June 12, 1939, as part of a celebration commemorating Baseball's Centennial. With all the shuffles worthy of a major event—including bands, banners, and a parade—highlights of the day included the introduction of the 11 living members voted into the Hall of Fame and a speech given by Baseball Commissioner Kenesaw Mountain Landis who said, "Since for a hundred years this game of baseball has lived and thrived and spread over all our country and a large part of the world, it is fitting that it should have a National Museum. And nowhere else than at its birthplace could this Museum be appropriately situated." With that definitive statement, Landis officially opened the doors to the National Baseball Hall of Fame and Museum.

Since that June day 70 years ago, more than 14 million visitors have entered those doors opened by Commissioner Landis, drawn by the magnetic pull of the nostalgia and memories inside that make baseball fans out of all of us.

★ ★ ★ ★ ★

When the then-named National Baseball Museum filed its original articles of incorporation in 1936, they listed "upwards of one hundred articles" including "the original Abner Doubleday baseball; the Shibe baseball collections showing the evolution of baseball to the present; a collec-tion originally exhibited at the Philadelphia Exposition; a collection of gloves, mitts, and uniforms of famous players; a very rare (collection of) Currie (sic) and Ives prints; oil portraits of Abner Doubleday; and many articles pertaining to the origin and history of baseball."

By the time the National Baseball Museum opened its doors three years later, delighted visitors could get a close-up look at dozens of cases and walls filled with artifacts including a baseball from Cy Young's 500th win, Ty Cobb's game-worn uniform, and a pair of Babe Ruth's spiked shoes—donated by the players themselves—along with hundreds of other artifacts. Today, over 70 years later, the renamed National Baseball Hall of Fame and Museum houses tens of thousands of artifacts in hundreds of exhibits which bring baseball's rich history to life. These rare treasures—from the familiar to the obscure—thrill, tease, and test even the most knowledgeable fan.

Through three major expansions and endless refurbishing—including a $20 million renovation that ended in 2006 in which the floor-plan was completely transformed—the Hall of Fame curatorial staff has painstakingly woven these priceless exhibits into a larger narrative, fusing them together in a contextual manner that transports the visitor on a magical tour through space, time, and event to tell the story of baseball from its earliest days to the present.

It is the very tour that all visitors to the Hall joyfully undertake that this book endeavors to duplicate; both as a remembrance for those fortunate enough to have been, and as an inspiration for those who hope to one day enjoy the pleasure of this once-in-a-lifetime experience.

Accompanying the hundreds of lush photographs that take the reader through a virtual tour of the National Baseball Hall of Fame and Museum is an engaging and informative detailed timeline of the history of baseball—our National Pastime.

COOPERSTOWN

ooperstown is a small town of unimaginable quaintness, strikingly suggestive of nineteenth century America and worthy of being called a "village."

It is nestled between the Adirondack and Catskill Mountains in the Leatherstocking Region of central New York, on the south end of Otsego Lake. The area surrounding Cooperstown is much like it was over 150 years ago when the son of the town's founder, James Fenimore Cooper, described the panorama of natural beauty framed by its rolling hills and shimmering lake in his epic novel *The Deerslayer* thusly: " 'Tis grand! 'Tis solemn! 'Tis an education of itself to look upon."

Cooper's description of the landscape surrounding early Cooperstown—along with his calling Otsego Lake "The Glimmerglass" in testimony to his witnessing bouncing glints of summer sunshine glistening off its quiet waters like a watercolor—still holds true. The Cooperstown of today is as picturesque as anything Cooper described, the town retaining the essence of a place and time long ago in a picture-postcard way.

Today's Cooperstown has the village-like look of a bygone era, almost as if it were a Hollywood set for the movie *It's a Wonderful Life*, with lovingly restored stately nineteenth-century homes reflecting a diversity of architecture along Lake Street, to small inviting storefronts with baskets of flowers and vines hanging from classic period lampposts on the aptly named Main Street.

While the town of Cooperstown evokes adjectives such as pastoral, bucolic, sylvan, and Arcadian, it is also a village of museums, featuring several jewels in its setting. Those many attractions include the National Baseball Hall of Fame and Museum, which has become synonymous with baseball and made the name Cooperstown famous the world over. Cooperstown is also the home of the Farmer's Museum, the Fenimore Art Museum, the New York State Historical Association Library, Glimmerglass Opera, and the Otesaga Hotel.

Put them all together—the beautiful surroundings of Cooperstown, its many attractions, and its classic definition of a long-ago village—and you will understand why, lo these many years later, what James Fenimore Cooper wrote still holds true: " 'Tis grand!"

THE ENTRYWAY

The first thing one sees upon entering the National Baseball Hall of Fame and Museum is a glimpse of the vaulted area illuminated in part by a great skylight that looks very much like a shrine. For many baseball fans, it is exactly that. This is The Hall of Fame Plaque Gallery, the centerpiece of every visitor's trip, where less than one percent of all players who ever played the game are honored. Bronze plaques adorn the walls of the Gallery, celebrating their immortality.

One glance into this shrine is enough to send the visitor hurrying through the entryway to begin the Baseball Hall of Fame and Museum experience. Once inside, the visitor may go wherever they so choose. But we will begin our tour in the room where the origin of the game itself is celebrated.

Sculptor Stanley Bleifeld's "Character and Courage" statue—honoring Hall of Famers (L to R) Lou Gehrig, Jackie Robinson, and Roberto Clemente—became a permanent addition to the Hall of Fame lobby on November 1, 2008.

CHARACTER AND COURAGE
Cast bronzes by Stanley Bleifeld, 2000

Hall of Fame takes more than just a great baseball
the-field challenges—and how those challenges are
as inner character that serves men and women
their lives. The life experiences of Lou Gehrig,
son, and Roberto Clemente stand out above all
personal and social obstacles with strength and
set an example of character and courage for all
here.

de possible through a generous donation by Robert Clary

THE COOPERSTOWN ROOM

The most frequently asked question by visitors to the Hall of Fame may very well be the simple two-word query: "Why Cooperstown?" The answer to that question is hardly simple. According to Mark Twain, the game of baseball had become "the very symbol, the outward and visible expression of the drive and push and rush and struggle of the racing, tearing, booming nineteenth century" of America. While the game proffered the perfect metaphor for a burgeoning nation, it also provided Americans some of its first sports heroes including Cap Anson, Charles Comiskey, King Kelly, Old Hoss Radbourn, and a whole raft of others celebrated in words and song. The Missouri Pacific Railroad even named four whistle-stops along its route for members of the St. Louis Browns starting

team! And yet, at the turn of the 20th century, there still existed a legitimate question as to the game's origin. That question is addressed in the Cooperstown Room.

The game Albert G. Spalding and others called "America's National Game" was, in reality, an extension of English children's games such as "rounders" which could be traced as far back as the age of Elizabeth I in the 16th century. The founders of the so-called America's Game were not comfortable acknowledging that *their* National Game was an import.

Caught in an upsurge of patriotism at the turn of the 20th century, and wishing to finally define baseball as an American invention, Spalding alone in 1905 established a national commission of seven men for the avowed purpose of determining the true origins of the

A portrait of Major General Abner Doubleday, who served at Fort Sumter and Gettysburg and was credited with "inventing" the game of baseball by Spalding's Committee. Although the exact origins of the game have become the stuff of legend, the fiction of Doubleday's creation has given birth to Cooperstown as the "Home of Baseball."

The Cooperstown Room on the second floor is a display of the history of the Hall of Fame and the Village of Cooperstown featuring exhibits on the founding of the Hall of Fame and previous induction ceremonies.

game. Actually, these seekers of truth viewed it as their solemn duty to promote—by whatever means necessary—evidence that would prove beyond a doubt that baseball was an American institution and disavow its rumored British origins.

Turning a deaf ear to all evidence to the contrary, the commission finally found the source they needed to promote their claim. It came in the form of a deceased Civil War hero: Abner Doubleday. The connection of Doubleday to the origin of baseball was made by the commission's chairman, Abraham G. Mills, former president of the National League (1882–84). The commission

claimed that Doubleday had "designated or christened" the game of baseball years before. Now Doubleday, well known for his heroism at Fort Sumter and Gettysburg, had not at that time been known for his contribution to baseball. Mills et al had grander plans for Doubleday's baseball legacy. His colleagues on the Commission, all early elders of baseball, eagerly agreed. Those founding fathers included Morgan G. Bulkeley, the National League's first president; Nicholas E. Young, the National League's fifth president; Alfred J. Reach; George Wright; Arthur P. Gorman, president of the Washington Base Ball Club; and James E. Sullivan, president of the Amateur Athletic Union.

Anxious to give the game an American provenance, the Commission leaned heavily on the testimony of one Abner Graves, who had attended school in Cooperstown in the 1830s with a fellow student named Abner Doubleday. Graves claimed Doubleday had introduced the game to his classmates back in 1839. With no unconditional surrender to undeniable facts, the

The famous "Doubleday Ball," the supposedly irrefutable evidence that Abner Doubleday had "invented" baseball, was found in a trunk near Cooperstown in 1935 and became one of the first displays in the Hall of Fame.

Mills Commission, committed to finding that baseball was an American game, relied heavily on Graves' account. In 1907 the Commission proclaimed that: "First—baseball had its origin in the United States; Second—that the first scheme for playing it, according to the best evidence to date, was devised by Abner Doubleday, at Cooperstown, New York, in 1839."

The unwitting inventor of the National Game was supposed to have "standardized the game in 1839 by drawing up a set of rules and designated a playing field." Dead for fourteen years and in no position to contest his posthumous honor, Doubleday had never given any indication that he "designed" or "christened" the game; nor ever alluded to his brush with sports history in any of his correspondence nor in the sixty-seven diaries he had compiled during his lifetime.

All this despite the fact that the game of "baseball" had previously been referred to in *A Little Pretty Pocket Book,* published in London in 1744 and republished in New York in 1762. Robin Carver's *Book of Sports*, printed in 1834, featured a

woodcut of the game being played on Boston Common and included a set of printed rules. The rules attributed to Abner Doubleday are found in the rule book for the English game of rounders, published in London in 1827. These were all ignored by the Commission. An American inventor was needed and Doubleday filled the bill.

Despite the meager evidence, the Doubleday connection congealed into baseball folklore, furthered in large part by the discovery in 1935 of an old tattered baseball, its cover torn along the seams, gathering dust in a trunk found in a home near Cooperstown in Fly Creek. The ball not only "legitimatized" Graves' claim but became baseball's "Golden Chalice." The baseball was purchased by a civic-minded local philanthropist named Stephen C. Clark who put it on display with other baseball artifacts in the Village Club of Cooperstown—the first home of the new baseball museum—as a proud exhibit of Cooperstown's part in the history of baseball. Soon, encouraged by the public attention given to the exhibit, Clark paid for and erected a museum in Cooperstown to

A Cooperstown Room display featuring recently donated items including a woman's uniform from a 1930s barnstorming club, and a uniform from a 1955 youth team.

The crowd at the official opening of the Hall of Fame in 1939.

commemorate baseball's founding. By 1935, plans had been drawn up for a building to house the memorabilia and a name given to the planned-for edifice: The Baseball Museum.

Even though the question of Abner Doubleday's provenance was held up to the light by later baseball historians and found to be independent of history, Cooperstown nevertheless became part of baseball's fabric. For although the story of Doubleday's "founding" may have had as much to do with baseball as Santa Claus to Christmas, without the Doubleday story, along with its propagation by Albert Spalding and the Mills Commission and the efforts of Stephen C. Clark, the Baseball Hall of Fame and Museum would not be in Cooperstown. That would be a shame, for Cooperstown is the perfect place for the Hall of Fame, a picturesque little town that

serves as a stand-in for baseball's Garden of Eden. To paraphrase Red Smith giving directions to a nearby locale in upstate New York, "Go up the New York State Thruway and turn left a hundred years," for that is where you will find the Baseball Hall of Fame and Museum, right where it should be, in this wonderful little town that looks today as it must have 100 years ago.

Here, in the Cooperstown Room, you'll find that old baseball—the "Doubleday Ball" as it is known—as well as an oil painting of General Abner Doubleday, a hero of Gettysburg if not the real hero of baseball, as well as documents and pictures pertaining to the founding of the Hall of Fame and Museum and its opening in 1939.

After walking through the room, ask yourself whether it really matters if Abner Doubleday was an historic reconstruction or not.

Ten of the eleven living members of the first four classes of inductees at the Hall of Fame opening in 1939: (Front row, L to R) Eddie Collins, Babe Ruth, Connie Mack, Cy Young; (Back Row) Honus Wagner, Grover Cleveland

THE GRANDSTAND THEATER

There is no better way to start your trip through the Hall of Fame than by witnessing the riveting presentation of "The Baseball Experience" in the 200-seat Grandstand Theater at the top of the stairway on the second floor.

The theater, made to resemble Chicago's old Comiskey Park, envelops you in much the same way a ballpark does as you watch real and "reel" snippets of film woven into a stirring fabric conveying the excitement of the game itself.

Courtesy of three digital, high-resolution video projectors shown on a giant 9 x 27-foot screen, the film captures the magic of the game featuring some of baseball's greatest moments and stars—including Hank Aaron's record-breaking 715th home run, Willie Mays' amazing 1954 World Series play simply known as "The Catch," Ozzie Smith's patented back flip, and other iconic moments. Interspersed are clips of Babe Ruth, Ty Cobb, Jackie Robinson and Kirk Gibson, along with J.F.K. throwing out an opening day ball and even the San Diego Chicken. Then there are some "reel" moments from the Silver Screen, including Gary Cooper in Pride of the Yankees, Robert Redford in The Natural, and Ronald Reagan in The Winning Team, plus a cut of the Three Stooges hamming it up, baseball style.

As if that weren't enough—just when you think you've seen everything—the show closes with a finale worthy of a post-game fireworks spectacle. Above, a state-of-the-art light display illuminates giant replicas of baseball cards on the ceiling—including those of Hank Aaron, Lou Brock, Roberto Clemente, Ty Cobb, Lou Gehrig, Kirk Gibson, Walter Johnson, Sandy Koufax, Mickey Mantle, Stan Musial, Jackie Robinson, and Babe Ruth.

The Baseball Experience is so magnetic that by its end you will think the only thing missing are some peanuts and Cracker Jack to make the experience complete.

Billy Earle

At the top of the stairs you will find yourself at the exhibit titled, *Taking the Field: The 19ᵗʰ Century*. This exciting exhibit, part of the Hall of Fame's three-year, $20 million renovation completed in 2006, pulls you back to another time, a time when America sought an outlet unique to its spirit, one reflecting the enthusiasm and vitality of the still-young country.

From the colorful display of trophy balls that were presented to the winners of those early games of "base ball" (then two words) that greet you at the door, to the woolen uniforms worn by early clubs—like the Baraboo, Wisconsin nine—to the artifacts, nearly 200 of them, that celebrate the growth of the game from its regional beginnings to its honored place as "The National Pastime," this room brings to life the beginning of the game in words and artifacts which work together to pay tribute to the sport's infancy.

And it is the place to begin your time travel through baseball's evolution from its earliest decades right up to the present.

★ ★ ★ ★ ★

The emergence of baseball, in many ways, paralleled the growth of America. Dating back to the first three decades of the 19ᵗʰ century, when the United States was first stretching its newfound muscles, its inhabitants sought an outlet unique to its identity. Not the game of cricket—played mostly by those born to privilege by their English forebears—nor other early stick-and-ball games played by children, but a game which

A collection of gilded game balls, called "Trophy Balls," dating back to the 1850s and '60s, each marked with the score and date of the game won by the Eckfords of Brooklyn.

The entrance to the 1Taking the Field1 exhibit—and the beginning of baseball's historic timeline—presenting the heritage of the game from the "Trophy Balls" won by the Eckfords of Brooklyn on the left to exhibits on early-day artifacts from a time we've only heard about shown in descriptive detail.

reflected the enthusiasm and vitality of a rollicking America that could be played by Everyman.

The games then played, called everything from "base" to "cat" to "town ball" to "soak," hardly bore a resemblance to the game we know today, but instead looked like a group of truants out on a romp, rowdy and noisy like the country itself. The field itself was without foul lines and laid out square. A single out retired the side—an out made by a ball being caught on the fly or on one bounce; a runner was also out if he was

"soaked" or hit by the ball thrown at him while he was running the bases.

The first set of written rules was issued in 1838 by the Philadelphia Olympic Ball Club. Their rules decreed that members shall be "persons above the age of twenty-one," that "each member will provide himself with a uniform similar in all respects to the pattern uniform owned by the Club" and that "They shall have Bats, Balls and all the implements belonging to the Club under their particular care, and it shall be their

The man in the top hat, along with everyone to the right of him, comprised the Excelsior Base Ball Club of Brooklyn. The players to the left comprised the Knickerbocker Base Ball Club—the first organized club that was devoted to the game of baseball that eventually became the game we know today. Photo taken August 2, 1859.

duty to have them kept in good order."

However, these rules were more cosmetic than substantive. It wasn't until seven years later that the New York Knickerbocker Base Ball Club, led by their president Alexander Cartwright, came up with a modified set of rules that helped shape the game. Their rules dictated that the infield be diamond-shaped, not square, that first and third bases be forty-two paces apart, and that there were to be "foul lines." Moreover, the batter got three missed swings before he was "out" and runners were to be tagged or thrown out, not thrown *at*.

The Knickerbockers were to play their first game on Elysian Fields over in Hoboken, New Jersey, in 1846, losing to the New York Base Ball Club, 23-1. Soon there were ballclubs throughout the New York area made up of young men anxious to play what was fast becoming America's game. From firemen to policemen to schoolteachers to actors and more, the game appealed to any band of young men who wanted to engage each other in competition, arranged by letters from club secretaries challenging other clubs to "base ball matches."

New York and the East Coast had become the center of the new game's universe. It wasn't until after the Civil War that baseball was being played in every hamlet and crossroads, from Baraboo, Wisconsin to Rockport, Illinois, a part of America's emerging character.

Even while base ball, as it was spelled then, was growing swiftly, it was far from a universal game. Its rules were different in different parts of the country and its language second only to the Tower of Babel.

Nevertheless, it continued to grow and, within a few short years, aided by two agents of change—railroad transportation and wireless telegraphy—the game was fast on its way to becoming part of America's popular culture with game accounts appearing in local newspapers and teams traveling from town to town by rail to challenge other clubs.

By the late 1860s America had become preoccupied with base ball. First labeled "The American Pastime" by newspaper writer Henry Chadwick, the story of America's growth became the story of baseball's as more and more Americans moved from small towns to the emerging larger population centers. These emerging metropolises began fielding teams as a matter of civic pride, playing for the glory and honor of the city and the trophy baseball that went with it. Teams like the Excelsiors of Chicago took on the visiting Nationals of Washington, the first eastern team to make a trans-Allegheny tour. The Atlantics of Brooklyn traveled to Albany,

This trophy bat was presented to the New York Giants' George Van Haltren by the New York Mercury newspaper after winning a paper-sponsored popularity contest among fans in 1894.

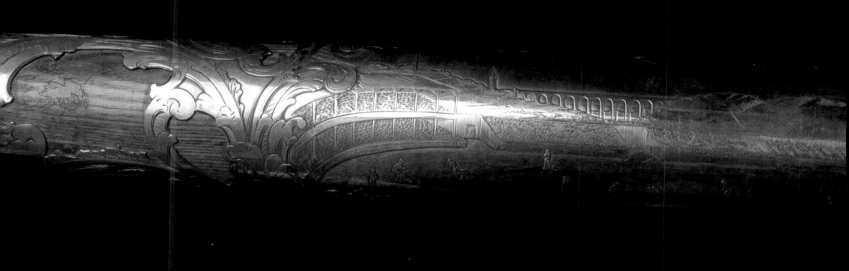

One of the earliest uniforms known to baseball, the uniform of Baraboo (Wisconsin) BBC (Base Ball Club) displayed along with relics of the earlier era.

In those rollicking, boisterous days of yesteryear, where anything went, nothing went farther than a slight, pouter-pigeon-proud man named John McGraw. Playing third base for the old Baltimore Orioles, McGraw would resort to anything to win—holding the belts of baserunners trying to get past his corner, obstructing the base, and unmercifully baiting the lone umpire. His underhanded ways on the field were matched by his sure-handed ways in the batter's box, where he batted over .300 in nine consecutive seasons. It was as a manager that he was to gain everlasting fame. Known as "Little Napoleon" to his legion of fans—and by any name that came to mind by his detractors, including the hated name "Mugsy"—McGraw constantly had run-ins with the so-called "establishment." As the player-manager of the new American League franchise in Baltimore, McGraw ran afoul of authority, in this case the president of the American League, Ban Johnson. He jumped from the Orioles in midsummer of 1902 to take over the reins of the National League New York Giants. Although his first edition would finish in last place, McGraw would go on to win ten National League pennants and three World Series in his 33-year managerial career—a career that saw him finish no lower than second place 20 times.

JOHN J. McGRAW

STAR THIRD-BASEMAN OF THE GREAT BALTIMORE ORIOLES, NATIONAL LEAGUE CHAMPIONS IN THE '90'S. FOR 30 YEARS MANAGER OF THE NEW YORK GIANTS STARTING IN 1902. UNDER HIS LEADERSHIP THE GIANTS WON 10 PENNANTS AND 3 WORLD CHAMPIONSHIPS.

The Chicago White Stockings of the National League along with a group of players from the American Association pose in Egypt during their around-the-world tour of 1888-89.

Uniform of Buck Ewing, of the Cincinnati National League club, circa 1897. Some say he was the best base ball player of the nineteenth century.

Troy, Utica, Syracuse, Rochester, Buffalo, Cleveland, Toledo, Detroit, Rockford, Freeport, Springfield, St. Louis and other cities. Everywhere there was a population center, so too was there a city baseball team.

Despite the price of admission they were all considered amateur teams in the beginning. With the population expanding, annual per-capita income and leisure time increasing, and interest in baseball growing, it wasn't long before someone in that good old American entrepreneurial way would figure out a way to profit from the game, replacing those high-prized trophy balls and silver trophies given to the winning team with something more valuable: cold hard cash.

And so it was that a group of investors in the so-called "Queen City of the West," Cincinnati, in 1869, decided to underwrite the first openly all-professional baseball team in America, the Cincinnati Red Stockings. The Red Stockings' manager was Harry Wright, the British-born son of a cricketer who had embraced the American game. Wright stocked his new team with the best players money could buy, mostly New Yorkers, with but one Cincinnati native. The highest-paid member of the team was his brother, George, who was paid the then princely sum of $1,400 in U.S. Grant dollars. The result: the Red Stockings toured the byways of America playing teams from other cities, a 12,000 mile cross-country odyssey that resulted in over 70 games without a loss and crowds of 3,000-plus.

Inspired by the success of the Red Stockings, other cities now rushed to join the play-for-pay movement, forming the loosely confederated National Association in 1871, baseball's first pro-fessional baseball league. The league consisted of the Philadelphia Athletics, Chicago White Stockings, Boston Red Stockings, Washington Olympics, Troy Haymakers, New York Mutuals, Cleveland Forest Citys, Fort Wayne Kekiongas, and Rockford Forest Citys.

The league, however, lasted only five seasons, finally succumbing to a combination of problems ranging from the Depression of the 1870s and '80s cutting into its attendance, its players jump-ing from franchise to franchise for bigger salaries, and public mistrust springing from rumors of players "hippodroming," or throwing games. But the groundwork had been laid and out of the National Association's ashes came a new league in 1876, the National League, with charter members in Boston, Chicago, St. Louis, Hartford, New York, Cincinnati, Philadelphia and Louisville, all sizable

In the early days of baseball, protective equipment—like that pictured here and displayed in the "Taking the Field" exhibit—was scorned by the players. One of the early players, Hall of Fame catcher "Orator" Jim O'Rourke, recalled, "There was no paraphernalia in the old days with which one could protect himself. Not mitts; no, not even gloves; and masks? Why you would have been laughed off the diamond had you worn one behind the bat." But all that began to change in the 1870s, though the exact origins are not known. One player, Charlie C. Waitt, braved the jeers of his teammates by donning a skintight buckskin driving glove to protect his injured hand. Eight years later Providence shortstop Arthur Irwin wore a glove to protect his injured hand, and New York Giant infielder John Montgomery Ward also adopted the fashion. Soon everyone was wearing one—except Jerry Denny, the last player to go barehanded—and by 1893 it had become accepted by baseball as a whole. Still, their use was derided by old-time players, including Tim Murnane of the Boston Globe, who played back in the gloveless days of the 1870s and lamented, "The real artist can play without gloves or mitts. Take the mitts off the present players and see how many great stars are left."

The next piece of protective equipment introduced after the glove was the catcher's mask, originally called the "bird cage." An adaptation of a fencer's mask, the catcher's mask was fashioned by Harvard student Fred Thayer with the help of a local Boston tinsmith, and patented by Thayer in 1878. Made out of light materials, the mask was sometimes a danger itself, with foul tips driving pieces of wire into the faces of catchers. Nevertheless, their usage was adopted by baseball in the 1870s, very soon after they were invented.

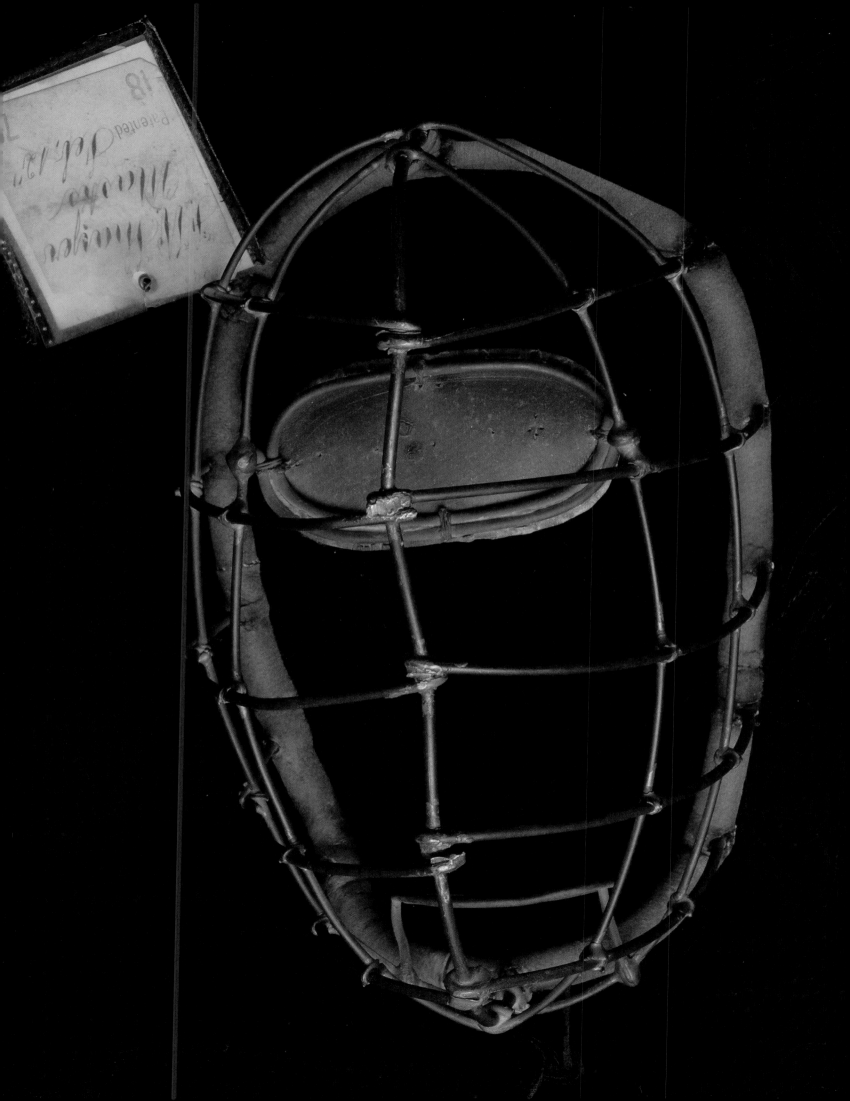

"WEE" WILLIE KEELER

WILLIE KEELER
"HIT 'EM WHERE THEY AINT!"
BASEBALL'S GREATEST PLACE-HITTER;
BEST BUNTER. BIG LEAGUE CAREER
1892 TO 1910 WITH N.Y.GIANTS.
BALTIMORE ORIOLES, BROOKLYN SUPERBAS,
N.Y. HIGHLANDERS, NATIONAL LEAGUE
BATTING CHAMPION '97-'98.

With a motto that read like a wall sampler—"Keep your eyes on the ball and hit 'em where they ain't"—five-foot-4½ inch, 140-pound Willie Keeler spent 19 years in major league baseball doing just that. Wielding his short bat like a toothpick with a choked-up hold, the man nicknamed "Wee Willie" punched the ball where the fielders "ain't" consistently, with over a 1,000 hits in his first five full seasons and 2,932 lifetime. Playing for the Baltimore Orioles back in the 1890s, Keeler posted astronomical numbers, hitting over .300 16 times in 19 seasons, batting over .400 once, collecting over 200 hits in a season eight times, and posting a 44-game hitting streak in 1897 that wasn't bettered until Joe DiMaggio hit in 56 straight 44 years later. An ideal leadoff hitter, Keeler regularly made contact with the ball. He was an exact bunter, master of the hit-and-run, and faultlessly executed the aptly named "Baltimore Chop"—a ball hit in front of home plate that bounced high off the hardened infield and gave him plenty of time to reach base safely almost before the fielder could attempt a throw. His lifetime .345 batting average serves as testimony to his playing maxim.

KEELER

cities with enough of a population base to support a team.

Other urban areas wanted a team of their own, and after petitioning the National League for franchises and being denied, they formed a league of their own in 1882, the American Base Ball Association, better known as the American Association, with franchises in Cincinnati, Philadelphia, Louisville, Pittsburgh, St. Louis, and Baltimore. Soon other cities replaced some of those that were failing—Detroit, Buffalo, and Cleveland joining the National League while Brooklyn, Columbus, and Syracuse fielded teams in the American Association.

Along with these new teams came new stars who were accorded kingly status, Cap Anson, Mike "King" Kelly, Charlie Comiskey, Dan Brouthers, Sam Thompson and others became holders of the original copyright as America's first great sports heroes. They took their place alongside the presidents, generals, and Indian fighters of previous generations as national icons. It was indeed the first time in the U.S. that professional athletes gained national acclaim and broad admiration. Their deeds were celebrated in song and story, their pictures featured on early trading cards and silks, their names headlined in these while-you-get-your-hair-cut weeklies of the time and given fanciful nicknames like "Death to Flying Things" Ferguson, "Silver" Flint, "Old Hoss" Radbourn, and "The

An exhibit of early baseballs manufactured by the J.D. Shibe Company of Philadelphia.

Apollo of the Box" Tony Mullane. Stories of their exploits didn't end at the 12-mile city limit but continued far afield. Four members of the St. Louis Browns even had remote railroad stops in Missouri named after them.

By the beginning of the "Gilded Age" of the 1890s baseball (now spelled as one word) was not just a game, it was a national passion with as many as three professional leagues (in 1890) playing in several cities. By 1892 the Depression of the early '90s had forced two of the financially strapped leagues to disband, leaving the National League as the only major league left standing. The Boston Beaneaters and the Baltimore Orioles, the rowdiest team in the history of baseball, dominated the National League. Led by third baseman John McGraw, the Orioles had little or no use for the rules of the game. He was, according to one write-up of the time, "the toughest of

the toughs . . . a rough unruly man (who) uses every low and contemptible method that his erratic brain can conceive to win a play by a dirty trick," which ran from holding a base runner by the belt to prevent him from advancing, to spiking his opponents through their shoes and baiting umpires. With McGraw, Wee Willie Keeler, Hughie Jennings, and Wilbert Robinson doing everything in their power to win, the Orioles won the National League pennant three years running, scratching and maiming their opponents.

Baseball had come a long way, growing from a freelance game to a structured one. From a group of anonymous players to teams consisting of recognizable heroes and stars. The US of A now had a B, baseball, as part of its culture. But as we entered the 20th century, the game still had a long way to go.

The By-Laws , Regulations and Rules of the Knickerbocker Base Ball Club from 1860.

EARLY RULES OF THE GAME

1845: Game to end when one team makes 21 aces (runs). Ball must be pitched underhanded. Only one base allowed when ball bounds out of the field of play. Ball caught on first bound is out.

1848: Baseman must hold onto the ball in order to put out a runner.

1857: Nine-inning game is introduced.

1859: Bat limited in thickness.

1864: Fair ball caught on one bounce no longer out. Pitcher's box to be 6x6 feet. Batter allowed to call for a high or low pitched ball.

1872: Pitcher allowed to snap delivery, though still restricted to below the waist motion.

1872: Ball reduced in size and weight to present 9-9¼ inches, 5-5½ ounces.

1873: Nine "balls" entitled batter to reach first base.

1876: Bat length limited to 42 inches. Substitute players allowed to enter the game before the fourth inning.

1877: Hitter exempt from time at bat if walked.

1880: Runner out if hit by batted ball.

1881: Pitching distance increased from 45 feet to 50 feet. Pitcher fined for hitting batter deliberately with ball. Eight balls entitled batter to reach first base.

1882: Three-foot baseline adopted. Umpire forbidden to reverse decisions on matters of judgment. Fine for pitcher deliberately hitting batter eliminated.

1883: Foul caught on one bounce no longer an out. Pitching allowed from anywhere up to shoulder height.

1884: All restrictions on pitching style lifted. Pitcher allowed to take only one step before delivery. Six balls entitled batter to reach first base.

1885: Portion of bat on one side allowed to be flat.

1886: Rule rescinded which allowed portion of bat on one side to be flat. Five balls entitled batter to reach first base. First and third base placed within foul lines. Batter hit by pitched ball exempt from time at bat.

1887: Base on balls counted as base hit. Number of strikes raised to four.

1888: Rescinded rule on base on balls counted as base hit. Number of strikes returned to three.

1889: Four balls entitled batter to reach first base.

1891: Substitutes allowed at any time during game.

1893: Pitching distance changed to 60 feet, six inches. Pitching box replaced by pitching rubber. Foul tip a strike if caught.

1894: Foul bunt ruled a strike. Sacrificing player exempt from time at bat.

1895: Infield pop fly rule adopted. Diameter of bat limited to 2¾ inches.

1899: Pitcher compelled to throw to base if he motions in that direction (the balk rule).

1900: Five-sided home plate introduced.

1901: Fouls called strikes up to two. Catcher required to position himself directly behind the batter.

1903: Pitching mound limited to 15 inches above plate.

1908: Pitcher prohibited from soiling new ball. Sacrifice fly rule adopted. (Abolished in 1931: restored in 1939 for scoring fly; abolished, 1940; restored 1954).

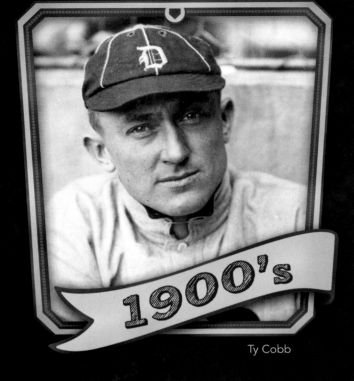

1900's

Ty Cobb

T he *New York World* began its editorial on January 1, 1900: "The 1800s are gone forever. . . ." But as the new century began, it looked strikingly like the old one. The dawning of the new century also brought the dawning of a new entity: the American League.

The new league had its roots in the Western League, a midwestern league with franchises in Detroit, Minneapolis, St. Paul, Indianapolis, Grand Rapids, Columbus, Milwaukee, and Kansas City. The head of the Western League, a former Cincinnati sports-writer named Ban Johnson, had a glimmer in his eye that the Western League could become a full-fledged competitor to the established National League. So in 1900 he changed the name of the league to the "American League" and, in advance of his

all-out assault on the National League, moved the St. Paul franchise to Chicago.

The National League had faced competition before from the American Association, the Players' League, and the Union Association, and in each case had faced its competition down by surviving as the dominant league. This time the new entity was better conceived and better marketed. Johnson promised "clean baseball, beer and"—trumping the National League's 50-cent admission charge—"plenty of 25-cent seats."

Taking advantage of the National League's $2,400 salary cap, American League president Ban Johnson—using part daring and cunning, part bluff and bluster, and plenty of cash on the barrelhead—cast a wide net for stars from National League rosters. By the start of the American League's first season in 1901, John-

A sweater emblazoned with a cap "D" worn by Ty Cobb in his later days with the Detroit Tigers.

son had taken established stars from the National League like Nap Lajoie for $3,500, Lave Cross and Win Mercer for $3,000, and Joe McGinnity for $2,500. What may now seem laughingly like small sums were no small amounts considering the income of the average American worker was less than $500 a year. The American League's first major league season opened with stars like Jimmy Collins and Cy Young in Boston, Clark Griffith in Chicago, and Nap Lajoie in Philadelphia—and everywhere a marquee name to ensure that teams in head-to-head competition with established National League teams would have a bona fide star or two, all the better to draw fans.

The investment in players paid instant dividends with Lajoie leading the American League, and all of baseball, in batting in 1901 with a .426 average, Cy Young leading the league in wins with 33, and Clark Griffith leading Chicago to the first-ever American League pennant.

The raids continued in 1902 with the American League signing National League stalwarts Ed Delehanty, Elmer Flick, and Bill Dinneen. Another important move was the moving of the Milwaukee franchise to St. Louis where the addition of familiar St. Louis players like Bobby Wallace and Jesse Burkett gave the franchise box-office clout. By the end of their second season, all American League clubs sharing cities with older National League teams had outdrawn their counterparts and, more importantly, the entire American League had outdrawn the National League by over half-a-million fans.

Inspired by the success of his teams in intra-city box-office competition with the established National League clubs, Johnson was now determined to place a franchise in the nation's largest city, New York. After a push-me-pull-you battle with the owners of the Baltimore franchise, a battle complete with more than a little finagling and maneuvering, the Baltimore Orioles team was moved to New York to take on the entrenched National League franchise, the Giants, for the 1903 season. The new New York team managed to steal away key National Leaguers like Wee

Willie Keeler, Jack Chesbro, and Jesse Tannehill, and to acquire players from other American League teams, like Clark Griffith from Chicago and Kid Elberfeld from Detroit. The alchemy worked, as the first edition of the team then called the New York "Highlanders" (later to be renamed the Yankees) finished fourth. The next season they finished second, losing on the final day of the season to Boston on a wild pitch by 41-game winner Jack Chesbro. Nevertheless, the move from Baltimore to New York had been a success with almost 439,000 baseball-crazed fans having passed through the turnstiles to see the recently transplanted New York team.

If the American League had gained almost immediate credibility by fielding teams with established stars, the newly minted league was to gain permanent credibility with Boston's stunning win over heavily favored Pittsburg (spelled without an "h" from 1890 to 1911) in the inaugural 1903 World Series. However, when the 1904 pennant-winning Boston Americans challenged the National League champion Giants to another post-season series the following year, Giants owner John T. Brush scornfully rejected the challenge, referring to the American league as "upstarts." By 1905, with a peace treaty signed between the leagues, the post-season "World Series" became part of the pact and the long tradition of the Autumn Classic began. The American League, once viewed as "upstarts," was now the equals to the National League.

By the middle of the first decade of the 20th century the American League had begun to develop some homegrown talent to go with the former National League players who filled their rosters—players like Ed Walsh, Eddie Plank, Rube Waddell and Ty Cobb. The premier player of the decade was Honus Wagner, the Pittsburg shortstop who, beginning in 1900, led the National League in batting and doubles seven times, stolen bases five times, RBI four times, runs scored and triples twice, and hits once in that first decade. Fittingly, his locker is the first exhibit the Hall of Fame visitor sees upon entering the beginning of

above. On May 10, 1913, more then 600 fans traveled from Troy, N.Y. to the Polo Grounds to honor hometown hero Johnny Evers, the new Cubs player-manager. Evers tripled in the eighth to drive in the run that beat the Giants, 2-1.

donated by Frank R. Boone

Glove used by second baseman Johnny Evers

donated by John J. Evers, Jr.

above. Joe Tinker's 1907 World's Champion gold watch fob

donated by Joseph B. Tinker, Jr.

Souvenir pennant picturing Joe Tinker

donated by Flora Moore

The Cubs wore this uniform in 1909. Catcher Johnny Kling, one of the era's best backstops, caught the

For most of the first decade of the twentieth century the dominant team was the Chicago Cubs. Anchored by the most famous double-play combination in history—immortalized in verse by Franklin P. Adams of the *New York Evening Mail* in his famous poem "Tinker to Evers to Chance"—the Cubs had an amazing .635 winning percentage for the 11 years the vaunted combo played together as a unit, and an even more amazing .693 percentage for the five-year period from 1906–1910 when the Cubs won 100 games four times and four pennants in five years. Together, the threesome of Joe Tinker, Johnny Evers, and Frank Chance were inducted into the Hall of Fame in 1946.

Honus Wagner, in the words of John McGraw, "was the greatest player in the twentieth century," his only contemporary rival being Ty Cobb. But in those early days of modern baseball Wagner often outshone his rival at bat, in the field, and on the base paths. Standing as far back in the batter's box as the rules and chalk lines allowed, Wagner skewered every pitcher he ever faced, including the best—batting .524 against Amos Rusie, .352 against Kid Nichols, .343 against Cy Young, and .324 against Christy Mathewson, future Hall of Famers all. Over the first 12 seasons of the 20th century he hit for an average of .347 and won eight batting titles. Wagner's stardom took on a stellar brightness in those early days with his exploits which were recognized as he became a member of the first class elected into the Hall of Fame, right behind his rival, Ty Cobb.

CY YOUNG

At the initial induction ceremonies at the Hall of Fame in 1939, a young reporter approached the 72-year-old figure ambling toward him and asked, "How many games did you win, sir?" At which the white-haired old man paused long enough to answer, "More games than you ever saw, son," and continued on his way. He had, too, for Cy Young had won 511 of them, spanning 22 years and bridging the evolution of the pitching game, pitching from a distance of 50 feet for the first three years of his career and from 60 feet, six inches the last 19. Then again, Cy Young—so named for the velocity with which he threw the ball, "as fast as a cyclone"—could win at any distance, against anyone, at any time. Young was already the winner of 285 games in the National League before he jumped to the new American League in 1901. Developing a curve to go with his howitzer-like fastball, Young quickly became the junior circuit's leading pitcher in the first three years of its existence, winning 33 and 32 in his first two seasons, the fourth and fifth times he had reached the 30-win level. The man for whom the coveted "Cy Young Award" is named would continue pitching, and winning, well into his 44th year when, unable to field bunts, he walked proudly off the mound forever, the winner of more games than anyone had ever seen before or since.

Led by the peerless Honus Wagner, the Pittsburg Pirates (then spelled without an "h") won an average of 94 games a season and four National League pennants between 1900 and 1909. Here is an image of the Honus Wagner locker exhibit on the 2nd floor.

The America of the early 1900s was confident and cocksure, certain of its place in history, yet still casting around for an identity. It found that identity in its heroes: Teddy Roosevelt in politics, Jack London in literature, and Christy Mathewson in sports (a glove used by Mathewson is pictured above). Baseball had other celebrities, to be sure, but in an age when baseball had a reputation for rough-and-tumble players Christy Mathewson was an idol, a Frank Merriwell character, who, in a field devoted to fashioning halos for its performers, wore a special nimbus. The mention of his very name was treated with such reverence by fans that if they wore hats, they would doff them every time it was spoken, such was his reputation. For the better part of 17 years Matty's concision and precision left other clubs probing at his offering with a dull resignation to their fate, the Cincinnati Reds in particular, Mathewson beating them 22 consecutive times. It got to the point that all he had to do was throw his glove on the mound, or, as Damon Runyon wrote: "Mathewson pitched against Cincinnati yesterday. Another way of putting it is that Cincinnati lost a game of baseball. The first statement means the same as the second."

the 20th century timeline on the second floor.

Other National League superstars included New York Giants pitching great Christy Mathewson—who captured 236 of his 373 career wins during the decade and pitched three shutouts in the 1905 World Series—and the Chicago Cubs' famous double-play combination of Tinker, Evers, and Chance, combined in verse by Franklin P. Adams as they were on the field. Adams wrote, "Trio of bear Cubs and fleeter than birds/ Tinker to Evers to Chance." (Unfortunately Mr. Adams couldn't fit the name of the third baseman, Harry Steinfeldt, who had more hits and more RBI than any of the three and led the league in fielding more times than either Evers or Chance. Today he has been relegated to being the answer to a trivia question.) Together these superstars would lead their three teams to pennants every year of the decade and to World Series wins in four of the six Series played.

Toward the end of the decade the following editorial appeared in *The Saturday Evening Post*: "It is important to remember, in an imperfect and fretful world, that we have one institution which is practically above reproach and above criticism. Nobody worth mentioning wants to chance its constitution or limit its power. This one comparatively perfect flower of our sadly defective civilization is—of course—baseball, the only important institution, so far as we can remember, which the United States regards with a practically universal approval."

The game of baseball had come of age, gaining its place in our society as "The National Pastime." Its solid foundation would form a natural base for the further evolution of the game, the enormity of which may not have been anticipated even in those glory days.

CHRISTY MATHEWSON

In a day and age when baseball had a reputation for the rough-and-tumble—its players were, in the words of one writer of the time, "tobacco-chewing, beer-guzzling bums"— Christy Mathewson was seemingly made of sunshine and clear weather. A beau idol with a blonde grassplot atop his head, Mathewson, a six-foot-one-inch-plus Adonis, quiet as a deacon and dangerous as a six-shooter, was called by the New York press "Big Six" after the famed New York City fire engine. He was treated with a reverence by the New York fans. His reputation was built on his famed "fadeaway"—a reverse curve, now called a "screwball," released with his hand turned over until the palm faced the ground instead of facing upward toward the sky, twisting off his thumb with a peculiar snap of the wrist and twisting away from the batter as well—and his uncanny control. Averaging about one-and-a-half walks per game, "Matty" had such remarkable control that sportswriter Ring Lardner rhapsodized, "Nobody else in the world can stick a ball as near where they want to stick it as he can." The cornerstone of Matty's fame lay in his three shutout wins over the Philadelphia Athletics in the 1905 World Series. The winner of 373 games in total, and the winner of 20 or more games 13 times and 30-plus four times, Mathewson was, in the words of Connie Mack, "The greatest pitcher who ever lived. It was wonderful to watch him pitch . . . when he wasn't pitching against you."

Ty Cobb stealing third against the Yankees in New York during the Tigers' 1909 pennant-winning season.

TYRUS RAYMOND COBB
DETROIT·PHILADELPHIA, A.L.·1905-1928
LED AMERICAN LEAGUE IN BATTING
TWELVE TIMES AND CREATED OR
EQUALLED MORE MAJOR LEAGUE
RECORDS THAN ANY OTHER PLAYER.
RETIRED WITH 4191 MAJOR LEAGUE HITS.

TY COBB

Subscribing to the theory that baseball was not unlike war, Ty Cobb played the game with an acid soul, endless spite, and burning rage. With every nerve exposed, Cobb waged a relentless war on the field and a continual assault on the record books. Still, even Cobb might admit that he was no better than a natural .300 hitter. It was his speed and daring that enabled him to beat out bunts and scratch out hits, adding another 50 points or so to his batting average. Combining speed, daring, and ability, Cobb staked his claim to nearly 90 records during his career, including most batting titles (12), highest career batting average (.367), most runs scored (2,245), most games played (3,033), et cetera, et cetera. When he retired after 24 seasons, according to Cobb, he had "many more hits left in my bat."

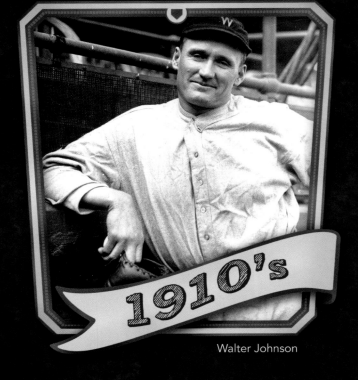

Walter Johnson

As you continue your time-travel trip down baseball's long memory lane on the second floor of the Baseball Hall of Fame, with the early New York Giants display, the differences between 1909 and 1910 seem very small indeed. Most of the same superstars, like Wagner, Lajoie, and Cobb, were still at the top of their games and the same dominant teams at the end of the last decade were still at the top of their leagues in the nineteen teens. By the end of the decade not only would the stars and the teams change, but so too would the game itself transform in one of the most turbulent eras in the history of baseball.

In 1910 the Tinker-Evers-Chance Chicago Cubs, winners of four of the last five National League pennants, were heavily favored to beat the American League champion Philadelphia Athletics in the seventh World Series. However, the underdog A's, behind the batting of Eddie Collins and Frank "Home Run" Baker as well as the pitching of Jack Coombs, easily coasted to a 4-1 Series win and, by repeating as league champion in 1911, 1913 and 1914, became the first AL dynasty of the decade. Over in the National League during those years, the Cubs, Giants and Pirates continued to dominate the league, finishing one-two-three—in one order of finish or another—as they had almost every year since 1903.

But the baseball landscape was to change, radically, in 1914. Not only were some of the superstars of yesteryear, like Cy Young, Frank Chance and Addie Joss, gone, replaced by new stars like Grover Cleveland Alexander and Tris Speaker, but the old order atop the National League was toppled by the former "have-nots," led by the most improbable of teams, the traditionally bottom-dwelling Boston Braves. The Braves, a team with minimal credentials, had come from last place on July 4th to win the

The Honey Boy Evans Trophy given to Ty Cobb For winning the American League batting title in 1911.

National League pennant by 10½ games, thus earning the nickname "The Miracle Braves." Then, against all perceived wisdom, they swept the mighty A's—they of the "$100,000 Infield" of Stuffy McInnis, Eddie Collins, Jack Barry and "Home Run" Baker—in the World Series.

The rest of the decade was colored by the glow of the Braves' victory, an unbelievable turn that served as the beginning of what might be called, for the lack of a better word, the "democratization" of the National League as, starting with the Braves in 1914, six different teams would win the National League pennant in the final six years of the decade—the Braves in 1914, the Phillies in 1915, the Dodgers (still referred to as the "Robins") in 1916, the Giants in 1917, the Cubs in 1918 and the Reds in 1919. The old order of Giants-Cubs-Pirates finishing one-two-three every year was no more as the Giants fell to the National League cellar in 1915 and the Pirates followed suit two years later.

There were other happenings that colored the decade as well, happenings off the ballfields. The first was the establishment of the Federal League, a third major league that began raiding the established American and National Leagues, taking a few marquee names like Eddie Plank, Joe Tinker and "Three Finger" Brown as well as several lower-tiered stars. Then there was the Depression of 1914, and finally

Three cases trace the early 1900s with vintage artifacts of the period featuring the three American League powerhouse teams of the era—(left to right) the Detroit Tigers, the Philadelphia Athletics, and the Boston Red Sox—combined winners of 14 of the first 16 American League pennants.

the outbreak of what was called "The Great War"—World War I—in the summer of 1914.

The off-the-field events affected all clubs, but impacted the Philadelphia A's the most. After losing Plank and Chief Bender to the Federal League, and "Home Run" Baker to retirement, Connie Mack began selling off the team's stars. The once-proud A's fell from a pennant-winning 99–53 in 1914 to a cellar-dwelling 43–109 the following season. But the stars Mack sold—like Jack Barry to the Red Sox and Eddie Collins to the White Sox—paid immediate dividends in pennants for their new teams, Boston winning in 1915 and '16 and Chicago in 1917.

It would be "The Great War" that would have the biggest effect on baseball. From the very day America entered the war in 1917, there was great concern that baseball itself might be a casualty as Secretary of War Newton D. Baker ruled that those ballplayers eligible for the draft would either have to enter the service or take "essential" jobs in the manufacturing sector. Several players, including Grover Cleveland Alexander, "Shoeless" Joe

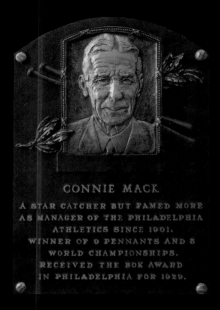

CONNIE MACK

A STAR CATCHER BUT FAMED MORE
AS MANAGER OF THE PHILADELPHIA
ATHLETICS SINCE 1901.
WINNER OF 9 PENNANTS AND 5
WORLD CHAMPIONSHIPS.
RECEIVED THE BOK AWARD
IN PHILADELPHIA FOR 1929.

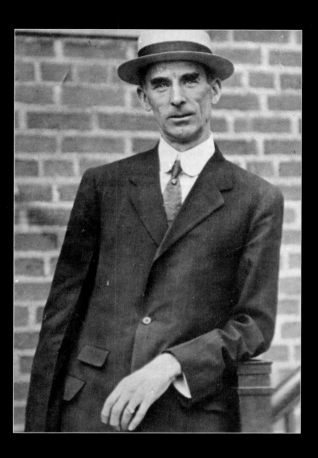

Architect of the American League's first dynasty, the Philadelphia Athletics—winners of six of the first 14 American League pennants—Connie Mack dismantled his great A's team in 1915 only to rebuild a second dynasty in the late 1920s and, in the process, become baseball's winningest manager. Below is the game ball from the last game he managed resting on a commemorative plate celebrating the Athletics' 1911 championship.

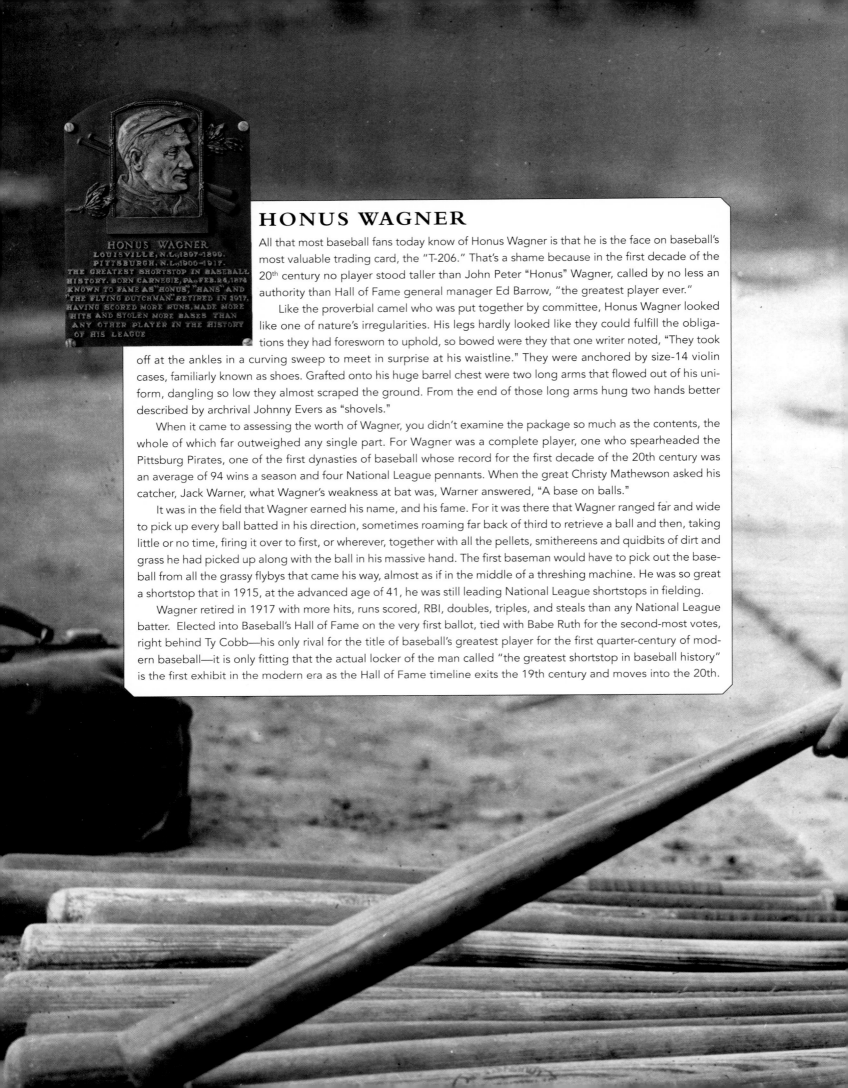

HONUS WAGNER

All that most baseball fans today know of Honus Wagner is that he is the face on baseball's most valuable trading card, the "T-206." That's a shame because in the first decade of the 20th century no player stood taller than John Peter "Honus" Wagner, called by no less an authority than Hall of Fame general manager Ed Barrow, "the greatest player ever."

Like the proverbial camel who was put together by committee, Honus Wagner looked like one of nature's irregularities. His legs hardly looked like they could fulfill the obligations they had foresworn to uphold, so bowed were they that one writer noted, "They took off at the ankles in a curving sweep to meet in surprise at his waistline." They were anchored by size-14 violin cases, familiarly known as shoes. Grafted onto his huge barrel chest were two long arms that flowed out of his uniform, dangling so low they almost scraped the ground. From the end of those long arms hung two hands better described by archrival Johnny Evers as "shovels."

When it came to assessing the worth of Wagner, you didn't examine the package so much as the contents, the whole of which far outweighed any single part. For Wagner was a complete player, one who spearheaded the Pittsburg Pirates, one of the first dynasties of baseball whose record for the first decade of the 20th century was an average of 94 wins a season and four National League pennants. When the great Christy Mathewson asked his catcher, Jack Warner, what Wagner's weakness at bat was, Warner answered, "A base on balls."

It was in the field that Wagner earned his name, and his fame. For it was there that Wagner ranged far and wide to pick up every ball batted in his direction, sometimes roaming far back of third to retrieve a ball and then, taking little or no time, firing it over to first, or wherever, together with all the pellets, smithereens and quidbits of dirt and grass he had picked up along with the ball in his massive hand. The first baseman would have to pick out the baseball from all the grassy flybys that came his way, almost as if in the middle of a threshing machine. He was so great a shortstop that in 1915, at the advanced age of 41, he was still leading National League shortstops in fielding.

Wagner retired in 1917 with more hits, runs scored, RBI, doubles, triples, and steals than any National League batter. Elected into Baseball's Hall of Fame on the very first ballot, tied with Babe Ruth for the second-most votes, right behind Ty Cobb—his only rival for the title of baseball's greatest player for the first quarter-century of modern baseball—it is only fitting that the actual locker of the man called "the greatest shortstop in baseball history" is the first exhibit in the modern era as the Hall of Fame timeline exits the 19th century and moves into the 20th.

WALTER JOHNSON

Walter Johnson had a physique made for pitching, with gangly arms and long wrists as loose as a man shaking them out. He threw his fastball in a whip-like motion, almost sidearmed by way of third base in that easy motion of his. Sam Crawford said the effect "reminded me of one of those compressed air machines . . . [it] comes in so fast when it comes by it swooshes. You hardly see the ball at all, but you hear it, swooooosh. . . ." It was the fastball that prompted writer Grantland Rice to nickname Johnson, "The Big Train." Rice added, "How do you know what Johnson's got? Nobody's seen it yet." That "swooshing" fastball won 417 games for Johnson, the most in modern baseball, with 12 20-plus-win seasons and two over 30, all with a mostly woebegone Washington club. He also holds the major-league record for most career shutouts with 110, most seasons (since 1900) leading the majors in strikeouts and shutouts and most seasons leading the American League in complete games, innings pitched, and games won.

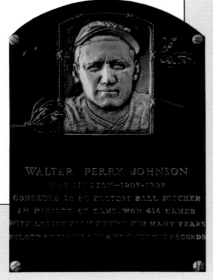

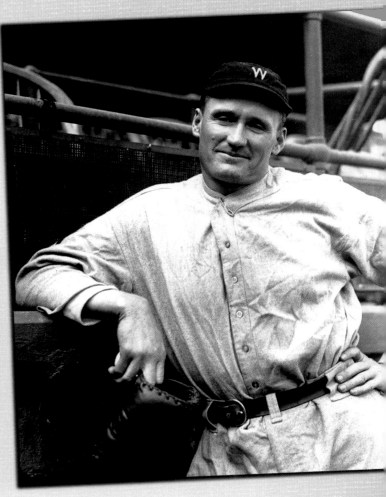

Jackson, Hank Gowdy, and Duffy Lewis traded in their flannels for other uniforms. It was Lewis— once part of the great Tris Speaker–Harry Hooper–Lewis outfield trio—whose absence was to indirectly help make baseball history. The Red Sox, having lost Lewis and most of the rest of their outfield for the duration of the war, were forced to press their star pitcher, Babe Ruth, into everyday duty in the outfield. Ruth responded by batting .300 and leading the league with 11 home runs in 1918 while also winning 13 games on the mound.

There was even some thought that baseball itself would not survive the War. With a shortened season, ending at the beginning of September, the leagues considered canceling the World Series. However, the owner of the American League champion Boston Red Sox, Harry Frazee, convinced all that the World Series should be played. With the Series starting on the earliest date in history, September 5, the Red Sox defeated the Cubs in six games with Babe Ruth winning two.

With the end of the war Americans turned from their rigors of problem-solving to the rituals of pleasure seeking, celebrating by spending all

their energies and money on any and all forms of entertainment, one of the first of which was the 1919 World Series. The Series between the Chicago White Sox and the Cincinnati Reds was expanded to a best-of-nine format, all the better to exploit the built-up excitement. Won by Cincinnati in eight games, the Series was memorable, but for all the wrong reasons. For the 1919 World Series would be remembered as the Series of the infamous "Black Sox" scandal, as seven members of the White Sox conspired to lose the Series to the Reds (an eighth was charged for not telling authorities). It was thought that their venality, which went to the very heart of the game, would leave a black mark that would take a long time for fans to forgive and forget.

Within a year, baseball fans would have reason to forget. In the last week of the last year of the decade, Boston Red Sox owner Harry Frazee sold Babe Ruth to the New York Yankees for $100,000 and other considerations. And, for the baseball world, to borrow the title of an Irving Berlin song, "Along Came Ruth. . . .

One of baseball's most tragic figures, the man called "Shoeless Joe," had one of the most fluid swings from the left side ever seen—one Babe Ruth admitted he copied. Batting .408 in his first full year in the majors, Jackson ended up with a lifetime average of .356, the third-highest in history. But Joe Jackson is remembered today less for his batting average than for the fact that although

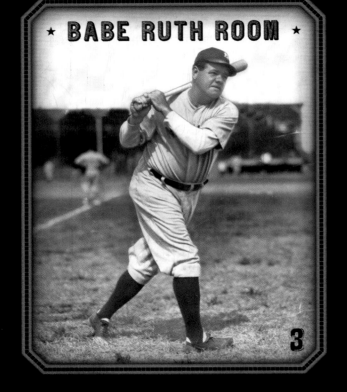

Babe Ruth. His very name brings back memories to the dwindling number of fans who saw this gargantuan figure on toothpick-thin legs boom colossal cloud-busters into the stands and then mince his way around the bases with catlike steps. To the older adult, he was a legendary figure who gave color to his era as John L. Sullivan had to his. To those of a younger generation, his name is spoken in reverential terms and used as a benchmark for modern home-run hitters, and as a metaphor for greatness itself.

Yet Babe Ruth was more than a mere name. He was an institution, almost a deity. One prominent Methodist minister even suggested at the time, "If St. Paul were living today, he would know Babe Ruth's batting average." Legions of sportswriters formed a cult, spreading the Ruthian gospel and calling him "The Sultan of Swat," "The Wizard of Whack," "The King of Clout," "The Behemoth of Big," and, of course, "The Bambino." He was the idol of American youth and the symbol of baseball the world over. He almost single-handedly saved the game of baseball after the Black Sox scandal and raised it to a new level of excitement, removing it from the suffocating bunt-and-stolen-base game of the deadball era to the new game of the longball.

Ruth had first come upon the scene as a talented 19-year-old left-handed pitcher for the Boston Red Sox in 1914. But even as he was setting the baseball world afire with his blazing fastball—leading the American League in ERA and shutouts in his second full season and winning 80 games by the age of 23, more than any left-handed pitcher in the Hall of

The hat, shoes, and famous #3 uniform of the Bambino, along with the historic 60th home-run ball hit off the Washington Senators' Tom Zachary, on September 30, 1927

Visitors are greeted at the entrance to the Babe Ruth Room by the outsized figure of the Babe and his equally outsized signature.

...aint at that young age—he was also creating some pyrotechnics with his massive bat, leading the American League in home runs in the war-shortened 1918 season with 11. By 1919 the Boston management had seen enough and converted their young pitching star into an outfielder, with a little pitching on the side. Many, like Tris Speaker, thought the conversion a mistake, Speaker saying, "Ruth made a grave mistake when he gave up pitching. Working once a week, he might have lasted a long time and become a great star."

But Ruth was to prove his detractors wrong by hitting a record-breaking 29 home runs in 1919. Suddenly, the home run had become the new currency of the game, courtesy of Ruth.

Sold to the Yankees after the 1919 season, Ruth, according to the headlines, "hit," "swatted," "clouted," or "whacked" a record 54 home runs in 1920, one every 11.8 times at bat, and more than any other American League *club*.

Every day brought new accolades and exaggerated stories about "The Bambino," his exploits the stuff myths are made of, including his supposed "Called Shot" in the 1932 World Series, a moment that will never be satisfactorily explained. With his every swing he continued his assault on the record books until, by the time he retired in 1935, he owned every line in those books under the categories of home runs, RBIs, and even strikeouts—his every missed swing bringing "ooohs" and "aaahs" from the fans.

Simply put, Babe Ruth was the greatest of all sports heroes in what was called "The Golden Age of Sports," the 1920s, and his feats made "The Roaring Twenties" roar that much louder. His name was the gold standard of the time, inspiring comparisons to superstars in other fields such as the famed tenor Enrico Caruso being called "The Babe Ruth of Opera."

Everyone, or so it seemed, was caught up in the Babe Ruth story, from songwriters like Irving Berlin, who wrote, "Along Came Ruth," to sports-

GEORGE HERMAN (BABE) RUTH
BOSTON–NEW YORK, A.L.; BOSTON, N.L.
1915–1935
GREATEST DRAWING CARD IN HISTORY OF BASEBALL. HOLDER OF MANY HOME RUN AND OTHER BATTING RECORDS. GATHERED 714 HOME RUNS IN ADDITION TO FIFTEEN IN WORLD SERIES.

writers like John Kieran of the *New York Times* who wrote a poem about Ruth containing the famous line, "From 'One Old Cat' to the last 'At Bat' was there ever a guy like Ruth?" To anyone who ever saw him, the answer was a resounding *No*. For there was only one Babe Ruth, and never again will there be anyone like him.

Proving that history does not relinquish its hold over men or monuments, the Hall of Fame has created a special exhibit to convey the full flavor and import of Ruth, with everything from displays of his massive bat to cartoons of the time, together with a video presentation of "The Babe" in action. After walking through this exhibit and experiencing the man's full glory, you will see why Babe Ruth's name has reverberated throughout the ages.

A young 19-year-old George Herman "Babe" Ruth, playing for the 1914 Providence Grays, also known as the Clamdiggers. That year, his first in professional baseball, he won nine games and lost three as a pitcher, and had 12 hits in 40 at bats with

The famous Number 3, given to Ruth for his spot in the Yankees batting order, hangs in his locker.

BABE RUTH

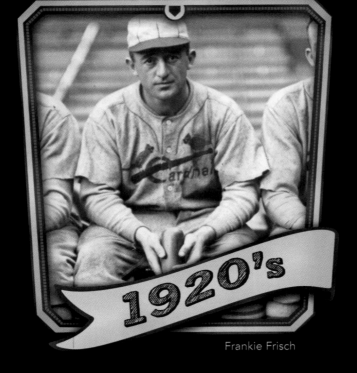

Frankie Frisch

The year 1920 was a watershed year for baseball. Described by the president of the Brooklyn Superbas (rechristened the Dodgers, as in Trolley Dodgers), Charles Ebbets, as being in its "infancy" back in 1908 when the combined two-league attendance was seven million, the attendance over the next 10 years had reached a plateau before declining during the war years, sagging to three million in 1918. The first postwar World Series of 1919 was the harbinger of great things to come. The Series—even with its dark hints of evil misdoings by the White Sox (later referred to as the "Black Sox")—had drawn almost a quarter-million more dollars than the previous record. The year 1919 also marked the legitimization of Sunday baseball in New York. With the addition of Babe Ruth during the winter of 1919-20 to the American League's showcase franchise, the New York Yankees, baseball was poised to take advantage of war-weary fans' rekindled interest in the sport.

The owners, sensing that a financial bonanza lay in the newly discovered long ball—there having been 447 home runs in 1919, including Ruth's record-breaking 29—made some changes to ensure that they could tap into the fan's renewed interest in the game. For one, they tightened the construction of the ball itself, reducing the raised stitching and making the rubber center thicker. The effect, described by sportswriter Westbrook Pegler, holding the new ball between his thumb and forefinger, "was like hearing a rabbit's heartbeat." Along with the newly named "Rabbit Ball" was the quicker replacement of baseballs in play, with newer,

A Lou Gehrig bat autographed by the New York Yankee team of 1942.

The St. Louis Cardinals of the late 1920s and early '30s were baseball's preeminent team. Known by many names, including "The Gashouse Gang," they were a rowdy group of hustling, fun-loving, and, not incidentally, winning players. Here is a Cardinals showcase featuring artifacts belonging to several of the future Hall of Famers who made the team so great: Joe Medwick's jersey; Dizzy Dean's socks and button; Frankie Frisch's cap, glove, silver bowl and autographed bat; Chick Hafey's glove and shoes; a picture of the great Dizzy Dean broadcasting; Rogers Hornsby's glove; and a silver game pass, watch, and 1925 MVP medal presented to Hornsby.

cleaner, and fresher (read: livelier) balls, exchanged for the discolored or damaged balls that had previously been used for the entire game. After the 1920 season, to further minimize the advantage pitchers had, the Rules Committee outlawed the spitball, the emery ball, the shine ball, and other so-called "freak" pitches.

The shift in emphasis from pitching to batting wrought immediate results as the high-octane ball, combined with the elimination of trick pitches, changed the dynamics of the game. Sud-

denly baseballs were rocketing off bats, so much so that Chicago Cubs manager Johnny Evers complained that the ball was "so full of rubber it goes at a fearful rate when hit."

With players from both leagues clouting, swatting, smiting, and whacking home runs at a theretofore unimaginable rate—630 in all in 1920, led by Babe Ruth's 54—baseball, suffocated for so long by the bunt and stolen base "inside" game, exploded. Attendance figures soared even higher than one of Ruth's parabolic shots, with more

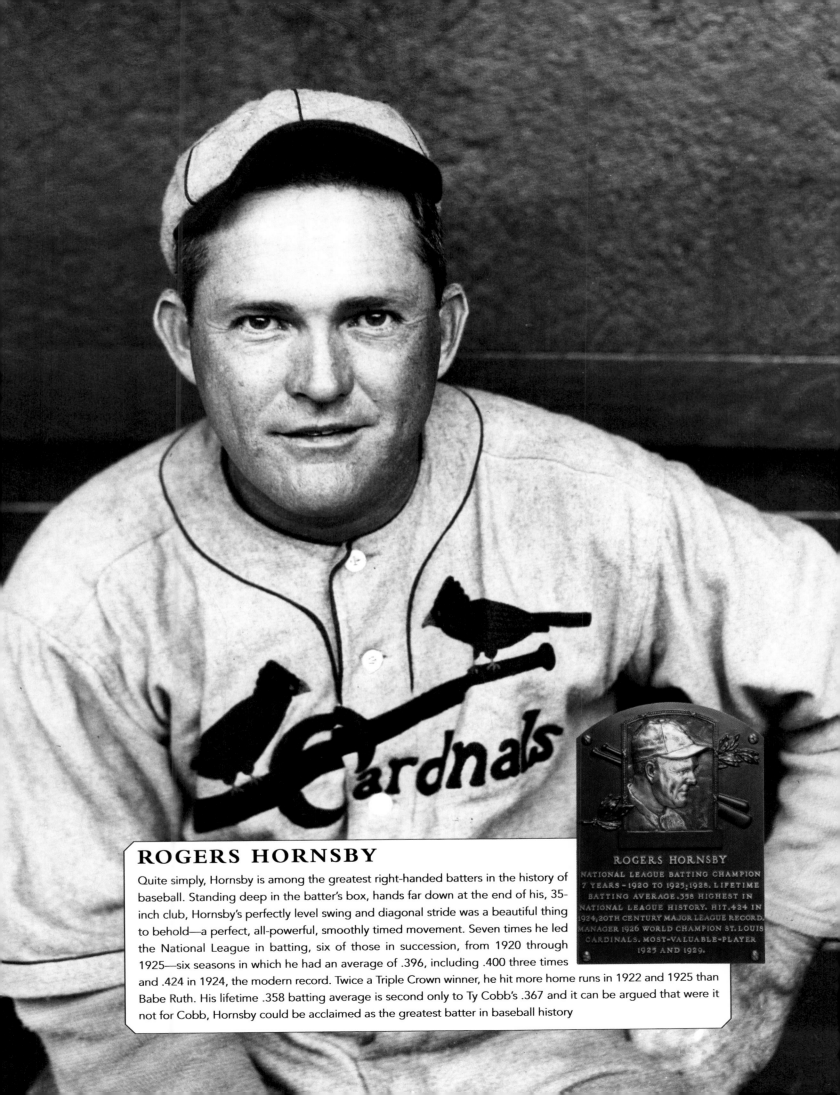

ROGERS HORNSBY

Quite simply, Hornsby is among the greatest right-handed batters in the history of baseball. Standing deep in the batter's box, hands far down at the end of his, 35-inch club, Hornsby's perfectly level swing and diagonal stride was a beautiful thing to behold—a perfect, all-powerful, smoothly timed movement. Seven times he led the National League in batting, six of those in succession, from 1920 through 1925—six seasons in which he had an average of .396, including .400 three times and .424 in 1924, the modern record. Twice a Triple Crown winner, he hit more home runs in 1922 and 1925 than Babe Ruth. His lifetime .358 batting average is second only to Ty Cobb's .367 and it can be argued that were it not for Cobb, Hornsby could be acclaimed as the greatest batter in baseball history

ROGERS HORNSBY
NATIONAL LEAGUE BATTING CHAMPION
7 YEARS - 1920 TO 1925; 1928. LIFETIME
BATTING AVERAGE .358 HIGHEST IN
NATIONAL LEAGUE HISTORY. HIT .424 IN
1924, 20TH CENTURY MAJOR LEAGUE RECORD.
MANAGER 1926 WORLD CHAMPION ST. LOUIS
CARDINALS. MOST-VALUABLE-PLAYER
1925 AND 1929.

Between 1926 and 1934 the St. Louis Cardinals won more games than any other National League team, including five pennants, largely as a result of Branch Rickey's famed "Farm System." Here are four members of the second of those pennant-winning teams, the 1928 edition: (L to R) Chick Hafey, Frankie Frisch, Jim Bottomley, and George Harper.

than nine million fans flocking to the ballparks to see the "new" game. Baseball was no longer in its infancy; it had come of age with the arrival of Ruth and the home run.

While the old guard faded, it hardly surrendered. One of the most fervent advocates of the "inside" game, John McGraw of the old Baltimore Orioles and now manager of the New York Giants, was vocally contemptuous of both the home run and of Ruth. Making no unconditional surrender to undeniable facts, McGraw continued to field winning teams. Adhering to their manager's "inside" game—while also hitting the third-most homers in the National League in both 1921 and '22—the Giants bested their Polo Grounds rivals, the Yankees, in both years' World Series.

By 1922, the Yankees, like fish, had begun to take on the odor of guests who have overstayed their welcome. Especially to the nostrils of McGraw, whose salary was based, in part, on the Giants attendance and who saw his now-hated tenants outdrawing his home team as hordes of fans came through the turnstiles to see Ruth hit home run after home run. With McGraw snarling at the very mention of the words "Yankees" and "Ruth," he evicted the Yankees from the Polo Grounds and forced them to seek a stadium of their own. They soon found it on ten acres just across the Harlem River from the Polo Grounds. In just 248 construction days they had Yankee Stadium, which was properly christened on Opening Day by Babe Ruth's game-winning home run. Ruth would go on to hit 40 more in 1923, prompting one imaginative sportswriter to name the stadium "The House that Ruth Built" in honor of the star who had made it possible. The 1923 World Series, the third straight all-New York Series, was less a battle between the New York Yankees and the New York Giants than a battle between the titanic forces of baseball: John McGraw versus Babe Ruth; the old school versus the new; and "inside" baseball versus the long ball. After six games, the final tally read: the first World Series win for the Yankees, three home runs for Ruth, and a loss for John McGraw and the old style of "inside" baseball.

Batting averages, which started heading northward in 1920, now reached high up into the paint cards in 1923 as Ruth batted .393 only to finish second to Harry Heilmann's .403, while over in the National League Rogers Hornsby won his fourth straight batting title in a streak of six, averaging .396 during that run with three .400 seasons. Ty Cobb had hit .401 in 1922 and still finished second to George Sisler's .420. Everybody, it seemed, was part of the hit parade with pitcher Walter Johnson hitting .433 in 1925. And no less than 26 teams hit .300 or more as a club during the decade of the '20s.

Home runs were flying out of the park at a record rate. Not just Ruth's, but everybody's. Hornsby twice out-homered Ruth, and no less than 15 players hit more than Ruth's 1919 record of 29—not counting Ruth himself who did it every year of the decade save one. The combined batting average of all teams in the "live ball" decade of the 1920s was .286, 30 points higher than the 19-teens. There was little doubt that the "live ball" had added more than a little roar to a decade known as "The Roaring Twenties."

Statistics aside, the decade was best defined by the players who had compiled those numbers, as teams which had once ridden pitchers' arms to the top now rode bats full of hits to championships. Nowhere was that truer than in the case of the Yankees' Babe Ruth who, in an era of celebrity culture, became the biggest name with the biggest bat, propelling the Yankees to pennants in 1921, '22, '23. '26, '27, and '28. If faint cries of "Break up the Yankees" had first been heard in 1922, they had become a full-throated roar by 1927 as the Yankees, arguably the greatest team in baseball history and now known as "Murderer's Row," added additional firepower to the "row" with Lou Gehrig, Tony Lazzeri and Earle Combs combining to easily win the American League pennant by 19 games and sweep the Pittsburgh Pirates in the World Series.

The Pittsburgh Pirates (now with an "h" added to their name) were another success story with the addition of third baseman Pie Traynor in 1920, outfielder Kiki Cuyler in 1921 and brothers

The heart of the 1927 New York Yankees batting order, better known as "Murderer's Row" (L to R: Lou Gehrig, Earle Combs, Tony Lazzeri, and Babe Ruth). Combined they had 133 home runs, a .344 batting average, and a .634 slugging average, and led the Yankees to a then-record 110 wins and a four-game sweep of the Pittsburgh Pirates in the '27 Series.

Lloyd Waner in 1926 and '27, along with veteran Max Carey, all future Hall of Famers, the Pirates were the only Major League team to finish in the first division every year of the decade, winning National League pennants in 1925 and '27 and the Series in '25. Yet another National League team that achieved success in the '20s was the St. Louis Cardinals. From 1901 through 1919 the Cards had finished in the first division only thrice while finishing last six times. With Rogers Hornsby, Jim Bottomley, and Chick Hafey providing the offensive power and Pop Haines, and later Grover Cleveland Alexander, the pitching, the Cardinals became a National League powerhouse, finishing in the first division seven times in the decade, winning their first-ever pennant and World Series in 1926 and a second National League championship in '28.

The feel-good stories of the decade belonged to Walter Johnson and the Philadelphia Athletics.

Johnson, who had pitched for some of the worst baseball teams in baseball history, the Washington Senators—called by writer Charles Dryden, "First in war, first in peace, and last in the American League"—finally, after 18 years and 377 wins, got his chance to pitch in the 1924 World Series. After two losses to the New York Giants, it appeared that the player dubbed "The Big Train" would come away empty-handed. However, in the seventh and deciding game, Johnson got another chance, coming in to relieve in the ninth inning. As Giants' losing pitcher Jack Bentley said after the Senators won in extra innings on a ball that hopped over third baseman Freddie Lindstrom's head, "I guess the Good Lord couldn't stand seeing Water Johnson lose again."

The Philadelphia A's, one of baseball's weakest teams—cellar-dwellers for seven straight years after Connie Mack had broken up his 1914

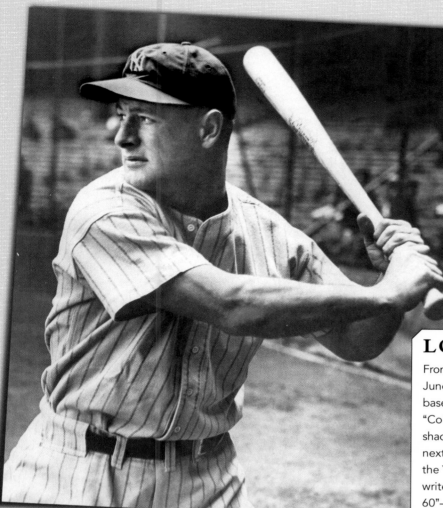

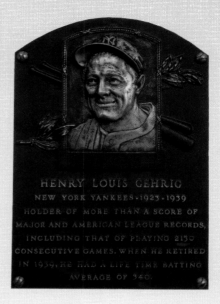

LOU GEHRIG

From the very first day Lou Gehrig took his place at first base—June 2, 1925, courtesy of the most famous headache in baseball history, suffered by Wally Pipp—the youngster called "Columbia Lou" was destined to play in the rather ample shadow of the man he called "The Big Guy," Babe Ruth. For the next ten years he was to bat number 4 to Ruth's number 3 in the Yankee batting order and even be called, by one sportswriter, ". . . the guy who hit all those homers the year Ruth hit 60"—hitting a runner-up 47 to Ruth in 1927, when the next-closest home-run total in the American League was fellow Yankee Tony Lazzeri's 18. However, 1927 was the season Gehrig proved he was a jewel in his own setting as he led the league in RBI's with 175 and was named the league's MVP. It seemed that Gehrig was forever doomed to stand in someone's shadow as when, in 1932, he became the first player in the 20th century to hit four home runs in one game but, unfortunately, it happened the same day John McGraw stepped down as manager of the New York Giants after 31 years at their helm and captured the headlines. It happened again when, in 1936, Joe DiMaggio came up and became the center of attention. Still, until the day he asked to be taken out of the line-up, May 2, 1939, Gehrig was baseball's "Iron Man," playing in 2,130 consecutive games. Two years later, the man who had called himself "the luckiest man on the face of the earth" died from the disease that carries his name. He is survived by his records, many of which still stand such as most career grand-slam home runs and most RBI for a season in the American League. And as the legend of the quiet man who put in an honest laboring man's effort, albeit with extraordinary results, each and every game.

club—began climbing the standings in 1922, and finally, with the addition of future Hall of Famers Jimmie Foxx, Mickey Cochrane, Al Simmons, and Lefty Grove, reached the top of the American League mountain in 1929 to begin their second mini-dynasty.

So the feverish decade of the '20s ended, a decade in which the Lords of Baseball, more than making up for bookkeeping arrearages, had switched the emphasis of the game from pitching to batting, opening it up like a piñata. The long ball had suddenly become the currency of the game, and dues-paying fans loved it, flocking to the ballparks in record numbers.

The era of excess and gaudy numbers would begin to come to a close on October 24, 1929, when the stock market fell with a resounding CRASH!, and everything would change, including the game of baseball.

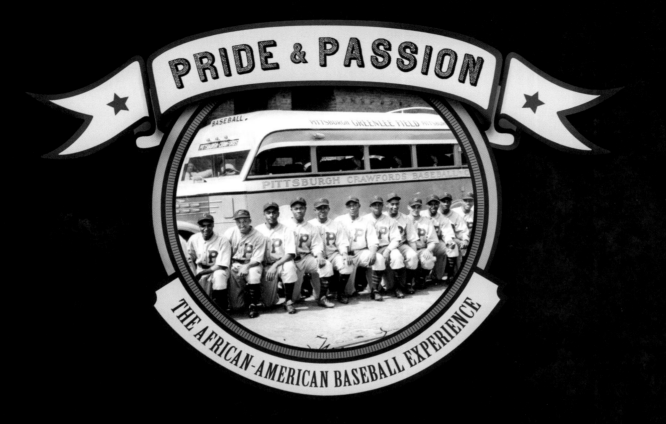

PRIDE & PASSION

THE AFRICAN-AMERICAN BASEBALL EXPERIENCE

One of the most inspiring exhibits in the Baseball Hall of Fame is Pride and Passion. No better title could have been designated for this moving exhibit that chronicles the African-American experience in and contribution to our national game.

The exhibit has its roots in the drawing of baseball's "color line"—that unwritten mandate to keep blacks out of major league baseball which began in the 1860s and lasted until 1947. The exact origin of this "gentleman's agreement" isn't clear: it came about over time and through the intense desire of baseball's white majority to keep "colored" players out of the game. One of the most vocal supporters of the color line was one

Adrian "Cap" Anson, who had numerous run-ins with opposing teams who tried to field back players.

While managing the Chicago White Stockings in 1883, his team took the field one August day for a well-attended exhibition game against the Toledo Blue Stockings. When Anson noticed Moses Fleetwood Walker, a black player, take the field as Toledo's catcher, he threatened to halt the proceedings. In this rare instance, however, Anson did not get his way. When Toledo manager Charlie Morton informed Anson that his team would not get their share of the gate money if they refused to play, Anson backed down. But he would never give up,

The Cuban X-Giants were champions of the integrated Tri-State Independent League in 1903. In 1905 they became the first black team to beat a major league team, outscoring the Brooklyn Dodgers 8-3 while taking one of two games.

The Pride and Passion exhibit is one of the most inspiring exhibits in the Hall of Fame. From the early days (as represented by the picture on the right of the entrance of the Philadelphia Giants, circa 1904), through the history of the Negro leagues (as shown left of the entrance in the photograph of the 1935 Pittsburgh Crawfords), and to blacks' ultimate entry into the major leagues, the Pride and Passion exhibit pays tribute in vivid and exacting detail to the contributions of African-Americans to the game of baseball.

and was even successful in some similar instances in forcing opponents to bench or fire black players. But Anson was hardly the sole architect of the color line, which would continue for another six decades.

Over the course of those 60 years, blacks, denied the right to play in organized ball, formed their own leagues and barnstormed against all-white teams. The Major League doors were closed to such greats as Satchel Paige, Josh Gibson, Cool Papa Bell, Double-Duty Radcliffe and many others, most equal in talent and some greater than many of those playing Major League ball. Some, like Satchel Paige, were so great that they served as a measurement for those playing in the Majors. Take, for example, the time the Yankees, anxious to try out their new rookie, Joe DiMaggio, put him into an exhibition game before the 1936 season against the Satchel Paige All-Stars. Facing the great Paige, DiMaggio struck out twice and fouled out once before hitting a single off Satchel's famous "Hesitation Pitch." The scouts were so ecstatic they sent a telegram back to Yankee headquarters reading: "DIMAGGIO ALL WE HOPED HE'D BE. HIT SATCH ONE FOR FOUR."

Throughout the intervening years, Baseball Commissioner Kenesaw Mountain Landis continued to release statements reading, "Each club is entirely free to employ Negro players to any extent it pleases." However, he rebuffed all petitions calling for blacks to play in organized baseball, telling journalists, like Wendell Smith of the Pittsburgh *Courier*, "The colored players have their own league, let them stay there." With the end of World War II, pressure mounted to allow blacks to take their place on the playing fields just as they had on the battlefields. Catching the temper of the times, new commissioner Albert B. "Happy" Chandler raised the bar to the door marked "Closed to Blacks" by saying, "If a black boy can make it at Okinawa and go to Guadalcanal, he can make it in baseball."

The man who was the architect of removing the bar was Wesley Branch Rickey, a color-blind man who had never paid full faith and credit to baseball's

The interior of the Pride and Passion exhibit, featuring displays of the early days of the African-American baseball experience and a timeline tracing baseball's place in historical context to the wider world of Civil Rights.

The 1935 Negro National League champion Pittsburgh Crawfords pose in front of their home field, Greenlee Field, and their new team bus which, in those days of Jim Crow baseball, served as their home-away-from-home—their dressing room, their dining room and their hotel.

HOMESTEAD
GRAYS

FRONT ROW - Left To Right DUKES, JACKSON, CARLISLE, WELMAKER, DULA, HARRIS, ALLEN, BENJAMIN.

BACK ROW - LEONARD, WAITE, PEREZ, G. WALKER, PARKER, J. WILLIAMS, GIBSON, BROWN , E. WALKER.

LEADERS of the 1937 PENNANT RACE
— VS. —
PITTS. CRAWFORDS
— AT —
BUTLER, PA.
— ON —
THURS. NITE, JULY 8

FOR GAMES WRITE, WIRE

~~~~ stead, Pa.

ADM.   ANY SEAT IN PARK    55c

asons for the Cleveland
World Championship in
e ageless Satchel Paige
24-year-old Larry Doby.
6–1 during the 1948
ding two shutouts, and
first African-American
World Series. Doby, the
American to play in the
eague, hit .301 for the
on and batted a team-
the 1948 World Series.

OBERT PAIGE
TCHEL
UES   1926-1947
          1948-1949
          1931-1953
 A.L.   1969
F THE GREATEST STARS
RO BASEBALL LEAGUES
NS OF PEOPLE AND WON
ES STRUCK OUT 21 MAJOR
XHIBITION GAME, HELPED
D INDIANS TO THE 1948
FIRST BIG LEAGUE YEAR
TCHING WAS A LEGEND
R LEAGUE HITTERS.

SATCHEL PAIGE

Finally brought to the Majors in 1948 at the advanced age of, supposedly, 42—nobody knew his exact age—Satchel Paige brought with him an amazing arsenal of pitches, all with descriptive nicknames. His most famous one was his "hesitation pitch," delivered sidearm with first his leg stammering down, then a delay and an out-of-synch follow-through. Other Paige pitches included his "two-hump blooper" (a moving change-up), "the little Tom" (a medium fastball), "the long Tom" (a hard fastball), "the looper" (a "nothing pitch"), the "bat dodger," "the trouble ball," and the "bee ball." For two decades in the Negro Leagues and in barnstorming exhibitions before he made it to "the bigs," Paige was estimated to have pitched as many as 125 games a year, pitching as frequently as five to seven times a week, for a total of 2,500-plus appearances. The first African-American pitcher in the American League, Paige worked 21 games for the pennant-winning Cleveland Indians, winning six games, two of them shutouts, with a 2.48 ERA. Paige played five more seasons in the Majors, ending his career in 1965 at the "guessed-at" age of 59, going on Social Security, to pitch one last game for the Kansas City Royals—becoming, in the process, the oldest player in Major League history to appear in a game.

murky traditions. While all others meekly accepted the "Gentleman's Agreement" as unalterable, Rickey knew that, like all other such "truths," it was blasphemous and determined to challenge it by putting a black in Brooklyn Dodger blue.

Rather than confront the Lords of Baseball directly, Rickey threw up a smoke screen, forming something called the United States Baseball League with the entry from Brooklyn to be called the Brown Dodgers. In August he sent Brooklyn's head scout, Clyde Sukeforth, out to Chicago to watch the Kansas City Monarchs play the Lincoln Giants with instructions to "Go up to that fellow Robinson and introduce yourself."

"That fellow Robinson" was Jack Roosevelt Robinson, an exceptional athlete and person. The younger brother of Mack Robinson, who had finished second to Jesse Owens in the 200-meter dash in the 1936 Berlin Olympics, young Jackie had been introduced to sports at an early age and found he could excel in almost any sport he tried.

At Pasadena Junior College he broke the record in the long jump, set by his brother, and gained such fame as a football star that crowds ranging from thirty to sixty thousand came out to see the wing-footed running back. Robinson would go on to even greater stardom at UCLA, where he became the school's first four-letter athlete. Called by one rival coach "the best basketball player in the U.S.," Robinson led the Pacific Coast Conference in scoring as both a junior and a senior. On the gridiron he led the nation in average yards gained from scrimmage in 1939, and in punt returns. To cap his collegiate career, Robinson won swimming championships, reached the semifinals of the national Negro tennis tournament, and won the 1940 NCAA long-jump title. Then came World War II.

Robinson applied for admission to the officer candidate school at Fort Riley, Kansas, where he won his commission as a second lieutenant. He won something else as well: a reputation for being a fiercely proud man. Although military

A St. Louis Stars uniform, hat, and sunglasses of outfielder "Cool Papa" Bell, one of six Negro League teams the Hall of Famer played for from 1922 to 1946. Known as the fastest man ever to wear spikes, "Cool Papa," according to teammate Satchel Paige, "could turn off a light switch and jump into bed before the room got dark."

Jackie Robinson: 1949 Bowman Baseball Card

buses had recently been desegregated, he was court-martialed for his failure to "move to the back of the bus." Army brass decided they could not control his pride nor his iron will and gave him a general discharge in November of 1944, happy to be rid of him.

Mustered out of the service, Robinson signed on with the Kansas City Monarchs. When Sukeforth went up to "that fellow Robinson," Robinson was skeptical of Rickey's intentions and pressured Sukeforth to repeat Rickey's instructions, word-for-word. Sukeforth could only say, "Jack, this could be the real thing." Following the rest of Rickey's orders to "bring him in," Sukeforth booked two berths on the train back to Brooklyn.

As Sukeforth ushered Robinson into Rickey's inner chambers, he began to make the customary introductions. But it was useless, for Rickey at once commenced speaking. It was obvious at the outset he was not only looking for an outstand- ing athlete with the ability to play the game at an exceptional level, but was also looking for some- one with the strength of character to endure the pressure and abuse sure to accompany his pio- neering effort. Rickey, never one to pull his punches, launched into a monologue: "Jack, I've been looking for a great colored ballplayer. But I need more than a great player, I need a man who will accept insults, take abuse . . . in a word, carry the flag for his race." Then, without waiting for Robinson to answer, he went on, "I want a man who has the courage not to fight, not to fight back. . . . If a guy slides into you at second base and calls you a black son of a bitch, I wouldn't blame you if you came up swinging. You'd be right. You'd be justified. . . ." Here Rickey paused. "But you'd set the cause back twenty years. I want a man with courage enough not to fight back. Can you do that?"

Determined to, as Rickey called it, "carry the flag for his race," Robinson did so admirably

Subjected to imprecations impossible to brook or overlook, Robinson kept his equanimity. His air connoted a quiet but conscious force and dignity. He answered the only way he could: with his bat and his feet.

Ever dangerous at the plate, it was on the basepaths that Robinson made his greatest mark, dominating the field like no player since Ty Cobb. Running with a pigeon-toed gait, Robinson dared to challenge fielders with a will-he-or-won't-he hesitation move, taking off for the next base when they threw the ball behind him. Other times this most artful Dodger would get into a rundown and, figuring it was a bad bargain that couldn't run both ways, jockeyed between the rundown men and before they knew it would be safely hugging the base he had set out for. Described by one writer as "a man of many facets, all turned on," Robinson was one of the greatest players of his era and the most socially significant figure in its long history.

At the end of his first year, 1947, Robinson was named "Rookie of the Year"; in his third he won the National League batting title and was named its Most Valuable Player. By his fourth season he had become the leader of the Dodgers team, leading them to six pennants in ten years—a National League record for success that eclipsed the one set back in the nineteenth century by none other than Cap Anson and his Chicago White Stockings.

Baseball's "Noble Experiment" had worked. Starting with Larry Doby, who became the American League's first African-American player just 11 weeks later, Robinson's example was followed by team after team as the game of baseball truly became the all-encompassing "National Pastime."

But Robinson's achievement wasn't merely a baseball achievement. It foreshadowed the Civil Rights movement of the 1950s and '60s. To honor both Robinson and his ground-breaking accomplishment, the Baseball Hall of Fame has dedicated their Pride and Passion exhibit—along with a timeline detailing the history of African-Americans in baseball from the Civil War through their integration into the game, tracing notable events in both African-American cultural history as well as the history of black baseball.

Beyond the insults, bench jockeying, strike threats, and overall ugliness from players and fans that Jackie Robinson had to endure during his rookie season of 1947, he also received menacing hate mail. But, turning the other cheek, Robinson answered with his play on the field, leading the National League in stolen bases and sacrifices, finishing second in runs scored, and leading the Brooklyn Dodgers to the National League pennant, all while winning Rookie of the Year honors in the process.

The Pride and Passion exhibit takes into account modern historical sensibilities with computer-based interactive features, three-dimensional artifacts, such as Cool Papa Bell's St. Louis Stars uniform, and Robinson's Dodger warm-up jacket, glove and bat, along with information on many of the black pioneers of the game.

For Robinson, Larry Doby, Monte Irvin, Satchel Paige and many, many others, the dream was a long time coming. It is that dream-turned-into-a-reality that the Baseball Hall of Fame honors with its Pride and Passion exhibit.

The interior of the Pride and Passion exhibit marking Jackie Robinson's historic entry into the major leagues in 1947.

One of Jackie Robinson's famous number 42 jerseys. The number 42 was retired by Major League Baseball permanently—for all marjor league and minor league teams—in 1997, the 50th anniversary of his debut.

JACK ROOSEVELT ROBINSON
BROOKLYN N.L. 1947 TO 1956
LEADING N.L. BATTER IN 1949. HOLDS
FIELDING MARK FOR SECOND BASEMAN
PLAYING IN 150 OR MORE GAMES WITH .992.
LED N.L. IN STOLEN BASES IN 1947 AND
1949. MOST VALUABLE PLAYER IN 1949.
LIFETIME BATTING AVERAGE .311. JOINT
RECORD HOLDER FOR MOST DOUBLE PLAYS
BY SECOND BASEMAN, 137 IN 1951.
LED SECOND BASEMEN IN DOUBLE
PLAYS 1949-50-51-52.

ADVERTISING AND BASEBALL

The 20th century brought mass production, and with mass production came its natural extension: mass advertising. Called "salesmanship in print," advertising was quick to tie in with what was then becoming part of America's culture—the sport of baseball.

One of the first baseball players to capitalize on his fame and supplement his income through endorsements was King Kelly, whose handsome, mustachio'd countenance beamed down from billboards in every city recommending everything from streetcar companies to baby foods to cigars. Cap Anson and Buck Ewing lent their names and images for a Burke Ale poster in 1889. They were compensated with $300 and a case of ale each.

The next recorded instance of a baseball player leasing his name came in 1905 when Honus Wagner gave the J. B. Hillerich & Son Company the right to use his name on its Louisville Slugger bats for a consideration of $75. Pursued by commercial suitors, Wagner was careful of what he endorsed. He lent his name to the Gillette Razor Company for an ad quoting him saying, in the quaint manner of the day, "I shave with a Gillette. I know of nothing that could induce me to change the system."

Even though he chewed tobacco, he was a non-smoker and sued the American Tobacco Company for putting his image on a Sweet Caporal tobacco card without his permission, believing it constituted his implicit endorsement not only of the product but of smoking itself. Wagner's act won him a bonus and the praise of Pirates owner Barney Dreyfuss, who tolerated no smoking on his ball club—Dreyfuss having previously sold a promising young outfielder named Tris Speaker who smoked rather than compromising his standard.

In 1907 J. B. Hillerich & Son signed Nap Lajoie to endorse its bats, and in 1908 they approached Ty Cobb, the 21-year-old phenomenon who had led the American League in batting for the second time. Even then displaying a keen understanding of the counter-offer, Cobb wrote back, "I'll give you my name for nothing if you'll provide me with selected bats. I want you to agree to set aside the best wood that comes into your plant. I want my own bin right at the factory. And I'd like the privilege of specifying the kind of lumber to be used." Counter offer accepted.

Advertising tie-ins in those early days of both baseball and advertising took many forms. Coca-Cola introduced a series of ads in 1907 heralding "The Great National Drink at the Great National Game," and pictured Wagner and Cobb drinking a modification of what had been called French Wine Cola. Bull Durham Smoking Tobacco bought all the outfield signs in both the majors and minors and offered a $50 prize to any player who "hits the giant 'Bull' sign with a fairly batted flyball in a league game." One sadistic manufacturer of female wraps marketed the Snodgrass Muff, named for the unfortunate Giant outfielder who dropped a flyball in the 1912 Series, costing the Giants the championship. Everyone, so it seemed, wanted their products associated with baseball.

As Babe Ruth began making headlines with his home runs, advertisers raced to hitch their products to the new star and his parabolic cloud-busters with a staggering variety of merchandise including Babe Ruth cigars, Babe Ruth underwear, and Babe Ruth candy—which the Curtiss Candy Company disingenuously tried to explain as having nothing to do with the Babe himself even though the candy was introduced in 1920, the year Ruth hit 54 home runs, by saying in press releases, "although millions associate Babe Ruth with the great baseball figure, it was named for President Grover Cleveland's daughter Ruth" whom, they claimed, "visited the Curtiss Candy Company plant years ago when the company was getting started." This despite the fact that Cleveland's daughter had died of diphtheria twelve full years before the company first opened its doors!

By the 1940s radio and baseball had become what columnist Walter Winchell called an "item," with radio announcers dubbing a home run a "Ballantine Blast" in New York, an "Old Goldie" in Brooklyn and a "Chesterfield Satisfier" in Washington, and around the rest of the majors a "Wheaties Wallop." The biggest advertiser was the Gillette Safety Razor Company which signed a long-term contract in 1939 to sponsor the World Series. In the early 1940s Gillette decided to add a little fillip to its advertising by having Series participants give their personal endorsements for the razor. When St. Louis Cardinals manager Billy Southworth was asked by a staff announcer whether had had shaved with a Gillette razor that morning, Southworth quipped, "You know bloody well I did!"

Yet with all the flubs and mishaps, throughout the years the connection between advertising and baseball has been, well, as the automobile commercial said, "Baseball, hot dogs, apple pie, and Chevrolet. They go together in the good ol' USA."

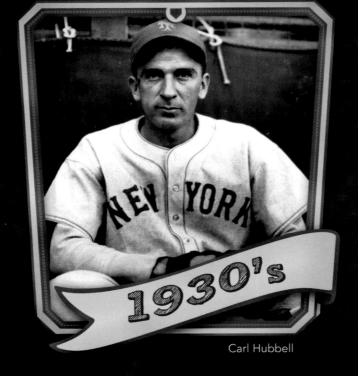

Carl Hubbell

With the crash of the stock market the feverish twenties imploded into the troubled thirties. As what was to become known as "The Great Depression" worsened, men without hope trudged the streets, soup kitchens opened, and shantytowns known as "Hooverville" (referring to presiding President Herbert Hoover) sprung up on many open lots. Everywhere people with little money to spend and only despair to look forward to, looked for a tonic for their sagging spirits, something that would allow them to live vicariously.

Movies filled this desire for entertainment with Depression-alleviating songs like "Who's Afraid of the Big Bad Wolf" and double-features for cash-strapped millions who could barely afford food, let alone luxuries, but attended movies in record numbers as an escape from their economic woes.

Baseball also provided escapism for millions, but it had to shed its traditional bonds to do so. With several franchises on the brink of collapse and attendance sagging to its lowest since the war-shortened season of 1918, it tried to win back its fans with several untried promotions, like doubleheaders. Once scheduled only as a part of rain-out make-up contests, they became as commonplace as double-feature movies. Sam Breadon, the owner of the St. Louis Cardinals, became so enamored with Sunday doubleheaders that,

Mickey Cochrane's A's jacket and shinguard. Cochrane was rated the key man in the three-year string of Philadelphia pennants, contributing batting marks of .331, .357 and .349.

CARL HUBBELL
NEW YORK N.L. 1928-1943
HAILED FOR IMPRESSIVE PERFORMANCE IN
1934 ALL-STAR GAME WHEN HE STRUCK OUT
RUTH, GEHRIG, FOXX, SIMMONS AND CRONIN
IN SUCCESSION. NICKNAMED GIANTS'
MEAL TICKET. WON 253 GAMES IN MAJORS.
SCORING 16 STRAIGHT IN 1936. COMPILED
STREAK OF 46⅓ SCORELESS INNINGS IN
1933. HOLDER OF MANY RECORDS.

CARL HUBBELL

Carl Hubbell was known for one of the most vicious pitches ever thrown, a left-handed variant of Christy Mathewson's famed fadeaway, one that had the opposite effect of a normal lefty's curve, breaking down and in on left-handed batters and outward and away from right-handers. The pitch—called, for reasons never fully explained, the "screwball"—became the inspiration for Larry Clinton's popular song of the '30s, The Dipsy-Doodle. Hubbell alternated his villainous screwball with a breaking curve thrown with a slow, cartwheel-like and excellent delivery, winning 20 games five years in a row and twice being voted the National League's MVP. He holds the record for most consecutive wins, 24, 16 of those in 1936 and eight more to open the '37 season, and led the National League in wins and winning percentage both years. Winner of more games in the Senior Circuit than any other pitcher during the '30's, Hubbell's greatest moment—and one of baseball's—came in the 1934 All-Star Game when he struck out, in order, five of the most feared batsmen in baseball—Babe Ruth, Lou Gehrig, Jimmie Foxx, Al Simmons and Joe Cronin, all future Hall of Famers. These five greats found out, just as did everyone who ever faced Hubbell, that they couldn't find his offerings with a Geiger counter, especially his "screwball."

according to Red Smith, then a writer for the *St. Louis Journal*, "Breadon would call off a weekday game if he so much as spat."

Breadon was one of the first, along with Chicago Cubs president William Veeck Sr., to come to the realization that radio was an effective promotional tool and began broadcasting weekday games as a come-on for those Sunday doubleheaders, which were *not* broadcast. Aware of the fact that most of the fans attending Sunday games came from within a 100-mile radius of St. Louis, Breadon "papered" the countryside with posters heralding the appearance of "DIZZY DEAN" who, it was announced in much smaller type, would "pitch against the Giants Sunday." Doubleheaders, radio, and advertising worked so well that a large proportion of Cardinal attendance every season was accounted for by Sunday's attendance.

Soon other clubs were trying the same formula. However, the Cardinals had one thing the other clubs didn't, American tintypes the fans could identify with, like Dizzy Dean and a dirty-faced, hungry-looking player hailing from the Oklahoma Osages who had entered baseball on

the rods of a freight train and whose nickname was almost as picturesque as his exploits: "Pepper" Martin. Each would play a major part of the Cardinals' World Championship wins: Martin in 1931 and Dean in 1934.

There would be other promotions during the Depression, like the first All-Star Game in 1933, staged as a part of Chicago's Century of Progress. With 17 future Hall of Famers playing, the game was won by the American League on Babe Ruth's two-run homer, 4-2.

The biggest promotion of all was a new phenomenon: night baseball. Knowing that 90 percent of all entertainment dollars were spent at night, E. Lee Keyser, president of the Des Moines team of the Class A Western League, announced at the 1930 National Association winter meeting that his would be the first team in organized baseball to play a regular league game at night. Keyser's idea took hold throughout the minor leagues as team after team tried what was then called "a scheme." Each profited because of it.

One club president who joined in the light at the end of baseball's tunnel was Larry MacPhail, president and general manager of St. Louis's

Mickey Cochrane
As field boss of the Athletics, Mickey Cochrane was a "take charge" catcher who handled pitchers with authority while manager Connie Mack pondered strategy from the dugout. Cochrane was rated the key man in the three-year string of Philadelphia pennants, contributing batting marks of .331, .357 and .349. Cochrane later led Detroit to two flags (1934-35) as player-manager. He ended a 13-year career in the majors in 1937 with a batting average of .320.

Mickey Cochrane's A's jacket, chest protector and shinguards

Lefty Grove
Athletics fans wondered if manager Connie Mack had been badly taken when he paid $100,600 to the Baltimore Orioles of the International League for pitching sensation Robert "Lefty" Grove in 1925. The grouchy ex-coal miner from Maryland went on to gain recognition as the greatest left-hander in American League history. He won 79 games for Philadelphia from 1929 to 1931, with a 31-4 mark in 1931, but was sold to the Red Sox

Watch given to pitcher George Earnshaw following the 1929 world championship season during which he won 24-8

Baseball autographed by pitching sensation Lefty Grove

The Philadelphia Athletics of 1929–31, led by future Hall of Famers Lefty Grove, Mickey Cochrane, Jimmie Foxx, and Al Simmons, were the first team to put together back-to-back-to-back 100-win seasons in their run of three consecutive American League pennants.

Chuck Klein owed his statistical greatness as much to his booming bat as to the clubby confines of Baker Bowl, that little bandbox of a ballpark the Phillies played in. With its corrugated right field fence only 280 feet from home plate, the left-handed Klein found it an inviting target, rattling hit after hit off, and over, the wall. In his first five seasons in a Phillies uniform, Klein stroked a total of 1,118 hits, most of those off that great wall, twice leading the league in hits, an equal number of times in doubles, four times in homers, twice in RBI, and once in batting, while also winning the Triple Crown and the MVP trophy (pictured) in 1933 and 1932, respectively.

DIZZY DEAN

Dizzy Dean was an American original, the most popular player of the 1930s, a brazen, I-can-do-it player who put his arm where his mouth was decades before Muhammad Ali ever did. A member of the St. Louis Cardinals' ragtag band of renegades known as "The Gas House Gang" with fancifully nicknamed comrades like "Pepper," "Ducky" and "The Lip," Dizzy dominated National League batters for five years with a blazing fastball and a dazzling curve. The last National League pitcher to record 30 wins, Dean's career was cut short when, in the 1937 All-Star Game, Earl Averill's line drive gave him a fractured toe to go with his fractured English. Coming back before his toe had completely healed, Dean altered his delivery and injured his arm. Traded to the Chicago Cubs before the '38 season, Dean relied on a slow curve and a tantalizing change-up to chalk up seven wins and helped Chicago win the National League pennant. After two more seasons Dean retired—only to come back for one more appearance in 1941—before turning to the microphone where he delighted a whole new generation of fans with his mangling of the English language, saying things like "he slud into second" and "the Spat of St. Louis," as in "Spirit of St. Louis."

Columbus farm club. MacPhail, taking advantage of Depression prices, built an all-new ballpark with a complete high-level lighting system, and completely revamped the doormat of a league into a winner, winning the American Association championship in 1933.

A funny thing happened on his way to the championship: he was fired, the result of his extravagance. No sooner was he "at liberty" than MacPhail bounced back to land the job of vice president of the Cincinnati Reds, a terribly downtrodden team, both in the standings and at the bank where the Central Trust Company had repossessed the team. Hooking up with financier Powell Crosley, Jr., MacPhail took over the team from the bank in 1934 and began looking for something, anything, that would draw fans to old Redlands Field. Obviously it was not going to be the ballclub, a perennial last-place club. So MacPhail, like an old tiger, returned to the place of his last-remembered beauty: night baseball. On the night of May 24, 1935, just one day before Babe Ruth's last major league home run, the lights went on at the newly named Crosley Field

for the first night game in Major League history, passing the torch from one great "promotion," Babe Ruth, to another: night baseball.

The '30s would be remembered for happenings on the field as well, like the Detroit Tigers of 1934 and '35, led by the "G" men—Hank Greenberg, Charlie Gehringer and Goose Goslin; and the "Homer in the Gloamin'" by another "G," the Chicago Cubs' Gabby Hartnett, giving his club their fourth pennant in 10 years; and, finally, by another "G," Lou Gehrig; who, after 2,130 games, suffered what he called "a bad break" and was forced to retire by a fatal illness known as amyotrophic lateral sclerosis, now more commonly known as "Lou Gehrig's Disease."

By the end of the decade, with Joe DiMaggio having filled the sizeable void left by the departure of Babe Ruth by leading the Yankees to four straight championships, and Ted Williams leading the American League in RBI in his rookie year, the 1930s, which had started out, to cop a phrase from Charles Dickens, in "the worst of times," now had some of "the best of times" to look forward to.

DIAMOND DREAMS

WOMEN IN BASEBALL

Edith Haughton

Another favorite destination for many visitors to the Baseball Hall of Fame is the exhibit entitled Diamond Dreams, which celebrates the achievements of women in baseball.

Even the most casual moviegoer remembers the splendidly lighthearted movie *A League of Their Own*, the story of a women's baseball league whose players, according to one newspaper montage in the film, "traded their oven mitts for baseball mitts." The film was based upon the founding of the All-American Girls Professional Baseball League by industrialist Philip Wrigley during World War II to fill the void left by the wartime call-up of hundreds of players from the Major and minor leagues. The film tells the tale of the Rockford Peaches, one of four original teams in the league (along with the Kenosha Comets, the Racine Belles, and the South Bend Blue Sox), the female group-dynamic of the fifteen players and their relationship with their manager, Jimmy Dugan, loosely patterned after Hall of Famer Jimmie Foxx (who actually managed in the AAGPBL along with Max Carey, Dave Bancroft and Bill Wambsganss). The film ends with a scene of the women who had played in the league, several of whom were the league's real, as opposed to reel, alumnae, gathering at the Hall of Fame to attend the special ceremonies for the opening of the exhibit.

The uniform worn by Alta Weiss, who performed before crowds of more than 3,000 in the Cleveland area when she pitched. Describing her uniform, "The Girl Wonder" said, "I found that you can't play ball in skirts. I tried. I wore a skirt over my bloomers and nearly broke my neck. Finally, I was forced to discard it and now I always wear bloomers . . . but made so wide that the fullness gives a skirtlike effect."

Women have played a part in the game as far back as the 1860s, when students at Vassar College formed two clubs. In the years that followed, a handful played with and against men—like Alta Weiss, "The Girl Wonder," back in the first decade of the twentieth century, and Ila Borders, who became the first woman to win a college baseball game and then went on to play in men's professional games as a member of various independent professional teams in the 1990s. Their remarkable exploits, and those of others, are celebrated in this colorful "In the Game" display.

While the pioneering efforts of the AAGPBL and its players are honored in Diamond Dreams with numerous intriguing artifacts—including uniforms of the teams—the real pioneers of women's baseball go back almost to the beginning of the game itself.

As early as 1866 freshmen women at Vassar College founded two teams, the Laurel and the Abenakis clubs. The next year the first African-American women's baseball team, the Dolly Vardens, was formed in Philadelphia. It was also in Philadelphia where, in 1883, promoters fielded two teams, the Blue Stockings and the Red Stockings, young women in flowing skirts who called themselves the "Blondes" and the "Brunettes" and played a series of exhibition games, traveling as far away as Newark and New

York City. The *New York Times*, writing about their game in New York, called it "a ridiculous exhibition," and went on to write, "When five innings had been played, the game was called. The girls heaved long sighs of relief." The final score was Brunettes 54, Blondes 22.

In 1890 the *National Police Gazette* reported that a women's baseball club, which they dubbed simply as "Young Ladies' Baseball Club No. 1," was not only "competent," but also played men's clubs. The novelty of women playing against men soon caught on and in 1891 a team of Washington, Ohio society girls challenged a team of men. The men, chivalrously playing left-handed, won by a score of 22-15.

Soon there were clubs everywhere calling themselves "Bloomer Girls" although, truth be

DIAMOND DREAMS

Diamond DREAMS

"Take me out to the ball game," sang Katie Casey in the famous baseball anthem. Katie was not alone. Women have always loved and played the game and have worked hard to fulfill their baseball dreams. Stories of exceptional women and their achievements on the field, in the press box and in the front office pepper baseball history.

What positions will today's girls play in tomorrow's game?

WOMEN IN BASEBALL

The entryway for "Diamond Dreams, Women in Baseball."

told, there was occasionally a man or two wearing women's clothing on the team. There were "Bloomer Girls" teams in Missouri, Texas, Massachusetts, New York, and all points North, East, South, and West, roaming the highways and byways of America challenging men's semi-pro and amateur teams from the local areas. One of the so-called "Bloomer Girls" teams featured "the famous lady pitcher" Lizzie Arlington who actually pitched part of an inning for Ed Barrow's Reading, Pennsylvania Atlantic League team, giving up two hits and a walk. The local paper gave her performance a semi-rave, writing, "Miss Arlington might do among amateurs, but the sluggers of the Atlantic League would soon put her out of business." The article added, in a condescending manner, "But, for a woman, she is a success."

Other women soon joined the ranks of baseball; more specifically, men's baseball. M. E. Phelan played with the theretofore all-men's Flora Baseball Club of Indiana in 1903, and Alta Weiss, the "Girl Wonder," pitched for the semi-professional Vermillion, Ohio, Independents in 1907. Other female players who played on previously all-male clubs included Carita Masteller, Irma Gribble, two sisters, Irene and Ruth Basford, who pitched for opposing men's teams and 14-year-old Lizzie Murphy, known as the "Queen of Baseball," who played with a number of teams throughout New England and signed with the semi-professional Providence, Rhode Island, Independents in 1918.

Perhaps the most famous woman ever to take the field was Jackie Mitchell. Mitchell was the stuff of local legend, having once struck out nine men in

Lou Gehrig and Babe Ruth watching 17-year-old Jackie Mitchell, who, pitching in an exhibition game for the Chattanooga Lookouts on April 2, 1931, struck out both fabled Yankees.

Cap worn by Edith Houghton
of the Philadelphia Bobbies, 1922

donated by Edith Houghton

**Jersey and belt worn by Edith Houghton on the
Philadelphia Bobbies tour of Japan, 1925**

Before World War II, women's barnstorming clubs
the Philadelphia Bobbies toured the country play
local men's teams. In 1922, 10-year-old Edith Hou
joined the Bobbies as their starting shortstop. Sh
worked for the Philadelphia Phillies, becoming ba
first professional female scout.

donated by Edith Houghton

a row in an amateur game. Claiming she was taught to throw a baseball by none other than future Hall of Fame pitcher Dazzy Vance "when he lived next door to us in Memphis," Mitchell became the first female professional baseball player when she signed a contract with the Chattanooga Lookouts of the Southern Association in 1931. She made her first appearance in a Lookout uniform on April 2nd in an exhibition game against the New York Yankees, striking out Babe Ruth and Lou Gehrig and then walking Tony Lazzeri before being taken out to the cheers of the four thousand-plus fans who had come to watch her. Unfortunately, it was also her last appearance, as Commissioner Kenesaw Mountain Landis ruled within days that baseball was "too strenuous" for women and disallowed her contract.

Jackie Mitchell's "first" would be followed by so many other "firsts"—such as Bernice Gera becoming the first woman umpire in professional baseball, Mary Shane the first major league play-by-play announcer, Yvonne Burch the first girl to play in the Babe Ruth League, Edith Houghton the first female scout for a men's team (the Phillies)—that by the new millennium the "Diamond Dreams" of the few had become the diamond realities of the many.

Artifacts from the movie, *A League of Their Own*.

As the All-American Girls Baseball League grew with the addition of more teams—including the Grand Rapids (Michigan) Chicks, the Fort Wayne (Indiana) Daisies, the Kalamazoo (Michigan) Lassies, and the Peoria (Illinois) Red Wings, represented here by pictures of their stars—attendance at AAGBL games also grew, reaching nearly a million fans in 1948.

Bob Feller

The beginning of the fifth decade of the 20th century was thought by all those professional weight-guessers known as pundits to be but a mere extension of the '30s with the Yankees, winners of the last four World Series, picked to win yet again. However, in a season that caused baseball fans to wonder if their faith in Gibraltar had been misplaced, the 1940 edition of the Yankees finished third, two games behind the pennant-winning Detroit Tigers who, in turn, lost the Series to the Cincinnati Reds.

But the stars aligned in 1941 and the Yankees reclaimed their usual perch atop the American League for the fifth time in six years, winning by a 19-game margin over second-place Boston.

However, it wasn't so much the Yankees' year as it was the year of the man teammate Red Ruffing called "The Great DiMaggio," the year of his 56-game hitting streak, a feat that captured the headlines and the imagination of the nation as no athlete had since the heyday of Babe Ruth. It was also the year of Ted Williams who, during the period of DiMaggio's streak—from May 15th through July 16th—actually outhit DiMaggio, .412 to .400, finishing with a season-ending average of .406, the first American Leaguer to bat .400 since 1923—and the last Major Leaguer to do so.

The Yankees' opponents in the '41 Series were the Brooklyn Dodgers, a colorful cast of characters who had gone through the season awhooping and ahollering and akicking everyone else out of their way, edging the Cardinals by 2½ games on the National side during a boisterous stretch drive. However, the Series was less classic than catastrophic

A jacket of Enos "Country" Slaughter, a member of the St. Louis Cardinals for 13 years (1938–42; 1946–53).

for the Brooklyn faithful. The first bit of misfortune befell the Dodgers in Game Three when, with the Series tied at one game apiece and Brooklyn pitcher Freddie Fitzsimmons pitching masterfully, a line drive broke his knee in the seventh inning and reliever Hugh Casey gave up two runs in the eighth to lose, 2-1. Then, in Game Four, calamity struck as the Dodgers, just one strike away from tying the series, lost when catcher Mickey Owen let a third-strike pitch get away and the Yankees capitalized on Owen's muff to score four times for a heart-breaking Dodgers loss; the Yanks finished them off to win the Series the next day.

The Yankees repeated as American League champs in 1942 and '43, splitting World Series wins with the St. Louis Cardinals. But by then the winds of war were sweeping the country and

STAN MUSIAL

Take one part corkscrew, two parts carpenter's rule bent double, and add a pinch of what Hall of Fame pitcher Ted Lyons called "the look of a little boy peeking around the corner of a door," and you have Stan Musial's batting stance, less that of a classicist than a contortionist. That odd batting stance achieved an eye-popping list of accomplishments in his 22-year career, which included seven batting titles, six times leading the National League in hits, five times in triples and runs scored, eight times in doubles, twice in RBI, and three MVP Awards. The story is told of how one day in 1947 Cincinnati pitcher Ewell Blackwell threw one of his sidearm sizzlers past Musial for a third strike. Unfortunately, he threw it past the catcher as well, allowing Musial to go all the way to second on the passed ball. In the Reds' dugout the manager could be heard moaning, "That guy Musial is so good that even when he fans, you're lucky to hold him to two bases." That was the man called "Stan the Man."

JOE DIMAGGIO

The Great DiMaggio was Hemingway's definition of "grace under pressure," a player with no fault lines. Casey Stengel, who had seen them all, said, "Joe never threw to a wrong base in his career. And he was thrown out trying to take an extra base only once . . . and the umpire was wrong on that one. He made the rest of the players look like plumbers." From the moment he first appeared in pinstripes, leading the New York Yankees to four pennants and four World Series in his first four years in a Major League uniform, through his incredible 56-game hitting streak in 1941, down through his immortalization by Paul Simon as a long-lost hero in the song, "Mrs. Robinson," the legend of the great Joe D. has grown with each passing year.

Joe DiMaggio's 1951 Championship ring.

TED WILLIAMS

In one of his rare unguarded moments Ted Williams drew back the curtain and gave the world a brief glimpse of what motivated the man called "The Splendid Splinter," saying, "All I want out of life is that when I walk down the street folks will turn and say: 'There goes the greatest hitter who ever lived.' " And to many who saw this spindly six-foot-three-inch figure with the shape of a baseball bat with a severe thyroid condition, he was. Six times he led the league in total bases, six times in batting, six times in runs scored, four times in home runs, and nine times in slugging average. The last man to hit over .400 with a .406 batting average in 1941, and the oldest man ever to win a batting title at the age of 39 in 1957 when he won his fifth title with a .388 average—a record he would break the next season at the age of 40 when he won his sixth title—Williams ended his 19-year career with a lifetime .344 batting average and a .634 slugging average. He might just have been what he always wanted to be: "The greatest hitter who ever lived."

many Major Leaguers were caught up in the draft—71 players in 1942; 219 in 1943; 342 in 1944; and 384 in 1945.

Even though many players, including Bob Feller, Hank Greenberg, Joe DiMaggio and Ted Williams, would go marching off to fight for Democracy, baseball, given the "green light" by President Roosevelt, would soldier on. For the duration of the War the rosters were filled with draft-deferred players as scouts scoured the countryside looking for beardless puppy-youths and bearded grizzlies well past their-sell-by-dates. The talent that remained was, for the most part, so inexpressibly dreary that the St. Louis Browns—led by 34-year-old pitcher Sigmund Jakucki, who had an 0-and-3 record his last time around, some eight years before—won the American League pennant for the first and only time in their history. Unfortunately, they met their intracity rivals, the Cardinals, in the World Series, losing in six games.

The last wartime World Series in 1945 pitted the Detroit Tigers against the Chicago Cubs. Asked by someone who would win, Chicago sportswriter Warren Brown could only look at the line-ups, shake his head and answer, "I've seen 'em both play and I don't think either team can win it." Despite Brown's less-than-enthusiastic appraisal of the talent, or lack thereof, the Tigers, behind pitcher Hal Newhouser, out-lasted the Cubs in seven rather uneventful games.

With the end of the War in '45, Johnny came marching home, along with Bob, Joe and Ted. New York manager Mel Ott, sizing up the situation, cautioned his now expendable troops, "You were all right when we had nothing better, lads, but the pros are back now." And as the "pros" were mustered out of the service, their replacements were mustered out of baseball, casualties of the peace.

The team that benefited most from veteran returnees was the Boston Red Sox, their ranks swollen with 17 returning servicemen including Ted Williams, Bobby Doerr, Johnny Pesky and Dom DiMaggio. Together the 17 contributed 65 percent of Boston's 104 wins and 59 percent of their 1,441 hits to lead Boston to its first pennant since 1918, winning by 12 games.

Over in the National League the pennant race was a two-team cakewalk as the teams with the most returning veterans in the National League, the St. Louis Cardinals and the Brooklyn Dodgers, finished in a flat-footed dead heat for the pennant. Playing an unprecedented playoff series to settle the matter, the Cardinals, with 15 returning veterans, beat the Dodgers, with only 13, by the same margin, two games, winning the playoff, two-games-to-none.

The handicappers, figuring the Red Sox had more firepower, installed them as 20-9 favorites. But the Cardinals had batting champion Stan Musial and RBI leader Enos Slaughter. However, it wasn't a run batted in by Slaughter that won the Series, but a run scored, his feet hollering "Gangway, here I come!" as he raced around the basepaths like a greyhound on a two-out liner over short, sliding into home well ahead of the throw to

.300 .320 .320 .330 .330 .315 .310
.310 .340 .340 .350 .340 .340 .320
.310 .340 .340 .350 .340 .340 .320
.340 .380 .380 .400 .390 .390 .320
.360 .390 .390 .400 .390 .390 .320
.360 .390 .390 .400 .380 .380 .310
.320 .340 .340 .330 .300 .300 .280
320 .340 .340 .330 .275 .270 .260
280 .300 .300 .300 .260 .250 .250
.270 .290 .300 .300 .250 .240 .240
250 .270 .270 .260 .240 .240 .230

THE SCIENCE OF HITTING

In the long history of baseball there have only been two superstars who have been reputed to have had the ability to read the signature on the ball as it made its way to the plate. One was Rogers Hornsby; the other Ted Williams, whose "eye" was legendary. Once, in a game in Cleveland, umpire Hank Soar decided to test Williams' claim that he knew the strike zone better than any umpire and deliberately called a strike on a pitch that was six inches outside. Williams said nothing at the time, but on his next at bat turned to Soar and said, "You know, that strike you called on me last time was six inches outside." All Soar could say was, "You're absolutely right."

That "eye" is on display in this special exhibit which illustrates what Williams called "The Science of Hitting," a science that enabled him to gauge each and every pitch and its potential for a safe hit. Using that science, and his "eye," Williams, who called hitting a ball "the hardest single feat in sports," won six battling titles—including hitting .406 in 1941, the last time the magic mark of .400 was achieved—and six times led the league in total bases, four times in runs batted in, and nine times in slugging average, finishing his 19-year career with a lifetime .344 batting average and .634 slugging average.

score the winning run in the seventh and deciding game for the Cardinals' third World Series title in five seasons.

The year 1946 would prove to be not just the season Slaughter broke baseball's base-running sound barrier, but also the year that Jackie Robinson broke a more important barrier: the color barrier. The man responsible for that was Branch Rickey, the man who had been responsible for the Cardinals' "farm system," one that had produced several great players, including Slaughter, and seven National League pennants in 16 seasons. Now the president of the Brooklyn Dodgers, Rickey sought the player who could break the color line and have the courage to hold it. The player he chose was Jackie Robinson. Asking Robinson, "I want a man with courage enough not to fight back . . . can you do that?" Rickey got his reassurance from Robinson, who answered, "Mr. Rickey, if you want to take the gamble, I promise you there'll be no incidents."

Brought up from Montreal in 1947, Robinson proved to be worth more than just a "gamble," as he called it. He proved to be the necessary piece that would carry the Dodgers to the pennant, batting .297, scoring 125 runs, leading the league in

stolen bases, and being selected as baseball's first "Rookie of the Year."

Their opponent in the Series that year was the New York Yankees, winners of their fourth American League pennant in the decade, but first in four years. Their World Series would be remembered as the Series three men, cameo players all, crowded the stars off the stage and, in their final hurrahs, gained timeless fame: Bill Bevens, Al Gionfriddo and Cookie Lavagetto.

In Game Four, Yankee pitcher Bevens stood on the cusp of greatness, only one out away from the first no-hitter in Series history. With two men on base, courtesy of Bevens' ninth and tenth walks of the game, Dodger pinch-hitter Cookie Lavagetto stepped into the batter's box. After swinging and missing on the first pitch, Lavagetto caught Bevens' 137th pitch of the game, smiting it on a line toward right field where it hit one of those little patches of advertising high on the Ebbets' Field wall and caromed at an angle back past Yankee outfielder Tommy Henrich. The two base runners scampered around the bases with the tying and winning runs, tying the Series at two games apiece.

After Joe DiMaggio's heroics won Game Five, the Series switched back to Yankee Stadium. With the Yankees threatening to tie the game in the sixth inning, DiMaggio hit another one of his shots, this one headed into the bullpen in faraway left field. But, at the last second, little Al Gionfriddo reached out his right gloved hand and made a fully extended catch of the ball at the 415-foot mark. Up in the broadcast booth Red Barber was in the process of calling DiMaggio's "home run," telling the nationwide audience, "Swung on and belted. It's a long one, deep to left-center. Back goes Gionfriddo . . . Back . . . Back . . . Back. . . . He makes a one-handed catch against the bullpen! Ohhhhhhhh, Doctor. . . ." Down on the field, DiMaggio, almost at second, for one split second allowed people a glimpse behind the normal curtain hiding his feelings by kicking at the dirt in frustration.

The Dodgers held on to win and force a seventh game which the Yankees, coming from behind, won in the most excitement-packed Series in years, thanks to the efforts of three players at

ROBERT WILLIAM ANDREW FELLER
CLEVELAND A. L. 1936 TO 1941
1945 TO 1956
PITCHED 3 NO-HIT GAMES IN A.L., 12 ONE HIT GAMES.
SET MODERN STRIKEOUT RECORD WITH 18 IN GAME.
348 FOR SEASON. LED A.L. IN VICTORIES 6 (ONE TIE)
SEASONS. LIFETIME RECORD: WON 266, LOST 162, P.C.
.621, E.R. AVERAGE 3.25, STRUCKOUT 2581.

BOB FELLER

Signed by the Cleveland Indians for a bonus of $1 and an autographed baseball, young Bob Feller, at the age of 17, made his Major League debut as a starter by striking out 15 St. Louis Browns to come within one strikeout of the American League record and two of the Major League record. Feller was to use his superhuman speed, along with what teammate Willis Hudlin called "the hardest and best curveball I ever saw," to record strikeout after strikeout and set record after record, leading the American League in K's seven times and 348 K's in 1946, one shy of Rube Waddell's all-time record, striking out every American Leaguer to face him with the exception of Barney McCosky. Even though his final career stats read 266 wins and 2,581 strikeouts, who knows what this pitching great's statistics would have been if, at the peak of his career, he hadn't served four years in the military during World War II. The author of three no-hitters—including the only Opening Day no-hitter in history—Feller became the first pitcher since Walter Johnson and Christy Mathewson to be elected to the Hall of Fame in his first year of eligibility.

their journey's end—Bevens, Gionfriddo and Lavagetto, three players who would never play another game in the Majors.

For the fifth time in five years the American League had a different pennant winner in 1948, this time the Cleveland Indians, who won in a one-game playoff with the Boston Red Sox. The Indians had an outstanding pitching staff which included Bob Feller, Bob Lemon, and rookie phenomenon Gene Bearden as well as late-season acquisitions Satchel Paige (described in press releases as "40 or older") and Sam Zoldak, plus an airtight defense in shortstop-manager Lou Boudreau and second baseman Joe Gordon. They also possessed an explosiveness at the plate in the bats of Boudreau, Gordon, Ken Keltner and Larry Doby. Their opponent in the '48 Fall Classic was the Boston Braves of "Spahn and Sain and Two Days Rain," appearing in their first World Series since the "Miracle" Braves of 1914. Both Spahn and Sain won a game, but it wasn't enough as Cleveland won its first world championship in 28 years in six games.

The 1949 American League pennant race was the most exciting since 1908 with the Boston Red Sox, winners of more games over the previous three seasons than any other team in baseball, and the preseason favorites to win, facing, who else, the Yankees. Very few thought the New York Yankees

posed a threat, especially after suffering through a season with an injured-reserve list that approximated a WWII body count with no less than 71 injuries, from torn tendons and facial lacerations to severed nerves and injured heels. Still, due to the imaginative platooning by new manager Casey Stengel and the timely hitting of the oft-injured Joe DiMaggio and the newly acquired Johnny Mize, along with that of Tommy Henrich, Yogi Berra, and Phil Rizzuto, the Yankees managed to limp into the final day of the season in a 96-57 tie with the Red Sox. In the first head-to-head battle for the American League supremacy on the last day of the season since 1908, the Yankees prevailed 5-3.

Over in the National League the Brooklyn Dodgers again won the pennant, like the Yankees, in their final game. For the third time in the decade the two intra-city rivals faced off in what was becoming an annual event, a "Subway Series." The result, unfortunately for the team now affectionately called "Dem Bums," was the same as the previous two times—a victory for the Yankees.

As the '40s came to a close, the two most dominant teams in baseball, the New York Yankees and the Brooklyn Dodgers, had met in the World Series three times. Who could predict that these two rivals would, like the watering of last year's crops, meet again, and again, and again, and yet again during the coming decade?

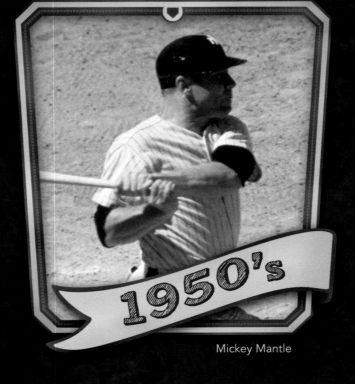

1950's

Mickey Mantle

The 1950s were a decade of change. Not on the field where the Yankees were winning with monotonous regularity, but off the field where franchises were realigning baseball's map.

Since 1903 baseball teams had maintained their headquarters and hindquarters in the same place. The first hints of wanderlust came in 1953 as the Boston Braves began dropping hints they were Milwaukee-bound. Even though plans for the Braves' movement were already afoot, many, including those in the Boston press, refused to believe that the Braves would abandon the town they had called home since 1871. One day, when the Braves were in Vero Beach, Florida, to play the Dodgers in a preseason exhibition game, two sets of sportswriters showed up to cover the game, one set from Boston wearing caps

with "B's" on the front and the other from Milwaukee wearing caps bearing the letter "M." One Boston writer, pointing to his cap, said "We're the Boston Braves. The other thing, the 'M', stands for 'Maybe.'" But, by opening day, the "M" had come to mean "Matter of Fact" as the Braves moved, lock, stock and players, to Milwaukee.

As soon as the owners of other troubled franchises saw the Braves strike gold in Milwaukee by setting Major League baseball's best attendance mark, U-Hauls began pulling up next to stadiums as others joined in baseball's version of the gold rush—the St. Louis Browns moving to Baltimore in 1954, and the Philadelphia A's transferring their franchise to Kansas City in '55. By the end of the decade other teams would pull up

Although it always seemed to observers that Willie Mays's feet were outfitted with wings, like those of Mercury, the god of speed, he wore these mortal-looking shoes outrunning the ball on the basepaths and in the outfield. Pictured here are the shoes he wore when he scored his 2,000th run.

The uniform of Duke Snider who, in his 11 years in Brooklyn as the only regular left-handed hitter in the Dodger line-up, hit 316 home runs, scored 994 runs, drove in 1,003 runs, and helped "Dem Bums" win five National League pennants and one World Championship.

The 1950 Philadelphia Phillies, better known as "The Whiz Kids," winners of only their second pennant in their long

their roots as well, following Horace Greely's advice to "Go West, young man."

The 1950s was also the era of big bonuses paid to highly touted but untried prospects. Within three months of Bob Feller signing a contract for $45,000, the Cleveland Indians signed a 17-year-old high school pitcher named Floyd Penfold, called by the Indians "the best prospect since Feller," for $150,000. Meanwhile the Boston Red Sox gave 19-year-old infielder Dick Pedrotti a three-year, $75,000 contract. Neither so-called "Bonus Baby" saw action in the Majors.

One "Bonus Baby" who would begin to make it after the Dodgers moved to L.A. in 1958 was Sandy Koufax, who joined other future superstars such as Whitey Ford, Mickey Mantle, Willie Mays, Hank Aaron, Roberto Clemente, Brooks Robinson, and Frank Robinson in a long chorus line of newcomers who helped make the 1950s one of baseball's great decades.

On the field the New York Yankees, in a stop-me-if-you've-seen-this-before manner, with the help of a few of those newcomers like Ford and Mantle along with stalwarts Yogi Berra, Billy Martin and Gil McDougald, gave new meaning to the word "dynasty" as they won World Series after World Series. It became so routine that Yankee veterans would greet rookies with "Don't screw up my World Series check" on the first day of spring training. In 1950 they defeated the "Whiz Kid" Phillies; in 1951, the miracle Giants of Bobby Thomson's "Shot Heard 'Round the World"; and in 1952 and '53, those perennial bridesmaids, the Brooklyn Dodgers, who would again have to, as their faithful chanted, "Wait 'till Next Year."

In 1954 the Yankees' seemingly permanent residency atop the American League standings was interrupted by the Cleveland Indians who won an American League-record 111 games and went into the World Series a heavy favorite to beat the National League champion New York Giants. The story of the Series was the story of the first game, which went into extra innings, courtesy of Willie Mays' back-to-the-plate catch of Vic Wertz's towering 425-foot fly in the eighth inning, forever known as just "The Catch." In the

bottom of the tenth, with the score tied 2-2 and two men on base, Giants manager Leo Durocher inserted Dusty Rhodes into the line-up to bat for Monte Irvin, instructing Rhodes to "get up there and hit one out." Rhodes, who had every intention of taking the first pitch, watched as Cleveland starter Bob Lemon hung a curve ball for his first offering. That did it! Rhodes less swung than merely browsed the ball with the bat, sending it 257 feet, eight inches into the shortest right field stands in the majors for a home run and a 5-2 Giant win. As Rhodes rounded first, he chanced a look over at Lemon who had just flung his glove high in the air in disgust. As Rhodes remembered it, "Lemon's glove went farther than the ball." The rest of the Series was anti-climatic as the Giants won the next three games for the National League's first Series sweep since the "Miracle" Braves won four straight from the Philadelphia A's back in 1914.

The Yankees reclaimed their usual perch in 1955, while over in the National League the Dodgers reclaimed theirs, setting up the fifth Series meeting in nine years between the two rivals. In baseball-mad Brooklyn, rooting for the Dodgers was both an obsession and a religion—so much so that when Hodges went 0-for-21 in the '52 Series, Father Herbert Redmond of Brooklyn's St. Francis Roman Catholic Church told his parishioners "Go home, keep your Ten Commandments and pray for Gil Hodges." Every proud Brooklynite worth his "hard-berled" egg prayed that this would be "the year" they had long waited for, the year they would finally, after five times coming up short, beat their hated rivals. After two games and two Brooklyn losses, it began to look like another Dodger nightmare. However, with the next three games scheduled to be played in that old duenna of a ballpark, Ebbets Field, where dreams had been made and unmade in the past, the faithful were now about to witness their fondest dream as "Dem Bums" swept all three games. Now it was back to Yankee Stadium where winning for the Dodgers had always been akin to taking cheese from a set mousetrap and winning the Series from the Yankees even more

NEW YORK YANKEES   *1950 World Champion's*

Led by five future Hall of Famers—Joe DiMaggio, Casey Stengel, Yogi Berra, Whitey Ford, and Phil Rizzuto—
the New York Yankees won the second of their five consecutive World Championships in 1950, beating the
Philadelphia Phillies in four games.

difficult. After losing Game Six and tortured by such visions, Brooklyn fans finally had a chance to rejoice after 23-year-old Johnny Podres shut down the Bronx Bombers' bats—with an able assist by left-fielder Sandy Amoros, who ran down Yogi Berra's opposite-field drive in the sixth—winning on Gil Hodges' two RBI's, 2-0. This was that "next year" the Dodger faithful had been waiting for all their lives.

The next year the same two teams gathered again in concert assembled, only the results were reversed. This time the Dodgers won the first two games, only to fall to the Yankees in seven, with Don Larsen winning Game Five in the only perfect game in World Series history.

Even before the last out of the '56 Series had been made, rumblings could be heard by Brooklyn fans that they may have seen the last of their beloved "Bums." Dodgers president Walter O'Malley, having had enough of outmoded Ebbets Field, turned to New York Parks Commissioner Robert Moses for the land to build a new privately financed stadium at the corner of Atlantic and Flatbush Avenues. Turned down, O'Malley turned to the city of Los Angeles, which made him an offer he couldn't refuse: 350 acres, free of charge,

to build his stadium on. Meanwhile, Giants owner Horace Stoneham, having watched his club's attendance drop from 1.1 million in its championship season of '54 to sixth in the league the following season and last in 1956, begin casting wistful eyes west for a new location. After the '57 season, the two picked up their franchises and moved them to California. Suddenly the once geographically challenged Major Leagues had spread coast-to-coast, from sea to shining sea.

Back on the field, the 1957 and '58 World Series were split between the Milwaukee Braves and the New York Yankees—the Yankees, by beating the Braves in '58, having beaten every one of the original eight National League teams in the Series.

The year 1959 was only the second time in the decade in which a team not named the Yankees won the American League pennant, the Chicago White Sox, led by Nellie Fox and Luis Aparicio afield and Early Wynn on the mound, winning their first pennant since 1919. Despite winning the first game of the Series, 11-0, the Chisox fell to the Los Angeles Dodgers in six games.

The '50s had become the decade of change. But, as Jimmy Durante used to say: "You ain't seen nothing yet!"

LIE MAYS

Bankhead, the famed actress, once said, "There have been two geniuses in the
. Willie Mays and Willie Shakespeare." For anyone who ever saw the nearest thing
plete player the majors has ever seen—hitting for average and power, running
s with a devil-Mays-care verve and playing the outfield with flashy grace—he was
a genius in cleats. Playing baseball like a schoolboy out on a romp, Mays gave
to Roy Campanella's definition of a ball player: "You gotta be a man to play
for a living, but you gotta have a lot of little boy in you, too." From his legendary
f the bat of Vic Wertz in the 1954 World Series to his constant racing out from
s one-size-too-small cap to his rounding the bases with the daring-do of a Cobb
inson, the image of Mays is one of a player just having fun. That fun translated
3 hits, 660 home runs, 2,062 runs scored, and 1,903 lifetime runs batted in.

WILLIE HOWARD M
"THE SAY HEY K
NEW YORK N.L., SAN FRA
NEW YORK N.L., 1951
ONE OF BASEBALL'S MOST CO
EXCITING STARS, EXCELLED IN A
THE GAME. THIRD IN HOMERS (6C
AND TOTAL BASES (6,066) SEVE
(.285) AND RBIS (1,903) FIRST
, OUTFIELDER (7,095) FIRST
300 HOMERS AND 300 STEALS L
BATTING ONCE, SLUGGING FIVE
RUNS AND STEALS FOUR SEASO
MVP IN 1954 AND 1965. PLA
ALL-STAR GAMES - A

1960's

Roberto Clemente

Bill Veeck once said, "Baseball is the only thing besides the paper clip that hasn't changed." By the 1960s that was no longer true. That whirring noise you heard was the sound of change as the National Pastime's elders reinvented the baseball wheel.

The decade had started off in typical fashion with the New York Yankees winning the American League pennant for the tenth time in 12 years, but the Bronx Bombers lost the 1960 World Series to the Pittsburgh Pirates on Bill Mazeroski's ninth-inning home run in the 7th game even though the Yankees outscored the Pirates in the Series, 55 to 27. Mazeroski's home run was but the first olive out of the jar as the home runs kept rolling out in 1961 with the Yankees, led by Roger Maris's record-setting 61, hitting an all-time team high of 240 in a season in which eight major leaguers hit 40 or more. In 1962 over 3,000 balls flew out of big-league stadia, prompting one writer to remark, "we didn't sell our atomic bomb secrets to the Russians, we sold them to Spalding."

Baseball, like nature, abhors a vacuum. With vacuums left by departing teams in Washington and New York, and with several other cities unsuccessful in detouring one of the floating franchises to their hubs, baseball decided to rearrange its map in the most extreme way: by expanding. Their hand may have been forced when a new league, the Continental League, announced plans to create a third major league. Taking notice, the

The cap Tom Seaver wore on April 22, 1970, when he set a modern major league record by striking out 10 consecutive batters, and tied Steve Carlton's record of 19 K's in a 9-inning game. For 11 years (1967–77), Tom Seaver was the mainstay of the New York Mets' pitching staff, winning 189 games and posting a win-loss percentage of .632—in fact, every year his win-loss percentage was better than the team's.

Boston's "Impossible Dream" team of 1967, a team that went from a half-game out of last place in 1966 to the American League pennant in '67. The bat in the middle was used by Carl Yastrzemski on July 24, 1979, to hit his 400th career home run. Less than two months later, on September 12, Yaz would hit a single off New York's Jim Beattie for his 3,000th career hit, making him the first American Leaguer to have both 3,000 hits and 400 home runs.

With this swing of the bat Roger Maris breaks Babe Ruth's 34-year single-season home run record with his 61st home run off Boston's Tracy Stallard, October 1, 1961.

National League grabbed two of the choicest staked-out Continental League territories for expansion in 1962: Houston and New York. However, the American League jumped their planned start date, voting to expand into Washington and Los Angeles a year earlier. Created out of whole cloth, the newly named Los Angeles Angels and the anachronistically titled Washington Senators lived up, or down, to expectations their first seasons with the Angels finishing eighth and the Senators tenth in their newly formed ten-team American League—the first time since 1899 that any league had fielded more than eight teams. The following season the Senators, following the pattern set by their old namesakes, finished, as the old saying goes, "First in war, first in peace, and last in the American League." Los Angeles however, became, the poster team for expansion, rising to third place with their own homegrown hero, no-hit pitcher Bo Belinsky.

The National League had a success story of its own in the expansion New York Mets. In an irony of ironies, when the Dodgers and Giants left town after '57, leaving their fans with no team to cheer

Ticket for the seventh and final game of the 1960 World Series won by the Pittsburgh Pirates over the New York Yankees on Bill Mazeroski's bottom-of-the-ninth inning home run, 10-9.

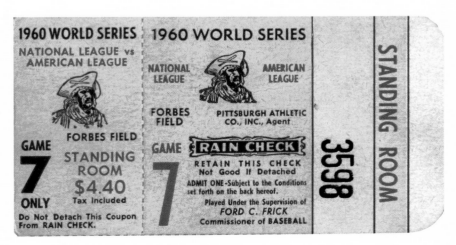

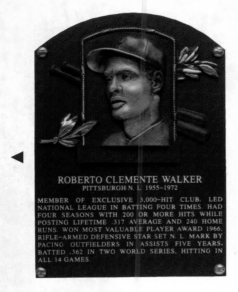

ROBERTO CLEMENTE WALKER
PITTSBURGH N. L. 1955-1972

MEMBER OF EXCLUSIVE 3,000-HIT CLUB. LED
NATIONAL LEAGUE IN BATTING FOUR TIMES. HAD
FOUR SEASONS WITH 200 OR MORE HITS WHILE
POSTING LIFETIME .317 AVERAGE AND 240 HOME
RUNS. WON MOST VALUABLE PLAYER AWARD 1966.
RIFLE-ARMED DEFENSIVE STAR SET N. L. MARK BY
PACING OUTFIELDERS IN ASSISTS FIVE YEARS.
BATTED .362 IN TWO WORLD SERIES, HITTING IN
ALL 14 GAMES.

ROBERTO CLEMENTE

"Roberto Clemente might have been as good a player as ever played the game," wrote Pulitzer Prize-winning sportswriter Jim Murray. And for one decade, the 1960s, Clemente was just that, playing with 100-watt excitement and lighting up the field as few before him had. With the most hits and highest batting average for the decade, Clemente won four batting titles in the '60s, including a .357 average in 1967, the highest season average for a right-handed batter since Joe DiMaggio's .381 in 1939. If Clemente was sparkling in the batter's box, he was absolutely incandescent in the field, cutting off balls hit into the gap and cutting down baserunners with his rifle arm, leading the National League in outfield assists five times. Clemente's life ended tragically when, on December 31, 1972, on a humanitarian mission to Nicaragua, his plane, carrying supplies for earthquake victims, crashed. The Hall of Fame honored Clemente the next year by inducting him.

for, it was only natural to think that their fans would somehow feed their baseball "fix" by switching their allegiance to the Yankees. However, such was not the case as the Yankees attendance actually dropped during yet another pennant-winning year in '58. Neither Dodger nor Giant fans showed the slightest interest in supporting their hated American League rivals. So it was that the National League filled this vacuum by creating a new entity, one which would appeal to National League fans bereft of a team in which they could invest their rooting interest. The Mets suddenly proved to be everything the Yankees weren't, a loveable underdog, creating a whole new fan base which viewed the Mets as an identifiable champion of lost causes, cheering for them when they won, which was infrequent, and supporting them when they lost, which was frequent. Even though the 1962 Mets set a modern record for futility, losing 120 games, 900,000 newly born Mets and old-time National League fans still showed up at the Polo Grounds to root for *their* team.

The talent available to the Mets was so unbelievably woeful that Mets manager Casey Stengel, drafting from a long laundry list of players found leaning against the job-wanted columns of *The Sporting News,* could only explain his selection of catcher Hobie Landrith as his first choice with: "If you don't have a catcher, you'll have all those passed balls." When asked the potential of two 20-year-old recruits, Casey pointed to one and said, "That one there . . . in ten years he has a chance to

be a star." Then, pointing to the other, he said, "And in ten years he has a chance to be thirty." Still, Casey called them, "My Amazin' Mets." Perhaps the most "Amazin'" of them all was a first baseman named Marvin Eugene Throneberry, whose initials, not incidentally, spelled "M.E.T."

Throneberry was the loveable prototype of ineptness as the Mets lost game-after-game, some in ways theretofore unknown to baseballkind, and some owing to Throneberry, who not only led National League first basemen in fielding errors, but made them on the basepaths as well.

One day the Mets were playing at home in the Polo Grounds and Throneberry chanced to hit what looked like a long triple. As he came roaring into third, there was the umpire holding his hands in the air calling Throneberry out for failing to touch first. As Stengel began his slow amble out of the dugout to do battle with the umpire, first base coach Cookie Lavagetto laid a hand on his arm to intercept him, "Forget it, Case," Lavagetto whispered, "he didn't touch second either." It didn't matter to the Mets faithful, labeled "The New Breed," as they continued to come out to root, root, root for their home team, many carrying homemade banners made out of bedsheets expressing their undying affection for their loveable losers.

Across town the Yankees, per invoice, continued to win pennant-after-pennant, four more from 1961 to 1964, capping them off with World Series wins in 1961 over the Cincinnati Reds and in 1962 over the San Francisco Giants, who had won the National League championship in a post-season playoff against the Dodgers in a replay of their historic 1951 playoff. The Yankees' storied supremacy came to an end in the World Series of 1963 and '64 losing to the Dodgers in four games in '63 and the following year to the Cardinals in seven.

Meanwhile, concerned that "the pitchers needed help urgently" after the home run deluge of 1961 and '62, Baseball Commissioner Ford Frick persuaded the owners to "tweak" the rules favoring batting over pitching by increasing the strike zone back to its pre-1950 proportions, from the top of the armpit to the bottom of the knee. The effects were predictable: strikeouts increased, walks and ERAs decreased, home run totals and batting averages shriveled. The batting-average slump was most noticeable, sinking to its lowest level since the "Dead Ball" era back in the first decade of the century. In 1968, Carl Yastremski won the American League batting title with a .301 average, the lowest winning average in history, and the same year the New York Yankees posted a team batting average of .214, the lowest team batting average in over half a century.

The year 1968 became the Year of the Pitcher with Bob Gibson posting an ERA of 1.12, the lowest since Walter Johnson's 1.09 in 1931, and both leagues' pitchers having a combined earned run average of under three runs a game, the lowest since 1918. Denny McLain became the first American League pitcher since 1931, and the first Major League pitcher since 1934, to win 30 games. So the owners "re-tweaked" the rules in an attempt to restore the balance between pitchers and batters, lowering the pitcher's mound and restoring the strike zone to its 1962 proportions. The restoration of the balance between pitcher and batter not only brought back the home run, the number hit in '69 1,124 more than in '68, but also brought back the fans, major league attendance increasing in 1969 by more than four million over the previous season (due to expansion and increased popularity).

The 1960s was also a decade of continued movement, both on the map and in the standings.

Two franchises, the Braves and the A's, moved from their second cities, Milwaukee and Kansas City, to their third, Atlanta and Oakland. One team, the New York Yankees, their string of successes coming to an end with their 1964 pennant, dropped through the standings, free-falling from first for four years to sixth in 1965 and dead last in '66. While the Yankees were going one way, other teams were going the other: the Minnesota Twins won the American League pennant in 1965; the Baltimore Orioles in '66; the "Impossible Dream" Boston Red Sox won in'67; the Detroit Tigers in '68; and the Baltimore Orioles won again in'69. Over in the National League the pennant winners were the Los Angeles Dodgers in '65 and '66 and the St. Louis Cardinals in '67 and '68.

But the big story of 1969 was the New York Mets. For their first seven years the Mets had compiled one of the sorriest records in Major League history—a .348 "winning" percentage, five times passing the dreaded 100-loss mark and finishing last five times in the 10-team National League, and in 1962 finishing 60½ games behind the league leader and a mere 18 games behind the ninth-place finisher. All of that was behind them in 1969 as Gil Hodges' crew went from second-worst to first, storming back from 10 games behind the Chicago Cubs on August 13 to win the National League Eastern Division title by eight games. Then, in the new configuration of the leagues—two divisions of six teams each to accommodate the two expansion franchises, San Diego and Montreal—the Mets swept the Western Division champions, the Atlanta Braves, three games to none in the inaugural League Championship Series. That was nothing compared to what they did in the World Series as the "Amazin's" defeated the Baltimore Orioles in five games in as big a "Miracle" as that of the 1914 Boston Braves.

So the decade, which had started off with the addition of four new teams, had come full circle with one of those expansion teams winning the World Series in the decade's final year. Baseball, thought by some to be "irrelevant" in a decade of change and turmoil, had once again become relevant and reasserted itself as the National Pastime.

SANFORD KOUFAX
"SANDY"
BROOKLYN N.L. 1955-1957
LOS ANGELES N.L. 1958-1966
SET ALL-TIME RECORDS WITH 4 NO-HITTERS
IN 4 YEARS, CAPPED BY 1965 PERFECT GAME,
AND BY CAPTURING EARNED-RUN TITLE FIVE
SEASONS IN A ROW. 1962-1966. WON 25 OR
MORE GAMES THREE TIMES. HAD 11 SHUTOUTS
IN 1963. STRIKEOUT LEADER FOUR TIMES,
WITH RECORD 382 IN 1965. FANNED 18 IN A
GAME TWICE. MOST VALUABLE PLAYER 1963.
CY YOUNG AWARD WINNER 1963-65-66.

SANDY KOUFAX

No pitcher since Lefty Grove in the late '20s and early '30s has so thoroughly dominated batters as Sandy Koufax. Trying to hit the great Dodger pitcher was, in the words of Hall of Famer Willie Stargell, "like trying to drink coffee with a fork." Referred to by the press as "The Man with the Golden Arm," Koufax was well-nigh unhittable as he proved by throwing four no-hitters in back-to-back-to-back-to-back seasons, 1962-65, one of those a perfect game. The man known for being able to lift his game to uncharted heights finally retired after having trouble lifting his golden arm, suffering from painful traumatic arthritis in his left elbow. Before retiring in 1966, *all* Koufax had done was lead the National League in ERA five times, most strikeouts four, most wins three and most shutouts three—all in his last six seasons.

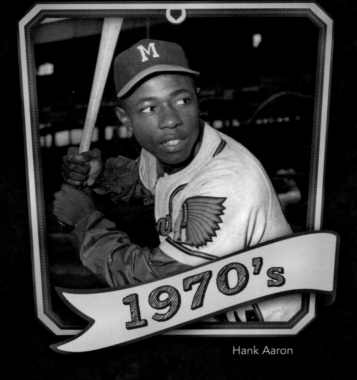

1970's

Hank Aaron

In many ways the decade of the '70s was reminiscent of that old rhyme, "something old, something new/something borrowed, something blue."

The "old" part was the Baltimore Orioles who became only the third team in American League history to put together back-to-back-to-back 100-win seasons, repeating as A.L. champions in 1970 and '71, defeating the Cincinnati Reds in the '70 World Series and losing to the Pittsburgh Pirates in the '71 Fall Classic despite four 20-game winners.

Another carryover from the '60s was the Major League Baseball Amateur Draft, a measure designed to equally distribute amateur talent between the "haves" and "have-nots," and to bring some sort of competitive balance to the game by enabling less deep-pocketed clubs to contend on an even footing with teams like the Yankees, Dodgers, and Cardinals. Adopted in 1964 and implemented in '65, the first selection belonged to the perennial cellar-dweller A's, who chose outfielder Rick Monday. In subsequent drafts the A's selected Reggie Jackson, Sal Bando, and Gene Tenace, who along with Vida Blue, Catfish Hunter, Joe Rudi, and Bert Campaneris formed the nucleus of the Oakland A's team that would win three World Series in a row from 1972 through 1974, the only club besides the Yankees to win three successive World Series Championships.

The "new" part of the equation was the advent of free agency. In October, 1969, the St. Louis Cardinals traded veteran outfielder Curt Flood to the Philadelphia Phillies, but Flood

The shoes worn and the bat used by Hank Aaron on April 27th, 1971, when, against the San Francisco Giants, he hit his 600th home run, becoming only the third player in history—along with Babe Ruth and Willie Mays—to reach that magic number. Also, the shoes worn by Aaron in 1974 when he hit home runs 714, 715 and 716 to surpass babe Ruth (714) as the all-time home run leader.

For 15 seasons, from 1969 to 1983, the Baltimore Orioles averaged 93½ wins a season—winning 100 games five times, including three seasons in a row (1969-71), to tie the Major League record—and won seven divisional titles, five pennants, and two World Series. Their success was, in large part, attributable to the contributions of five future Hall of Famers: #4, their manager, Earl Weaver, who won 1,480 games in his 17 years at the helm of the O's; #5, Brooks Robinson, "The Human Vacuum Cleaner," who won 16 straight Gold Gloves; #33, Eddie Murray, who averaged 99 RBIs a season in his 12 years with the O's; #22, Jim Palmer, who won 20 games eight times (including being one of four Oriole pitchers in 1971 to win 20 games); and #20, Frank Robinson, who won the Triple Crown, hit 179 home runs, and drove in 545 runs in his six seasons with the O's.

The four 20-game winners on the 1971 Baltimore Orioles pitching staff—only the second time in history one club has

refused to report to the Phillies. Expressing his feelings in a letter to Baseball Commissioner Bowie Kuhn, Flood wrote, "After 12 years in the Major Leagues, I do not feel that I am a piece of property to be bought and sold irrespective of my wishes. . . . I have received a contract offer from the Philadelphia club, but I believe that I have the right to consider offers from other clubs before making any decision."

In January of 1970 Flood filed a civil suit challenging Major League Baseball's reserve clause, contending the rule violated federal anti-trust laws. Flood's case made its way through the federal courts, finally reaching the Supreme Court. In June of 1972 they confirmed the lower court's ruling upholding baseball's exemption to the anti-trust laws and supporting the reserve

clause. After Catfish Hunter won his release from the A's in 1974, claiming that A's owner Charles Finley had not honored Hunter's contract, and pitchers Andy Messersmith and Dave McNally won arbitration decisions ruling them to be free agents, free agency became a reality after the 1976 season.

Almost immediately the gold rush was on. One owner, when asked if he thought free agents would lean toward playing in big cities, answered, "Not really, they lean toward cash." While most owners thought free agency would be the death of baseball with million-dollar contracts the new standard—compared to the salaries of just two decades before when the entire payroll for the 1955 champion Brooklyn Dodgers was just $510,000—one owner in particular welcomed it

HENRY "HANK" L. AARON
MILWAUKEE N.L., ATLANTA N.L.,
MILWAUKEE A.L. 1954-1976
HIT 755 HOME RUNS IN 23-YEAR CAREER TO BECOME MAJORS' ALL-TIME HOMER KING. HAD 20 OR MORE FOR 20 CONSECUTIVE YEARS, AT LEAST 30 IN 15 SEASONS AND 40 OR BETTER EIGHT TIMES. ALSO SET RECORDS FOR GAMES PLAYED (3,298), AT-BATS (12,364), LONG HITS (1,477), TOTAL BASES (6,856), RUNS BATTED IN (2,297). PACED N.L. IN BATTING TWICE AND HOMERS, RUNS BATTED IN AND SLUGGING PCT. FOUR TIMES EACH. WON MOST VALUABLE PLAYER AWARD IN N.L. IN 1957.

HANK AARON

Appropriately enough, the player whose name for years had appeared first alphabetically in *The Baseball Encyclopedia*, Hank Aaron, also is listed first in several of baseball's all-time statistical categories—including runs batted in and total bases. But it was one record he held for 33 years, that of baseball's all-time home-run leader, which gave him everlasting fame. For 39 years, Babe Ruth's mark of 714 home runs had served less as a catalogue of his achievements than the outline of uncharted waters no man had come close to eclipsing. While other muscled home run hitters, like Jimmie Foxx, had tailed off before coming near the so-called magic number, the man destined to replace him at the top of baseball's supposedly unattainable Everest was a trim line-drive hitter with a reputation for quick wrists, so quick that opposing pitcher Curt Simmons said of him: "Throwing a fastball by Hank Aaron is like trying to sneak the sun past a rooster." For 20 seasons, without any recognizable landmarks like 50 homers in a season, Aaron had quietly sneaked up on Ruth's record without the fanfare of others, like Willie Mays. Then, on April 8, 1974, he smote one of Al Downing's fastballs on a line into the Braves' bullpen at Atlanta Fulton County Stadium to become Number One on the all-time home run list—39 years after Ruth's last home run; which was only fair, Aaron having been born 39 years, less a day, after Ruth. By the time the man known as "Hammerin' Hank" retired, in 1976—one of the last Negro League alumni to play in the Majors—he held the all-time record in home runs, total bases, runs-batted-in, at bats, and games played, and was second in hits.

Cincinnati's "Big Red Machine" of the 1970s, winner of six division titles, four pennants, and two World Championships.

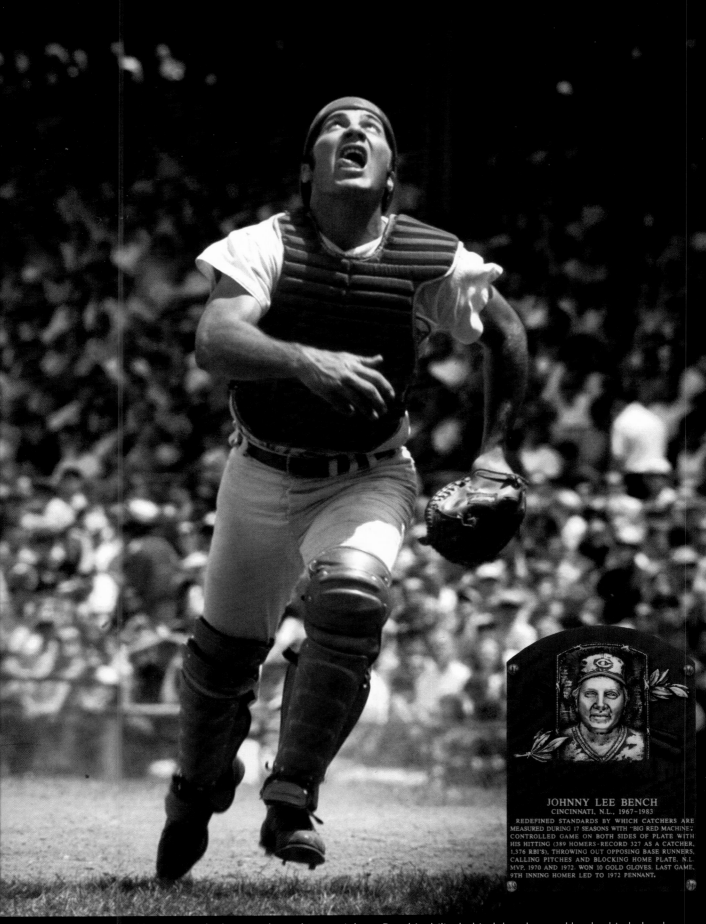

JOHNNY LEE BENCH
CINCINNATI, N.L., 1967-1983
REDEFINED STANDARDS BY WHICH CATCHERS ARE
MEASURED DURING 17 SEASONS WITH "BIG RED MACHINE".
CONTROLLED GAME ON BOTH SIDES OF PLATE WITH
HIS HITTING (389 HOMERS-RECORD 327 AS A CATCHER,
1,376 RBI'S), THROWING OUT OPPOSING BASE RUNNERS,
CALLING PITCHES AND BLOCKING HOME PLATE. N.L.
MVP, 1970 AND 1972. WON 10 GOLD GLOVES. LAST GAME,
9TH INNING HOMER LED TO 1972 PENNANT.

Acknowledged by most as the best catcher in his era, Johnny Bench's ability behind the plate and leadership helped make Cincinnati's "Big Red Machine" the outstanding team of the 1970s.

NOLAN RYAN

Nolan Ryan was baseball's version of Ol' Man River; for twenty-seven seasons he just kept rolling along, washing away records and the improbability of the calendar as well. With an arm so alive it vibrated even while he slept, every time he reared back and threw the ball he voyaged Columbus-like into new worlds. Consider his seven no-hitters, 12 one-hitters, et cetera, etc., etc. And then there were his strikeouts, 5,714—at the time he had retired 1,500 more than the second-best pitcher on the all-time list; eight times averaging 10 strikeouts a game over nine innings; the all-time record of 383 strikeouts in a season; and so many other strikeout records they became routine for the man with the fastball known as "The Ryan Express." In the ninth inning of his second no-hitter, Norm Cash of the Detroit Tigers came to bat brandishing a sawed-off table leg, figuring, "I wasn't gonna hit the guy anyway." If he was the hardest-throwing man in the league, he was also the most feared, Dick Sharon of Detroit summing it up by saying, "He is baseball's exorcist. He scares hell out of me!" Sandy Koufax, the pitcher with whom Ryan was most often compared, said, "Pitching is the art of instilling fear. But if your control is suspect like Ryan's is and the thought of being hit is in the batter's mind, you'll go a long way." Armed with his fastball and that fear, Ryan did go a long way, pitching for the longest stretch in baseball history, 27 seasons, and winning 324 games.

with open arms and an open checkbook, playing the new game better than anyone else: George Steinbrenner of the New York Yankees. Steinbrenner outbid other owners in signing free agents Catfish Hunter, Don Gullett, Goose Gossage and Reggie Jackson to multi-million dollar contracts and, in the process, created "The Best Team Money Could Buy," the pennant-winning New York Yankees of 1976, '77, and '78.

However, the Yankees would be swept in their first World Series appearance since 1964 by "The Big Red Machine," the Cincinnati Reds of Johnny Bench, Joe Morgan, Pete Rose, and Tony Perez. The Reds, after losing World Series in 1970 and '72, beat the Yankees in four games in 1976 after winning what was considered by many the greatest World Series in history in 1975 over the Boston Red Sox—highlighted by a Game Six that had great catches, perfect throws, clutch hits and, of course, the dramatic home run hit by Boston's Carlton Fisk in the twelfth inning; a game so exciting that when Pete Rose came to bat in the later innings, he turned to catcher Fisk and said, "This is some kind of game, isn't it?" It was!

But when free agent Reggie Jackson joined the Yankees in 1977 the self-proclaimed "straw that stirred the drink" helped lead the Yankees to a World Series victory over the Los Angeles Dodgers, hitting three home runs on three consecutive pitches off three different Dodger pitchers in the sixth and deciding game. The next year, after coming from 14 games behind to tie the Boston Red Sox and force a playoff game, won by Bucky "Bleeping" Dent's seventh-inning home run, the Yankees beat the Dodgers in what looked like Son of '77, again in six games.

There was something else "new" in the '70s: the designated hitter. Looking to inject more offensive firepower, the American League adopted the designated hitter in 1973—an idea that first had been introduced by National League president John Heydler five decades earlier. This time the National League declined to go along, and so it was that the American League introduced the "DH" on April 6 when

Ron Blomberg—who said, "With Bobby Bonds in right field and three first basemen, I might as well have donated my glove to charity"—came to bat against Boston's Luis Tiant. And walked.

The "borrowed" part of the aforementioned rhyme? That came when baseball, almost as if they had taken a page out of the "scientific baseball" book written by John McGraw at the turn of the century, dusted it off and reintroduced one of its early essentials: the stolen base. Once one of baseball's offensive staples, the stolen base had fallen into such disuse that in 1950 Dom DiMaggio had led the American League in steals with only 15—saying, "Pesky missed the hit-and-run that many times." But in the '50s and early '60s with first Luis Aparicio and then Maury Wills stealing their ways around the basepaths—and Lou Brock, Joe Morgan, Bert Canpaneris, Bobby Bonds, and Davey Lopes picking up on their lead—the stolen base had once again become an offensive weapon, with Brock stealing 551 bases and Morgan 488 in the decade.

And the "Blue"? That was for one of the two new expansion teams, the Toronto Blue Jays, which joined the American League in 1977 along with the Seattle Mariners. The name was the result of a "Name the Team" contest. With the National Hockey League's Maple Leafs wearing blue and white, the CFL Argonauts known as "The Double Blue," and their primary sponsor, Labatt's Beer, which marketed "Labatt's Blue," the predominant coloration of the entries was blue, as in Blue Caps, Blue Stockings, Blue Vulcans, Blue Ribbons and of course, Blue Jays—chosen as the winner although the name had been used by the Phillies back in the '40s as an alternate nickname.

The decade of the '70s ended as it had begun, with an "old" match-up between two teams that had faced one another in the World Series of 1971: Baltimore and Pittsburgh. This time around the "old" repeated itself as the "We Are Fam-A-Lee" Pittsburgh Pirates, led by Willie Stargell in their retro railroad conductor caps, beat the Orioles just as they had in '71, four-games-to-three.

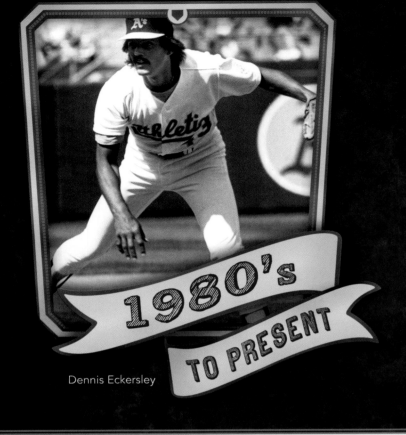

1980's TO PRESENT

Dennis Eckersley

M ost baseball fans of a certain age remember the era beginning in the 1980s, an era crowded to overflowing with a new order of winning teams, new superstars, new records, and newfangled innovations and variations on the theme.

Within their living memories come recollections of the 1980 Philadelphia Phillies, once one of baseball's most woeful franchises, shedding their back-of-the-pack image and on the bat of Mike Schmidt and the arm of Steve Carlton winning their first World Series. Following the Phillies' win, eight different teams won the remaining nine World Series during the decade, some winning for the first time. The long laundry list of those who staked their claim to the world championship after Philadelphia were the Dodgers,

Cardinals, Orioles, Tigers, Royals, Mets, Twins, and A's. The list of Series-winning teams became even longer going into the '90s with the Reds winning in 1990, and the Toronto Blue Jays, back-to-back in '92 and '93.

After the cancellation of the 1994 World Series due to a labor dispute, Major League Baseball introduced a new wrinkle into post-season play: the Division Series, a second round of playoffs added to the League Championship Series with three divisional winners and a "wild card" team facing off to determine each league's ultimate pennant winner. The Braves captured the first two-tiered playoffs in 1995, then beat the Cleveland Indians in the World Series for Atlanta's first world championship. The following year the New York Yankees won their two rounds of playoffs then defeated

The uniform that third baseman Mike Schmidt wore when he hit his 500th home run, against the Pirates, on April 18, 1987. In 18 years as a Phillie (1972-1989), he led the National League in home runs eight times, RBI and runs scored four times, and slugging percentage five times while also winning eight Gold Gloves in a row and three National League MVP awards.

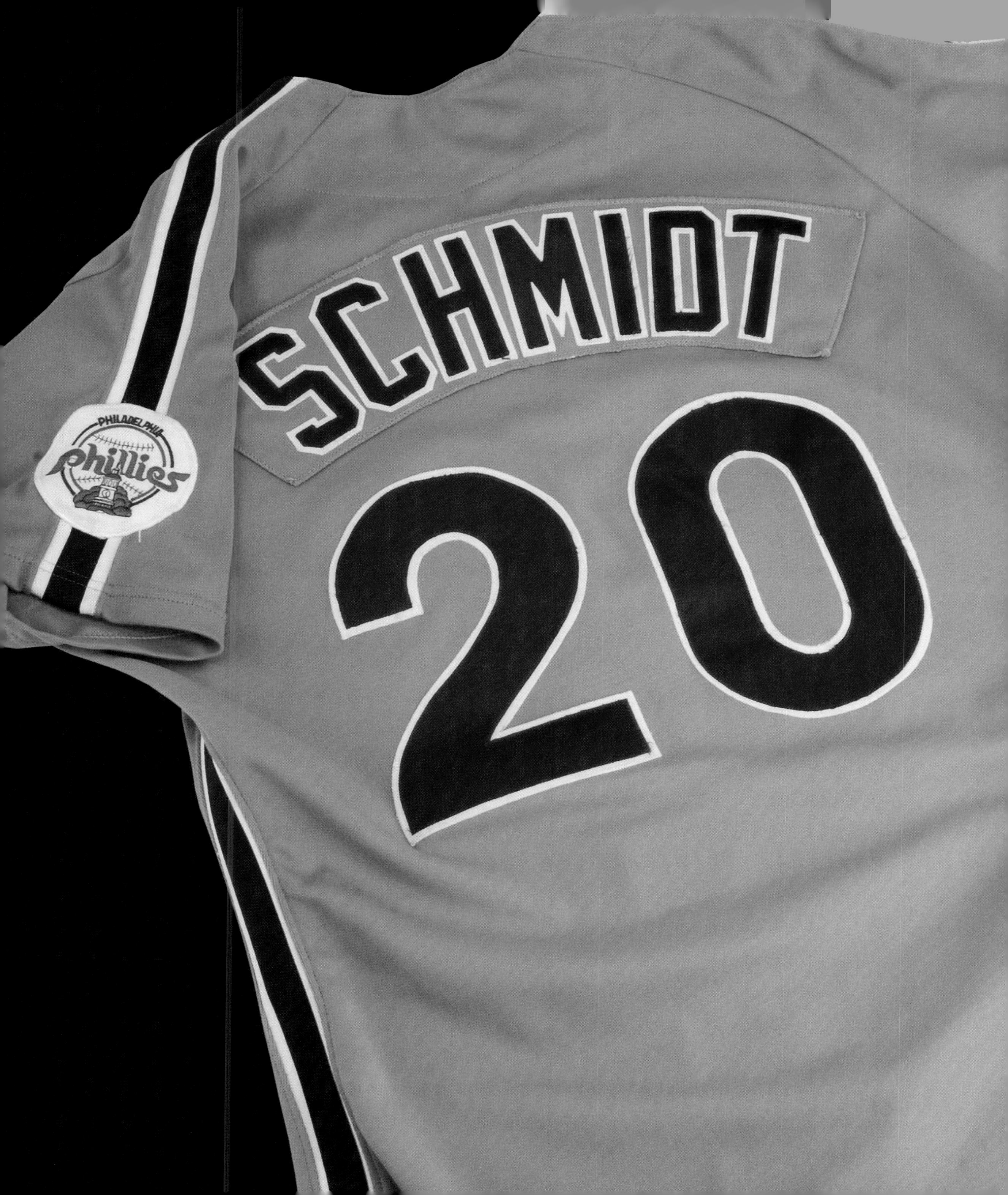
SCHMIDT
20
PHILADELPHIA
Phillies

defending champion Atlanta to win their first world title in 18 years. It was a scenario that would repeat itself in five of the next seven seasons as the Yankees made their way through both league playoffs to the World Series, winning three more in 1998, '99 and 2000. For Boston's perennially frustrated fans who had lived with the so-called "Curse of the Bambino" since 1918, 2004 was their year as the Red Sox, down three-games-to-none against their rivals, the Yankees, in the American League Championship Series, orchestrated the greatest comeback in postseason play to win the ALCS, and then went on to sweep the Cardinals to *finally* reverse "The Curse." Then, as if to prove it wasn't a once-in-a-lifetime aberration, they repeated in 2007 by sweeping the Series from the Colorado Rockies, making their first World Series appearance.

It was also an era when baseball's stage was filled with more superstars—past, present, and future—than at any other time in its history. On stage, taking their final curtain calls, were such future Hall of Famers as Jim Palmer, Rod Carew, Dave Winfield, Reggie Jackson, Joe Morgan, Johnny Bench and Steve Carlton. Doing their star turns in prime time were such greats as Mike Schmidt, Cal Ripken, Kirby Puckett, Dennis Eckersley, and Rickey Henderson. Waiting in the wings for their cue to come front and center were future All-Stars like Greg Maddux, Tom Glavine, Mark McGwire, Barry Bonds, and Roger Clemens.

If there was one constant during the era, it was the continued growth of home run numbers, the total hit in the 1980s going-going-going up some 11 percent over the number hit in the '70s and increasing another 25 percent in the '90s. Home run records began to fall as fast as exit ramps flying by on the

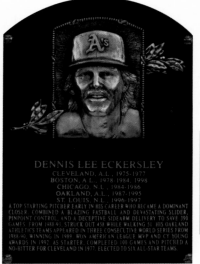

DENNIS LEE ECKERSLEY
CLEVELAND, A.L., 1975-1977
BOSTON, A.L., 1978-1984, 1998
CHICAGO, N.L., 1984-1986
OAKLAND, A.L., 1987-1995
ST. LOUIS, N.L., 1996-1997
A TOP STARTING PITCHER EARLY IN HIS CAREER WHO BECAME A DOMINANT CLOSER. COMBINED A BLAZING FASTBALL AND DEVASTATING SLIDER, PINPOINT CONTROL, AND A DECEPTIVE SIDEARM DELIVERY TO SAVE 390 GAMES FROM 1988-91. STRUCK OUT 458 WHILE WALKING 51. HIS OAKLAND ATHLETICS TEAMS APPEARED IN THREE CONSECUTIVE WORLD SERIES FROM 1988-90, WINNING IN 1989. WON AMERICAN LEAGUE MVP AND CY YOUNG AWARDS IN 1992. AS STARTER, COMPLETED 100 GAMES AND PITCHED A NO-HITTER FOR CLEVELAND IN 1977. ELECTED TO SIX ALL-STAR TEAMS.

As a starting pitcher, Dennis Eckersley achieved some fame, winning 20 games in 1978 and pitching a no-hitter in 1977. But it was as a reliever that he achieved lasting fame, compiling 390 saves in his incredible 24-year "two-career" career. ▶

The Milwaukee Brewers batting helmet worn by Hall of Famer Robin Yount when he hit his 3,000th hit on September 9, 1992. Only weeks later, his friend and rival George Brett reached the same goal.

San Diego Freeway as ball-after-batted-ball found its way to the bleacher seats, with season home run records set and set again, and the 500-career home run milepost, once the private preserve of Babe Ruth, which numbered just 12 members as the decade began, grew to double the number in the next two-plus decades. It was that home run explosion, most notably those hit, swatted and smote by Mark McGwire and Sammy Sosa—not without controversy over their alleged use of performance-enhancing drugs—that helped bring fans back to baseball after the disastrous players' strike of 1994, the long ball having become the coin of baseball's realm once again.

By the 1990s baseball had gone global. Before then there had been a trickle of non-Americans on

Major League rosters—dating back to the early 19-teens when Cubans Rafael Almeda, Armando Marsans and Dolf Luque made their Big League debuts—but nothing like the Niagara of talent that came with the 1990s and on into the 2000s. Every team now had one or two superstars from other countries on their rosters, stars like Hideo Nomo, Hideki Matsui, and Ichiro Suzuki from Japan; Albert Pujols and David Ortiz from the Dominican Republic; more than 17 shortstops from the small Dominican city of San Pedro de Macoris; Chein-Ming Wang from Taiwan; Rafael Palmeiro from Cuba; et cetera, etc., etc.—the et ceteras going on for about five pages or more. By the first decade of the new century the National Pastime had become the International Pastime.

ANTHONY KEITH GWYNN
"TONY" "MR. PADRE"
SAN DIEGO, N.L., 1982-2001

AN ARTISAN WITH A BAT WHOSE DAILY PURSUIT OF
PRODUCED A .338 LIFETIME BATTING AVERAGE, 3,141
NATIONAL LEAGUE RECORD-TYING EIGHT BATTI
CONSISTENCY WAS HIS HALLMARK, HITTING ABOVE .300
MAJOR LEAGUE SEASONS, INCLUDING .394 IN 1994. RE:
ABILITY TO HIT TO ALL FIELDS, FREQUENTLY COLLECTI
FIELD BASE HITS BETWEEN THIRD BASE AND SHORTSTOP.
JUST ONCE EVERY 21 AT BATS. A 15-TIME ALL-STAR AND FIV
GLOVE AWARD WINNER. HIT .371 IN TWO WORLD SERIES – 19

TONY GWYNN

One of the most gifted hitters in baseball history, Tony Gwynn won eight batting titles, tying him with Honus Wagner at second only to Ty Cobb. His .394 average in 1994—only three hits shy of .400—was the highest since Ted Williams' .406 in 1941. Wielding his bat like a toothpick, Gwynn had 3,141 lifetime hits and a .338 career average and is one of only a handful of players who played 10 or more seasons and never hit below .270 in any season—something not even Cobb, Wagner, nor Williams could duplicate. However, his prowess with the bat tended to obscure the fielding ability of this five-time Gold Glove outfielder. In short, Tony Gwynn was a com-

CAL RIPKEN JR.

Cal Ripken was a player's player, both afield and at bat. In his first full year with the Or 1982, playing both shortstop and third base, young Cal had 28 home runs and 93 RBI an selected American League Rookie of the Year. The next season, switching over to shortsto time, Ripken led the league in hits, runs, and doubles, led the Orioles to a World Serie and was rewarded for his efforts by being voted the American League's Most Valuable P For the next 15 years he was the mortar of the great Orioles teams, playing every day, game, until, in mid-season 1995, he had played in 2,131 consecutive games, breakin thought-to-be-impossible-to-break record of Lou Gehrig. With 3,184 lifetime hits and two awards, Cal Ripken was, to many, "The Greatest Baltimore Oriole of all time."

Cal Ripken breaks Lou Gehrig's 57-year-old "ironman" record by playing in his 2,131st consecutive game on September 6, 1995.

Known as "Mr. Oriole," Cal Ripken Jr. was also "Mr. Durability," playing in a record 2,632 consecutive games over 17

Today's Game

Time, like taffy, stretches out. The baseball timeline comes to an exhibit of today's game as you near the end of the second floor exhibits.

The exhibit is unlike that of previous decades—a recreation of a modern clubhouse. Unlike the posted sign on the visitors' clubhouse at old Tiger Stadium which read, "Visitors Clubhouse. No Visitors Allowed," this clubhouse warmly invites visitors to venture inside.

There, inside this replica clubhouse, the visitor will see 30 different lockers represent-ing each of today's 30 clubs, and each filled with a wide variety of articles from colorful team uniforms to bats, balls, caps, cleats, and all manner of "accessories" like batting helmets and batting gloves singular to the stars of each team.

Here can be seen living history. To look into your favorite team's locker can be somewhat like what James Earl Jones said in *Field of Dreams* when he described the feeling of the players: "It's as if they had dipped themselves in magic waters (and were) part of the past."

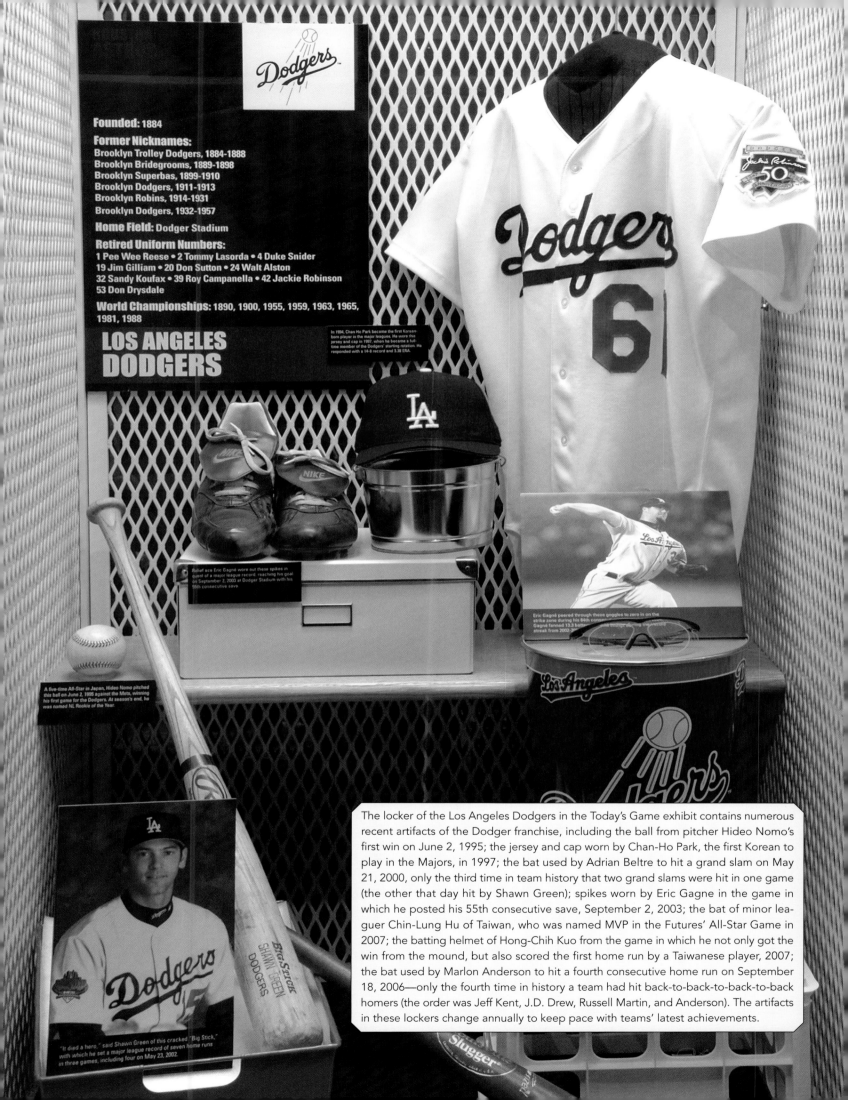

Founded: 1884

Former Nicknames:
Brooklyn Trolley Dodgers, 1884-1888
Brooklyn Bridegrooms, 1889-1898
Brooklyn Superbas, 1899-1910
Brooklyn Dodgers, 1911-1913
Brooklyn Robins, 1914-1931
Brooklyn Dodgers, 1932-1957

Home Field: Dodger Stadium

Retired Uniform Numbers:
1 Pee Wee Reese • 2 Tommy Lasorda • 4 Duke Snider
19 Jim Gilliam • 20 Don Sutton • 24 Walt Alston
32 Sandy Koufax • 39 Roy Campanella • 42 Jackie Robinson
53 Don Drysdale

World Championships: 1890, 1900, 1955, 1959, 1963, 1965, 1981, 1988

LOS ANGELES DODGERS

In 1994, Chan Ho Park became the first Korean-born player in the major leagues. He wore this jersey and cap in 1997, when he became a full-time member of the Dodgers' starting rotation. He responded with a 14-8 record and 3.38 ERA.

Relief ace Eric Gagné wore out these spikes in quest of a major league record, reaching his goal on September 2, 2003 at Dodger Stadium with his 55th consecutive save.

Eric Gagné peered through these goggles to zero in on the strike zone during his 84th consecutive save. Gagne fanned 13.3 batters... streak from 2002-...

A five-time All-Star in Japan, Hideo Nomo pitched this ball on June 2, 1995 against the Mets, winning his first game for the Dodgers. At season's end, he was named NL Rookie of the Year.

"It died a hero," said Shawn Green of this cracked "Big Stick," with which he set a major league record of seven home runs in three games, including four on May 23, 2002.

The locker of the Los Angeles Dodgers in the Today's Game exhibit contains numerous recent artifacts of the Dodger franchise, including the ball from pitcher Hideo Nomo's first win on June 2, 1995; the jersey and cap worn by Chan-Ho Park, the first Korean to play in the Majors, in 1997; the bat used by Adrian Beltre to hit a grand slam on May 21, 2000, only the third time in team history that two grand slams were hit in one game (the other that day hit by Shawn Green); spikes worn by Eric Gagne in the game in which he posted his 55th consecutive save, September 2, 2003; the bat of minor leaguer Chin-Lung Hu of Taiwan, who was named MVP in the Futures' All-Star Game in 2007; the batting helmet of Hong-Chih Kuo from the game in which he not only got the win from the mound, but also scored the first home run by a Taiwanese player, 2007; the bat used by Marlon Anderson to hit a fourth consecutive home run on September 18, 2006—only the fourth time in history a team had hit back-to-back-to-back-to-back homers (the order was Jeff Kent, J.D. Drew, Russell Martin, and Anderson). The artifacts in these lockers change annually to keep pace with teams' latest achievements.

SACRED GROUND

THE FANS

At the top of the staircase leading to the third floor the visitor is greeted by five of baseball's most storied fans. Here, flanking a Yankee Stadium kiosk and turnstile, are the fabric-mache figures of Hilda Chester of Brooklyn, Harry Thobe of Cincinnati, Lolly Hopkins of Boston, Pearl Sandow of Atlanta, and "Yoyo" of Philadelphia—five real-life superfans who have become as well known as some of the players down on the field. Together they represent the hundreds of drummers, dancers, bell-ringers, cheerleaders, flag- and sign-wavers and bullhorn shouters whose uninhibited passion for their home team has become part of the game's total experience in every ballpark nationwide.

Known throughout the ages by many names from "cranks" to "bugs" to "enthusiasts" to "fanatics"—later contracted to just plain ol' "fans"—they are the heartbeat of their home team. Sometimes they are more than just the heartbeat; sometimes they are the drum beat, or the toe-tap beat, or the cheerleading beat, making antic hay while their team shines and turning the stands into an Aeolian trumpet like choirmasters waving the choir of fans on and off.

Back in Boston at the turn of the twentieth century, the Red Sox were cheered on by a superfan named N. T. "Nuf 'Ced" McGreevey who led a group called "The Royal Rooters" in constant singing of the then popular song "Tessie." Yet this group of rabble rousers substituted their own barbed words for the song's traditional lyrics, striking fear into the opponent's ear while driving them to distraction. Then there was Brooklyn's own Hilda Chester and her ever-ready

The "Royal Rooters," a band of rollicking, roisterous, sometimes riotous Boston fans, led by tavern keeper "Nuf Ced" McGreevey, make their grand entrance into the old Huntington Avenue Grounds trumpeting their fight song before taking their seats down the left-field line for the opening game of the 1912 World Series.

Hall of Famer Tony Gwynn once said: "The beauty of the game is that people realize this is a fans' game. They're the ones who make this go." And here, at the top of the third floor stairs, complete with two concessionaries and a ticket kiosk and turnstile from Yankee Stadium, are five fabric-mache figures of quintessential fans who made "this go": (left to right) Hilda Chester, Brooklyn fan; Harry Thobe, Cincinnati fan; Lolly Hopkins, Boston fan; Pearl Sandow, Atlanta fan; and "Yoyo," Philadelphia fan (in sunglasses).

cowbell complementing the Dodgers' unofficial band, the Sym-Phony, which would lead off-key choruses of cheers, especially when they played "Three Blind Mice" in mock tribute to the umpires. There was John Adams of Cleveland who would play his weathered bass drum, called "Big Chief Boom-Boom," out in the upper reaches of Municipal Stadium (and later The Jake) to stir up the Indian crowds. And Baltimore's "Wild" Bill Hagy, who would mount the Oriole dugout in the seventh inning to lead the faithful in cheers of "O-R-I-O-L-E-S." There were so many others, their passions overflowing as they made the stadium a lively experience and the game an event.

Perhaps the quintessential fan was one S. D.

Reed who was in attendance at Detroit's old Bennett Park one fine day back in 1905. The game had gone into the eleventh inning when umpire Jack Sheridan turned toward the grandstand and raised his hand to command silence. "Is S. D. Reed in the stands?" he shouted, without benefit of a megaphone. "He is wanted at home . . . his house is on fire." There was a small commotion in the stands behind first base and then someone stood up. "I am S. D. Reed," he called out loudly. "But I'm not leaving. I couldn't get there in time to do anything about it. Let the house burn!"

Such is the fire that burns within every baseball fan. Especially within those superfans like Hilda Chester, Harry Thobe, Lolly Hopkins, Pearl Sandow and "Yoyo."

THE STADIUMS

urning past those colorful figures of the game's greatest fans, you enter an area covering all manner of artifacts relating to the ballparks and the ballpark experiences that we all know and love.

Some years ago Joe Raposo wrote a ballad to old ballparks with the words, when sung by Frank Sinatra, sounding like a funeral dirge for a world that once was:

"And there used to be a ballpark where the field was warm and green.

And the people played their crazy game with a joy I'd never seen.

And the air was such a wonder from the hot dogs and the beer,

Yes, there used to be a ballpark right here."

There used to be a Forbes Field and a Shibe Park and a Redland Field and a Sportsman's Park. And many, many others "right here"—before they were gone, all bulldozed into the past.

There used to be a Huntington Avenue Grounds, the original home of the Boston American League team. Situated on the south side of Huntington Avenue at the intersection of what is now Forsyth Street, the site was purchased in 1901 from the Boston Elevated Railroad and the wooden structure built in three months at a cost of $35,000, in time for the Americans' opening day—a game seen by a capacity crowd of 9,000, plus an equal number of standees behind ropes in the outfield, who paid 25 cents for the privilege of root, root, rootin' for their home team, which won its first

The scoreboard crew writing in the inning-by-inning scores at the third Chicago ballpark, called South Side Park, where the White Sox of the new American League played from 1901 to 1910 and the Chicago American Giants of the Negro National League played from 1920 to 1940. Notice the announcement on the scoreboard reading, "Detroit Saturday Sunday," Chicago being one of the few cities where Sunday baseball was played before the 1920s.

home game 12-4 behind Cy Young. With Young winning 33 games and player-manager Jimmy Collins batting .332, the Americans finished second that year and drew a reported total of 289,448 rabid fans through the turnstiles, almost twice as many as their National League intra-city rivals, and next-door neighbors, the Braves.

The Grounds were the site of two historic events: the first World Series (along with Pittsburgh's Exposition Park); and the first modern Perfect Game, pitched by Cy Young against the Philadelphia A's and Rube Waddell, in 1904.

By 1912, Huntington Avenue Grounds was no more, abandoned by the team now known as the "Red Sox" for their new headquarters at Fenway Park. Today the site is part of Northeastern University where its one-time presence is commemorated by a plaque on the outside wall of the University's Cabot Physical Education Center reading: "The site of the former Huntington Avenue American League Baseball Grounds, on which in 1903 four games of the first World Series were played. The Boston Americans defeated the Pittsburg Nationals five games to three." (The Grounds are further remembered by the magnificently detailed scale model of the ballpark that greets visitors to the third floor of the Sacred Ground exhibit.)

The reason for the move from Huntington Avenue Grounds to Fenway in 1912 was because the lease was about to expire and Red Sox owner John I. Taylor, on the cusp of selling the team, would collect rent from the new owner on the new ballpark he owned in Boston's Fens. The reason the Pirates moved from their Exposition Park home in 1909 was different. Seems that the old ballpark was proximate to Pittsburgh's red-light district and no "decent woman" would dare pass through this so-called "sinful area" to get to the ballpark, and so Pirate owner Barney Dreyfus decided to move to a new location, over to Schenley Park.

The opening of the new steel-and-concrete Shibe Park in Philadelphia in April 1909, and Forbes Field in Pittsburg two months later, sparked a stadium-building boom around the league, as 13 new "pleasure palaces," as they were then called, were built in the following six years.

Not only was it a case of "build a field and they will come," as new fans came to the new stadium, but it also brought "good luck," with both Pittsburg and Boston winning the World Series their first year in their new homes.

Fans of a certain age well remember the stadia of their youth and their irregular patterns and idiosyncrasies. Griffith Stadium and Fenway Park were both irregularly shortened to accommodate neighboring houses and streets. Crosley Field and Fenway originally had left-field embankments which served as warning tracks—the one at Crosley called "The Terrace" and the one in Fenway (before its 1933 renovation) called "Duffy's Cliff" for outfielder Duffy Lewis who mastered it, although a later outfielder, Smead Jolley, never did, once complaining that he had been taught how to go up the hill but that nobody had "taught me to come down again." Ebbets Field was most remarkable for its wonderful signage, like the one under the scoreboard reading: "Hit Sign Win Suit/Abe Stark/1514 Pitkin Avenue," or an earlier one for Tanglefoot flypaper: "Last year Zack Wheat Caught 216 flies/Tanglefoot Caught Thousands." Braves Field's "Jury Box" out in right-field was so named because a writer once counted the same number of fans out there as in a jury box.

Today, with the exception of two monuments—Fenway Park and Wrigley Field—those ballparks that once were "right here" are all gone, replaced by modern ballparks with names that have changed. For those who have their own memories of their favorite old stadium—retaining only the essential and rejecting the superficial, remembering things that were important to them like their first ballgame, their team's heroic comeback, and their favorite player's exploits—these were *terra sancta*. For, as baseball historian Larry Ritter wrote, "Most of yesterday's ballparks are gone. But they had magic, magic that will live for years in the memories of those who were lucky enough to have passed through their turnstiles."

Pictured here is a home plate from the visitors' bullpen at Ebbets Field; displayed behind it is a painting of the famed ballpark. ▶

South End Ground, home of the Boston Nationals (1888-1894), is featured in the dynamic computer interactive model.

The cornerstone of Brooklyn's famed Ebbet's Field is on exhibit in Sacred Ground. Located at Bedford Avenue (right field), Sullivan Place (first base), McKeever Place (third base), and Montgomery Street (left field), Ebbets Field was home to teams called the Dodgers and Robins for 45 years, from 1913 to 1957.

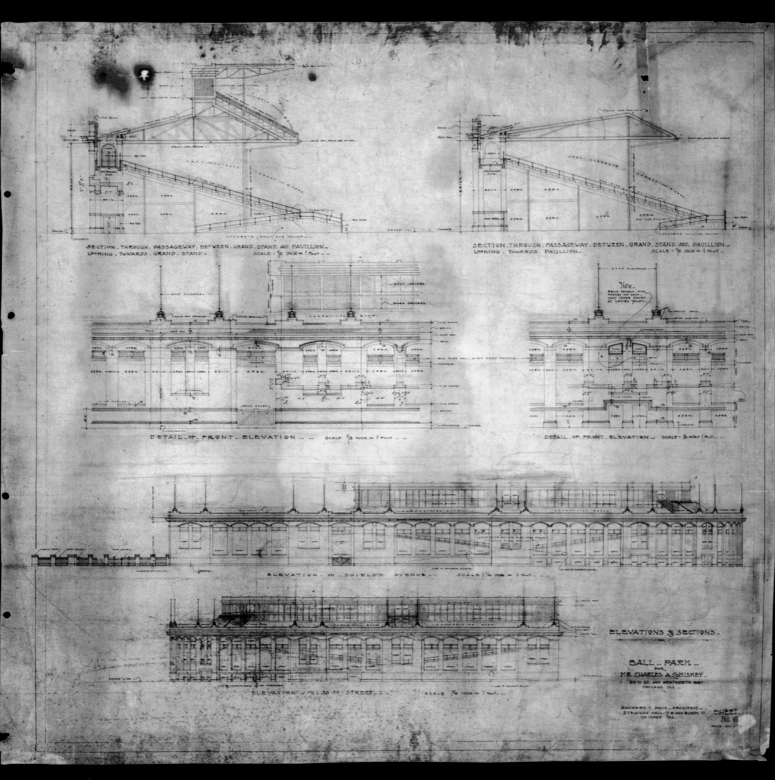

The original blueprints for Comiskey Park, a 32,000-seat stadium built in 1910 by Chicago White Sox owner Charles Comiskey at the cost of $750,000.

A typical New York mob outside
Yankee Stadium in the late 1950s.

Crowds forming on Clark Street in front of Wrigley Field for a 1946 Chicago Cubs afternoon game.

One of the eight giant lighted pinwheels that adorned Comiskey Park's famous "Monster Scoreboard," created by Bill Veeck in 1960.

MASCOTS

The word "mascot" derives from the French, meaning "a little sorcerer or magician," or in the alternative, a talisman or good luck charm. In the early days of baseball, that's what the mascot was—a little (as in an actual child) good luck charm as teams like the old New York Giants of the Buck Ewing days had a little kid serve as their combination good-luck charm and bat boy.

The "newer" version of the Giants adopted their own good-luck charm in 1911 when a tall, gangly individual showed up one day in St. Louis and introduced himself to Giant manager John McGraw, saying, "Mr. McGraw, my name is Charles Victory Faust. I live in Kansas and a few weeks ago I went to a fortune teller who told me that if I would join the New York Giants and pitch for them, they would win the pennant." McGraw, like most ballplayers of the time, was superstitious, and took Faust with the team, telling his players, "Gentlemen, we're taking Faust along to help us win the pennant." Sure enough, with Faust sitting on the bench in uniform, the Giants began winning, pulling away from their nearest rivals, the Cubs and Pirates. With the pennant clinched, McGraw even let Faust pitch part of two games.

Over the next five or six decades mascots were few and far between, with one of the few being Eddie Bennett, the good-luck charm and batboy for the "Murderer's Row" Yankees teams of the '20s. Then, perhaps inspired by H. Allen Smith's novel *Rhubarb*, the story of a cat that inherits a baseball team and helps them win the pennant by becoming their mascot, animals became the unofficial mascots of their teams—like Schottzie, a 170-lb. droopy-eyed St. Bernard owned by Cincinnati Reds' majority owner Marge Schott, and Charlie O., a mule named after Kansas City A's owner Charlie Finley.

The first mascot, as we know mascots today, came with the opening of Shea Stadium in 1964 when the New York Mets unveiled "Mr. Met," a humanoid wearing an oversized baseball head with

Considered by many to be one of the greatest team mascots in all of sports, the Phillie Phanatic is known for his entertaining antics on the field and in the stands.

a perpetual smile. Soon Major League fields were overrun with mascots. There were two of the best ever—the San Diego Chicken and the Phillie Phanatic—along with the Mariner Moose, the Expos' "Youppi!," Baltimore's "The Orioles Bird," Boston's "Wally the Green Monster," and a collection of other assorted beasties and fuzzy anthropomorphic characters all looking like escapees from a Halloween party, leading cheers and performing antics to the delight of young and old alike.

But of all of them, perhaps the most unusual mascot isn't one down on the field, but instead up on the stadium JumboTron: the Los Angeles Angels' "Rally Monkey." The Rally Monkey first made her appearance during the 2000 season

The Sacred Ground exhibit includes many of the added attractions which greatly enrich the fan's ballpark experience—from mascots to scoreboards, including the lighted pinwheel from Comiskey Park, to an audio station featuring several renditions of "Take Me Out to the Ball Game," sung by various artists.

when the Angels' stadium video crew, trying to exhort the Angels' faithful to cheer for a come-from-behind rally, threw a video of a capuchin monkey named "Katie" from Jim Carrey's "Ace Ventura, Pet Detective" up on the giant scoreboard with the words "Rally Monkey," adding the sound of rock band House of Pain's song "Jump Around." It worked; the Angels rallied to win. The Rally Monkey then became an Angels' fixture during the 2002 World Series, when, down again, little Katie was flashed up on the screen to the accompaniment of fans banging away on their noisemaking "Thunderstix." The Angels came back to defeat the Giants. Now, every time the Angels are tied or trailing after the sixth inning, Katie "The Rally Monkey"

flashes up on the JumboTron.

Whether cavorting around the field or standing atop their team's dugout leading cheers, today's mascots have added an element of entertainment to the game. By channeling a little of the antics of the Three Stooges, a little of the clownishness of an Emmett Kelly, and a lot of the good-luck charm of a Charles Victory Faust, mascots today are part and parcel of the "Fan Experience."

A collection of mascot-related artifacts, covering both human and humanoid mascots—from "The Clown Prince of Baseball" Al Schacht's famous top hat and tails to the San Diego Chicken, Montreal's Youppi!, and Boston's "Wally the Green Monster."

Top hat and tails worn by baseball clown Al Schacht when he performed as a solo act in ballparks across the country from 1935 to 1968.

Tattered jersey worn by famed baseball clown Max Patkin, whose on-the-painted antics on the ballfields from 1946 to 1995 earned him the nickname "The Clown Prince of Baseball."

Monster Crunch cereal box and bean bag doll of Wally the Green Monster, the Red Sox mascot named for Fenway Park's famous left field wall.

Coloring book featuring Youppi!, the beloved and bilingual Expos mascot who made his home at Montreal's Olympic Stadium from 1979 to 2004.

The comedy tandem of Nick Altrock and Al Schacht, partners from 1921 through 1934, clown prior to a World Series game at the Polo Grounds in the duo's first year together.

Foam visor featuring the head of Tremor, the dinosaur mascot who roams The Epicenter, home park of the California League's Rancho Cucamonga Quakes.

Richard King, better known as "King Tut," clowned from 1934 to 1959, primarily with the Indianapolis Clowns of the Negro American League.

After a mediocre three-year career with the Washington Senators—winning 14 games while losing 10 between 1919 and 1921—Al Schacht, wearing a top hat and tails, became known as "The Clown Prince of Baseball," entertaining the fans for many years, often with fellow pitcher and coach, Nick Altrock.

Part of all fans' ballpark experience is the sights and sounds surrounding them. And nothing says being at a ballpark more than hearing vendors hollering, "Programs . . . getcha programs . . ." and "Hot dogs heah. . . ." In these displays on the third floor the Hall of Fame recaptures the fan experience with displays of those ballpark pluses—the concessions, the souvenirs, and the tickets that begin the experience.

CONCESSIONS

A Chicago Cubs official once said, "The hot dog is king. For every dollar we get in paid admissions, our total cost of operating the club is $1.06. If we didn't have extra income from concessions in the ballpark, we'd have to lock our gates."

Now more than ever, astronomical salaries and expenses have forced clubs to look for additional sources of revenue. One source is concessions, which were once mere appendages of the action on the field. According to one veteran concessionaire, "arenas thought of food concessions like bathrooms—you had to have them."

Without concessions and the amounts of money they generate, there might not be a base-

ball team in Milwaukee or a stadium in St. Louis. Certain franchises wouldn't exist. Ever since Harry M. Stevens advanced money to Harry Frazee, and Louis M. Jacobs, the so-called Godfather of Sports, lent money to Connie Mack to save their faltering franchises in the 1920s and '30s, financial aid in the form of advances on long-term concessions contracts has been a standard practice of the baseball business.

In the 1960s Louis Jacobs' concern, Sportservice, guaranteed $12,000,000 in concession fees to insure that Busch Memorial Stadium would be built in St. Louis. In 1970, the firm advanced the Milwaukee Brewers $3,000,000 for conces-

Several of the many concessions sold in ballparks through history, beginning, in the lower left-hand corner, with the man who started it all, Harry M. Stevens. Next to Stevens is a popcorn holder that doubles as a megaphone, sold by the Washington Senators in the 1960s, then a sandwich concession basket. Above Stevens's picture is a hot dog container from Milwaukee's County Stadium and an advertisement found on the sushi containers sold at Seattle's Safeco Field. Above the hot dog container are stuffed doll replicas of the four "Sausages" that perform at Milwaukee home games, and a program in the form of a glove from 1908, along with caps and buttons worn by concessionaires.

The scorecard for the seventh All-Star Game, July 11, 1939, at New York's Yankee Stadium, won by the American League, 3-1. Ironically, the starting pitchers for the two leagues, Red Ruffing of the Yankees for the American League and Paul Derringer of the Reds for the National, were the starting pitchers in that season's opening game of the World Series, also played at Yankee Stadium, with Ruffing winning, 2-1.

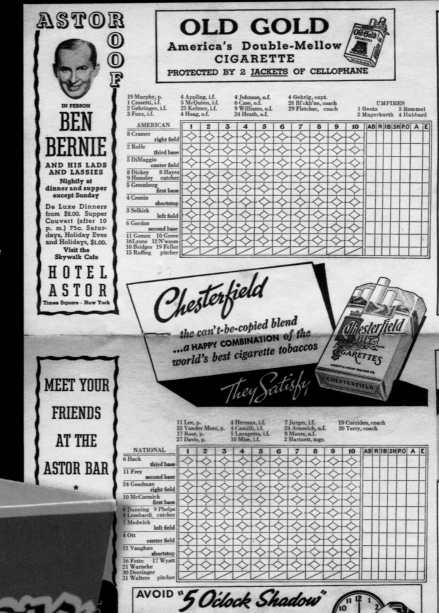

Popcorn and its derivative, caramel corn (i.e. Cracker Jack), became popular after their introduction at Chicago's Columbian Exposition in 1893 and soon found their way into ballparks, becoming, by the second decade of the twentieth century, baseball's unofficial snack food. Throughout the years it was sold in many different containers, like the one pictured, sold at Washington's RFK Stadium as a box that doubled as a cardboard megaphone.

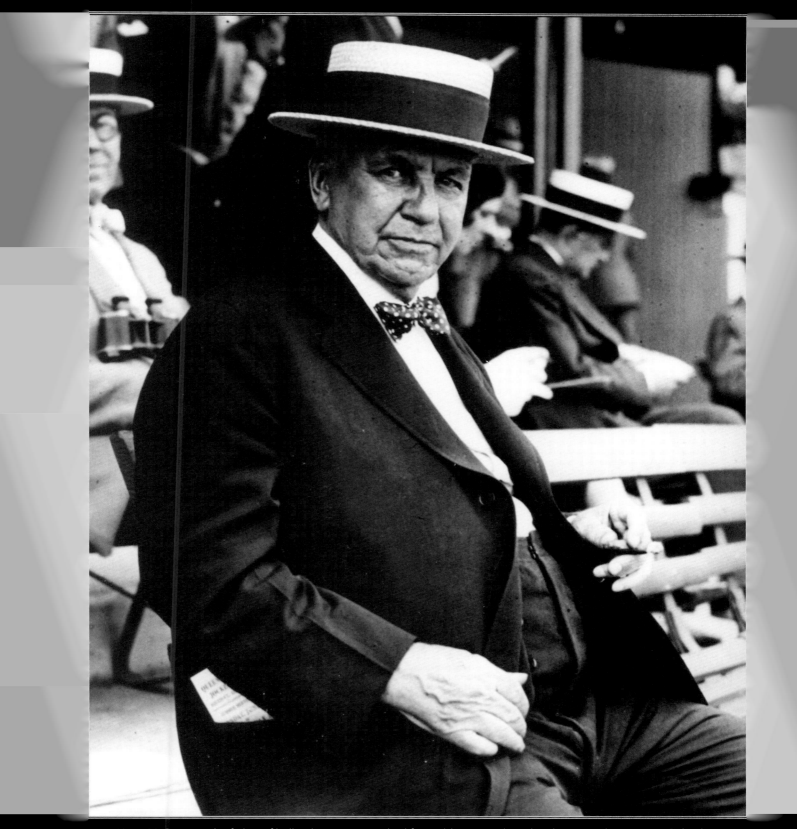

Harry M. Stevens, the father of ballpark concessions, had first sold scorecards and soda pop and peanuts in Columbus, Ohio, back in 1887. Moving into the Polo Grounds as the concessionaire for the New York Giants in the first decade of the twentieth century, he found that his soft ice cream was not selling well on one cold April afternoon. So he instructed his vendors to go out and buy all the frankfurters and rolls they could find in nearby stores. Boiling the franks and splitting the rolls to form a bed for the frankfurters, he had his vendors go out into the stands selling what he called "red hot daschund sausages," the frankfurters resembling small German dogs. The treats we now know as "hot

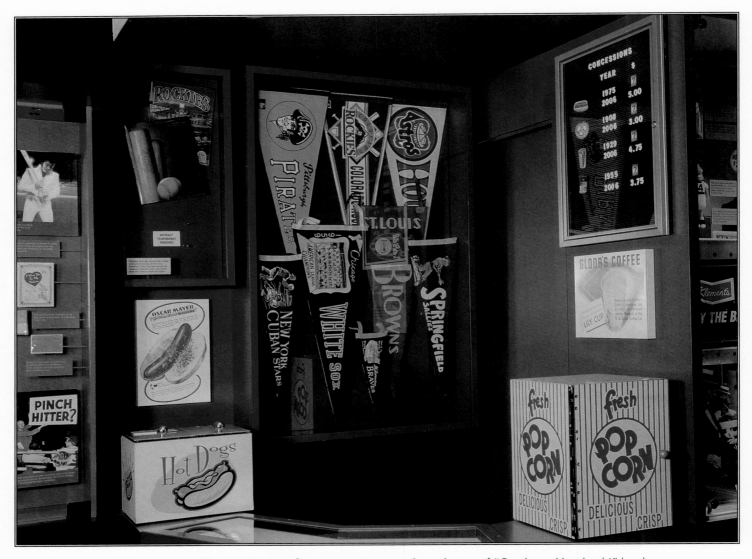

Ever since concessionaire Harry M. Stevens first put a weiner on a bun, the cry of "Getcha red hot heah!" has been heard at ballparks everywhere. Along with banners, bobblehead dolls, buckets of popcorn and more, it's part of the fan's total experience.

sion rights at Milwaukee County Stadium over a long period, providing them with the financial wherewithal to move the franchise from Seattle.

Concessions today are big business. Baseball crowds, like armies, travel on their stomachs. The average big-league ballpark accounts for a massive yearly consumption of hot dogs, slabs of ice cream, and bags of peanuts, all washed down with soft drinks and beers.

The amount of money churned can be enormous, for a team drawing a million fans.

The multimillion dollar concessions business started one hot summer's day back in 1887, in Columbus, Ohio, when a baseball fan named Harry Mosley Stevens went out to the local ballpark to escape the heat and watch the local nine play. Unable to decipher the garbled scorecard he

had purchased at the front gate, Stevens walked into the front office and offered the club the princely sum of $700 for the privilege of printing and selling an intelligible scorecard in the park. They accepted the offer and Stevens set to work. Improving the design and selling advertising in his "newfangled" scorecard, Stevens soon recouped his initial investment.

Soon afterwards, Harry M. Stevens branched out into the selling of peanuts and soda pop. He reached the big leagues, when he moved his concession business into the Polo Grounds. One day, during a cold and windy Giants' game, he noticed that his soft drink sales were lagging. Employing the same spur-of-the-moment creativity that had first launched his business, he sent his vendors out into neighborhood stores to buy up all the frankfurters and rolls they could find. He had the franks boiled, split the rolls to form a bed, and sold them to the chilled spectators with the slogan that still rings true to this day: "Get 'em while they're hot." His frankfurter sandwiches proved popular from that very first game and, despite the whimsical libel on the beef sausages, "hot dogs" became baseball's staple.

Throughout the years other concessionaires have copied the hustling methods of Harry M. Stevens, who founded the royal family of sports caterers. And here, "hustling" is the right word. Promoter extraordinaire Bill Veeck remembers that when the Wrigley Field concessionaires would run out of beef, they would dip dough-balls in beef blood. Placed on rolls, they were sold as "hamburgers."

Not only can a hot day in the midday sun work up a gigantic thirst, but vendors know what works up an appetite for their wares. One vendor, working the stands in Houston during a long-ago Dixie Series game, told a reporter, "Peanuts is tension food. People eat peanuts when the score's close and a lot's at stake. That's when they sit tight." (You can also throw in Cracker Jack in that regard, courtesy of Jack Norworth's famous phrase in baseball's anthem, "Take Me Out to the Ball Game.") The Houston vendor went on to explain that, "When a game is one-sided or a series ain't important, they eat popcorn. Ice cream, too. They're the stuff that relaxes you. You eat popcorn and ice cream when nothing makes no difference."

Concessions do make a difference, both in the enjoyment of the game and in the financial picture of the ball club.

PROMOTIONS

Bill Veeck was baseball's P.T. Barnum, its premier promoter. Believing that all promotions were successful if they increased attendance, he tried anything and everything, all in the name of upping attendance. After working for the Chicago Cubs and helping to plant the storied ivy on Wrigley Field's brick walls, Veeck became owner of the Triple-A Milwaukee Brewers in 1941 and loosed a steady stream of promotions on the fans, giving out such unlikely items as a thousand pounds of poultry, live guinea pigs and burros, a two-hundred pound cake of ice, a thousand cans of Chinese noodles, five hundred jars of iguana meat, and suntan lotion to bleacher fans. If that weren't enough, he staged Barbershop Quartet Day, Taxicab Drivers' Day, and Bartenders Night, just to name a few unlikely targets of celebration. He let all mothers in free and presented them with baby orchids upon presentation of baby pictures. He gave 50,000 assorted screws and nuts and bolts to one fan. He brought in strolling minstrels, contortionist Max Patkin and acrobat Jackie Price with their baseball hi-jinx, established morning "Rosie the Riveter" games for wartime night shift workers, and once presented a thousand cans of beer to one fan. With Veeck, it was a circus, a midway, a fair. Fans fully expected Milwaukee's starting battery to be Barnum & Bailey.

Veeck sold the Brewers and entered the service for the War—losing a leg at Guadalcanal—then returned almost five years to the day he had first taken over the Brewers with his first big-league team, the Cleveland Indians. He also took his acts with him. Convinced that baseball was the best entertainment buy, dollar-for-dollar, he went to work using his promotions to sell his product, while showering the fans with gifts and the field with fireworks. Everyone was fair game. Ladies were wooed with gifts like hard-to-get nylons, provided with baby-sitters, and generally made to feel at home at Cleveland's Municipal Stadium. Clowns, constant giveaways, and a winning team provided the rest of the inducement. Every game was a happening, and Bill Veeck made it all happen. And, not incidentally, the 1948 pennant-winning Indians set the all-time attendance mark as 2,620,627 baseball-and-promotions-mad fans flocked into the House that Veeck Promoted the Hell Out Of.

Veeck would sell the Indians in 1949 and resurface two years later as owner of the woebegone St. Louis Browns. Veeck immediately went to work digging deep into his endless bag of tricks. He hired Max Patkin as contortionist-coach, signed the ageless wonder Satchel Paige and installed him in the bullpen comfortably seated in a rocking chair, and initiated a Grandstand Managers Club where the crowd was called upon to give signals in response to questions held up on large placards, including such strategic points as "Shall We Warm Up the Pitcher?" and "Move the Infield Back?"

Veeck even added one outrageous twist that affected the game on the field. Believing that all promotional gimmicks were transferable ("you just change the gag line"), he resurrected an old James Thurber short story about a midget who played baseball and inserted his own into the Brownies' lineup in the person of three-foot, seven-inch Eddie Gaedel. Wearing elfin-sized cleats, the number 1/8 on the back of his uniform, and carrying a bat that looked like a conductor's baton, little Eddie took his place—or, at least, part of a place—in the batter's box. As home plate umpire Ed Hurley challenged Browns manager Zack Taylor on the propriety of sending a midget to the plate—not that it mattered; the Browns were already on their way to another hundred-loss season—Detroit Tigers catcher Bob Swift went out to the mound to visit with pitcher Bob Cain. Trying to keep a straight face, Swift imparted what little wisdom he could on how to pitch to a midget. "Keep it low," he said. Notwithstanding Swift's advice, Cain walked Gaedel on four pitches that couldn't have found his mini-strike zone with a pair of high-powered binoculars.

While that one moment cemented Veeck's legacy, he had other memorable moments as well.

Not to mention, some forgettable ones. Like the day in 1952 when a salesman, knowing Veeck's off-the-wall reputation and having something unusual to sell, came to see Veeck with "something" to sell. That "something" was the remnants of an out-of-business bat company, which he got Veeck to buy lock, stock and barrel. This of course led to the first "Bat Day," in which every fan entering the stadium was given a real baseball bat. Almost every club quickly adopted the gimmick, which proved a problem for several clubs, like the Yankees, who found that fans pounding the bats on the cement floor of the stands created "a structural problem" for the Stadium.

But not all baseball promotions sprung full-blown from the brow of Bill Veeck. In fact, in the 1880s the owner of the Cincinnati Reds discovered that when handsome Tony Mullane, known as "The Apollo of the Box," was scheduled to take his turn on the mound, the stands were filled with hundreds of female fans. Soon the local papers were carrying ads reading: "Mullane Will Pitch for Cincinnati Today!" And in small print underneath the ad came the hook: "Women Accompanied by Male Escorts Will be Admitted Free."

The Washington Senators took note of Cincinnati's success in wooing female fans and, having a handsome pitcher of their own in Win Mercer, decided to name one day each week "Ladies Day," with women to be allowed in free. During one of his last appearances in the 1897 season Mercer took exception to the umpire's call and walked in from the mound to hand the official a pair of glasses he had produced from his back pocket. The ladies in the stands shrieked in delight, but the umpire was not amused. He handed the glasses back to Mercer and forthrightly ejected him from the game. Now that the reason for their attendance had been removed from the game, the women unleashed all their fury upon the umpire who compounded his felony by calling a Washington player out on a close play to end the game. That did it! Hundreds of infuriated females surged onto the field intent on exacting revenge against the poor umpire who had ruined their afternoon. Seeing the sea of

BATS AND BOBBLE HEADS

To fans, nothing says "Come on in!" like a promotion. Minor league teams pioneered the practice of giving fans a small gift or special event to build excitement for certain games. Now, major and minor league games often feature free treats to lure fans and to give them something extra for their money. Businesses pay for the chance to reach baseball's audience, raising income for ballclubs in the process.

Some promotions reward specific spectators. Giveaways can target women, children or the first fans to arrive at the game. The best promotions build fan excitement for the team and for the experience of coming out to the ballpark.

GRANDSTAND MANAGERS

Even before Bill Veeck inaugurated "Bat Day" in 1952 baseball teams have sponsored promotional days, whether they be special days for players, fans, or giveaway days. Over the past half-century there have been cap days, jacket days, T-shirt days, bobblehead days, batting helmet days, tote bag days, and all manner of giveaway days designed to bring

Grandstand Managers Day was a promotion staged in 1951 by St. Louis Browns owner Bill Veeck. The promotion called upon "Grandstand Managers" seated in special sections in Sportsman's Park to hold up their "Yes" or "No" cards in response to signs asking questions like, "Shall We Move the Infield Back?" Somehow it worked, and after the lowly Brownies had defeated the Philadelphia A's, a pleased Veeck was heard to say, "I'm the only owner in the Majors who

parasol-wielding females descending, the umpire made a mad dash for the Senators' offices, leaving the female mob to hang around the office for hours afterwards, brandishing their weaponry in the hope of catching a glimpse of the miscreant.

Thus began—and almost ended—Ladies' Day. It would be another 20 years before William Veeck Sr., father of Bill and president of the Chicago Cubs, was to brave the obvious and introduce Ladies' Day again. Now an institution, the day has come almost full circle with some minor league clubs offering "Women's Lib Day" where the woman pays and her companion gets in free.

Team-sponsored promotions remained few and far between back in the early days of baseball. Most were generated not by the clubs themselves, but by the fans who, true to their roots and their root word, "fanatics," sponsored days for their favorite player, giving them a trophy or a watch or some-such. Sometimes that took on the form of spontaneous collections from the player's personal following in the stands, like the time little Miller Huggins, then the second baseman for the Cincinnati Reds, hit a home run off New York Giant great Christy Mathewson, the only one he hit in 1907, and the grateful fans rewarded him by presenting him with a pair of shoes, a five-pound box of chocolates, the traditional gold watch, a silk scarf and its accompanying scarf pin, and a Morris chair.

Teams also got into the act. A popular promotion in the '30s—borrowed from an idea conceived by minor league manager Abner Powell back in the 1880s—was something called "Knothole Gangs," a name reminiscent of the days when kids stood outside the wooden ballparks peeking through a hole in the fence. For a nominal fee kids were admitted into the game to root for this year's heroes and, hopefully, tomorrow's as well.

Then there were field days, with players engaging in pitching and batting and distance-throwing contests, along with foot-races. On the night in 1938 when night baseball came to Brooklyn, almost 40,000 Dodger fans pushed their way through the turnstiles at Ebbets Field to see night baseball and the pre-game fanfare with Olympian Jesse Owens running against the clock. It was also the night Johnny Vander Meer threw the second of his consecutive no-hitters.

One promotion that worked when it was first introduced (and still does today) is Old-Timers Day, appealing to the nostalgia of fans. The New York Yankees first "officially" introduced Old-Timers Day in 1946, but its antecedents go all the way back to 1911 when American League players gathered to pay tribute to and raise money for the widow of pitching great Addie Joss, who had died earlier that year at the still-young age of 31. Another such day was held in Boston in 1917 to commemorate the passing of the popular Tim Murnane who had played for Boston in the old-old National League and then had been a Boston sportswriter for three decades. There also was the "Day" for Lou Gehrig in 1939, and the game staged by the Philadelphia Athletics the same year to celebrate baseball's centennial, featuring the 1911 A's playing against the 1929 version. It became such a successful promotion that even the New York Mets got into the act, staging an Old-Timers Day the very first year of their existence, 1962.

The scenario for every Old-Timers Day is always the same. The team's old-timers are dusted off and trotted out, like the queen's jewelry, to the roars of an appreciative crowd. Everyone seems to share in this tribute to yesteryear. Well, almost everyone. One who had some reservations about Old-Timers Day was Casey Stengel, who said, "Old-timers weekends and airplane landings are alike. If you can walk away from them, they're successful."

Today fan appreciation and gift days dot the baseball calendar with more frequency than doubleheaders. There are bobblehead doll days, cap days, jacket days, batting helmet days, T-shirt days, tote bag days, and all manner of promotional material known to promotionkind, all the legitimate offspring of that first Bat Day introduced by baseball's all-time promotion king, Bill Veeck.

TROPHIES

Baseball has always rewarded success. The rewards given have come in more different varieties than Baskin-Robbins has flavors.

Back in the old-old days, when baseball was still in knickers, awards usually took the form of trophy balls given to the winning teams. Later, players were the subject of their fans' adoration, the recipient being presented with a basket of flowers or some other token of appreciation. Sometimes the gift given to the player evoked the old saying, "look a gift horse in the mouth," like the time back in 1894 when first baseman Perry Werden hit a home run to win the game for Minneapolis and, as he crossed the plate, a committee of fans greeted him and rewarded him with a gold watch. As Werden walked away he chanced to look down at the watch and screamed, "You sons-of-a-gun," or somesuch. For the gold watch presented to him was his own! He had given it to a friend at the start

of the game for safekeeping. Then there was the time the entire population of Wichita, Kansas, showed up to honor its favorite son, White Sox second baseman Frank Isbell, one of the heroes of the just-concluded 1906 World Series. Isbell, who sported the handle the "Bald Eagle" for obvious reasons, was presented with a live bald eagle, a bald-faced mustang, and a billiard cue ball.

Sometimes those awards took other forms, like the coin of the realm with which Pittsburg Pirates owner Barney Dreyfuss rewarded his team after the 1903 World Series, tossing his shares of the profit into the players' pool and making the share of the losing Pirates players more than that of the winners, the Boston Americans. Another award more substantial than the wee gifts doled out by adoring fans was the motor car offered by the Chalmers Auto Company to the winner of the league batting title during

CY YOUNG AWARD

PRESENTED TO
SANDY KOUFAX

MOST VALUABLE PITCHER
NATIONAL LEAGUE
1963

The Cy Young Award given to Sandy Koufax of the Los Angeles Dodgers in 1963. Koufax's record in '63 was 25-5, and he led the National League in strikeouts (306), and ERA (1.88), thereby winning pitching's "Triple Crown." He was also voted the National League's Most Valuable Player that year, only the eighth player ever to win both the Cy Young and MVP Awards in the same year.

Going back to the very first time a player was given an award for his on-the-field performance—a silver tray awarded to James "Deacon" White of the Boston Red Stockings of the National Association, inscribed WON BY JIM WHITE AS THE MOST VALUABLE PLAYER TO BOSTON TEAM 1875—baseball has honored its "best" with awards. Among those awards are its Most Valuable Player award, its award to the best pitcher (The Cy Young Award), its award to the best hitter (The Silver Slugger Award), its award to the best fielders (The Gold Glove Award), its award to the best relief pitcher (The Rolaid's Relief Man of the Year Award), the Rookie of the Year, and many other awards for both on-the-field and off-the-field performances. Here, in this magnificent exhibit, the Hall of Fame displays these prestigious awards, all inscribed with previous winners, for fans to see first-hand and grasp their significance as well as their beauty.

the early 1900s. The 1910 title race came down to the last day of the season with Ty Cobb batting .385 and Nap Lajoie .376. While Cobb decided to sit out Detroit's double-header against the White Sox, Lajoie played both games of the double-header in St. Louis and went eight-for-eight. However, when it was later discovered that the Browns' infielders had been under orders from the manager to play back on the edge of the outfield whenever the popular Lajoie came to bat—giving him six "gift" bunt singles—the Chalmers Auto Co., embarrassed by the controversy, decided to award both a car.

By the '20s awards had become far more standardized, with championship rings taking the place of the earlier watch fobs given to the winning World Series team, and trophies, like the Most Valuable Players Award, given to players for their accomplishments. Soon trophies, silver bats, and gilded baseballs became baseball's way of rewarding success. And fan awards became things of the past, reserved for players' special days.

Many of the more recent awards—like World Series rings, trophies, and all manner of valuable hardware given to commemorate a team's or player's achievement—can be seen in this wonderful award display case that would be the envy of any jeweler. But don't look for a Morris chair or a billiard ball; they're relics of the past.

One of three Most Valuable Player trophies won by Stan Musial of the St. Louis Cardinals. The Most Valuable Player Award given to Stan Musial of the St. Louis Cardinals in 1946, the season Musial led the National League in batting with a .365 average, as well as in hits, doubles, triples, runs scored, and slugging average. He also led the Cardinals to the World Series.

DF - CARL YASTRZEMSKI - 6th AWARD
THE SPORTING NEWS
AMERICAN LEAGUE ALL-STAR FIELDING TEAM

The Gold Glove Award, started by the Rawlings Sporting Goods Company in 1957, recognizes superior individual fielding performances. The first winners of the Award were: Bobby Shantz, New York Yankees, pitcher; Sherman Lollar, Chicago White Sox, catcher; Gil Hodges, Brooklyn Dodgers, first base; Nellie Fox, Chicago White Sox, second base; Frank Malzone, Boston Red Sox, third base; Roy McMillan, Cincinnati Reds, shortstop; and Willie Mays, New York Giants, Minnie Minoso, Chicago White Sox, and Al Kaline, Detroit Tigers, outfield. Down through the years many players have been awarded the trophy multiple times, with the following receiving Gold Glove Awards as many as ten times: Jim Kaat and Greg Maddux, pitchers; Johnny Bench, catcher; Keith Hernandez, first baseman; Brooks Robinson and Mike Schmidt, third baseman; Ozzie Smith, shortstop; and Willie Mays, Al Kaline, and Barry Bonds, outfielders.

Since 1976, the Rolaids "Relief Man" (or "Fireman's") Award has been given to the best relief pitcher in both leagues—beginning with Bill Campbell of the Minnesota Twins in the American League and Rawley Eastwick in the National. Down through the years three relievers have won it the most times (Dan Quisenberry, Rollie Fingers, and Mario Rivera), and four future Hall of Famers have been awarded the trophy (Goose Gossage, Rollie Fingers, Bruce Sutter, and Dennis Eckersley).

Rolaids
ReliefMan
AWARD

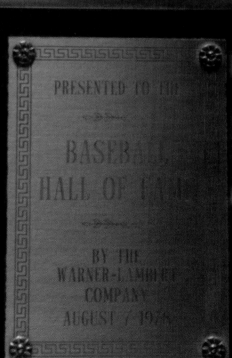

PRESENTED TO THE

BASEBALL
HALL OF FAME

BY THE
WARNER-LAMBERT
COMPANY
AUGUST / 1976

RECORDS

Records and the statistics behind them are the very mortar of the sport of baseball, allowing fans and statisticians alike to compare yesteryear's players with those of today.

Way back in the second decade of the 20th century *The Sporting News* trumpeted the accomplishments of superstars of the earlier era by writing, "Five great records have been placed on the tablet of baseball deeds by players of the present day, and they bid fair to remain for all time and never suffer effacement." *The Sporting News* then went on to cite those records they believed "would remain for all time" including, "The half-thousand victories credited to the mighty (Cy) Young; the ten-year record of Christy Mathewson, the famous New York pitcher; and the remarkable batting averages of Hans Wagner, the Pittsburg shortstop, and Napoleon Lajoie, the Cleveland second baseman, and the wonderful hitting of Ty Cobb during their major league careers (which) will be talked about while the genus fan continues to exist."

However, in the 80-plus years since *The Sporting News* listed those "five great records" that would "remain for all time," only those of Young and Cobb have withstood the test of time (so far) and escaped that old adage that "records are made to be broken." As the passing years have proven, the bookkeeper's mind has become more than rattled at the number of records that have been broken, from total home runs to total hits to total strikeouts as milestone-after-milestone has fallen by the wayside, with more predictably to fall in the years to come.

It is with that awareness that the Hall of Fame continually updates every home run hit by A-Rod, every strikeout thrown by Randy Johnson, every victory posted by Greg Maddux and every other individual statistical accomplishment of current players on multiple leader boards as they continue to mount assaults on all-time records.

Doubles

All-Time

Tris Speaker	793
Pete Rose	746
Stan Musial	725
Ty Cobb	724
Craig Biggio	668
George Brett	665
Honus Wagner	651
Napoleon Lajoie	648
Carl Yastrzemski	646
Hank Aaron	624

Active

Luis González	577
Jeff Kent	543
Iván Rodríguez	516
Frank Thomas	492
Manny Ramírez	483
Ken Griffey Jr.	480
Garret Anderson	471
Todd Helton	464
Carlos Delgado	450
Gary Sheffield	444

Tris Speaker
793 Career Doubles

Luis González
570 Career Doubles

Hits

All-Time

Pete Rose	4256
Ty Cobb	4191
Hank Aaron	3771
Stan Musial	3630
Tris Speaker	3515
Honus Wagner	3430
Carl Yastrzemski	3419
Paul Molitor	3319
Eddie Collins	3314
Willie Mays	3283

Active

Omar Vizquel	2607
Ken Griffey Jr.	2596
Gary Sheffield	2541
Luis González	2532
Iván Rodríguez	2437
Frank Thomas	2405
Derek Jeter	2369
Jeff Kent	2276
Álex Rodríguez	2259
Manny Ramírez	

Pete Rose
4256 Career Hits

Omar Vizquel

Runs Scored

All-Time

Rickey Henderson	2295
Ty Cobb	2246
Barry Bonds	2227
Hank Aaron	2174
Babe Ruth	2174
Pete Rose	2165
Willie Mays	2062
Stan Musial	1949
Lou Gehrig	1888
Tris Speaker	1881

Active

Ken Griffey Jr.	1564
Gary Sheffield	1552
Alex Rodriguez	1515
Frank Thomas	1481
Derek Jeter	1400
Luis Gonzalez	1393
Manny Ramirez	1368
Jim Thome	1358
Omar Vizquel	1343
Chipper Jones	1327

Batting Average

All-Time

Ty Cobb	.367

Active

NO-HIT GAMES

Grover Cleveland Alexander never did it. Dizzy Dean, ditto. Lefty Grove, as well. In fact more than half the pitchers elected to the Hall of Fame never did it—the "it" that of pitching a no-hitter.

Yet no-hitters, and that rarer-than-rare feat of pitching a 27-up-27-down perfect game, have been thrown by some of the least-known pitchers in baseball history. There have been no-hitters thrown by pitchers in their first Major League start (Bobo Holloman in 1953), perfect games by pitchers in their third start (Charley Robertson in 1922), pitchers with career losing records (Bo Belinsky in 1962), youngsters whose faces were still strangers to the razor (Jon Lester in 2008), fortysomethings (Warren Spahn in 1961), and collectively by a combination of pitchers (Vida Blue, Glenn Abbott, Paul Lindblad and Rollie Fingers for the A's in a 1975 contest). There have been those pitchers who have come *thisclose* to pitching perfection, retiring the first 26 men before the 27th and final batter spoiled their bid (Billy Pierce in 1958 and Milt Pappas in 1972).

To explain why some have pitched a legacy-making game while others haven't would be the subject of an expansive if not plausible essay, because nothing about their achievement is plausible. It undoubtedly has something to do with skill, but it might also lie in the pitcher being blessed by luck as much as skill in pursuit of his place in history.

Take Don Larsen's Perfect Game in the fifth game of the 1956 World Series, for instance. Larsen came close to losing his place in history in the fifth inning when Brooklyn Dodger first baseman Gil Hodges caught one of Larsen's change-of-pace curves and drove the ball into the outer reaches of Yankee Stadium's center field area known as "Death Valley." All of a sudden, there was Mickey Mantle running with all the speed at his command, outrunning the ball and, at the last second, sticking out his yawning glove and making the catch to preserve Larsen's gem.

Whatever the reason for their effort, whether it be skill and luck or pure skill alone, there have been over 260 no-hitters thrown since the first recorded one in major league ball back in 1876 by George Bradley. To commemorate this rare pitching performance, the Baseball Hall of Fame has gathered a ball from every one of these history-making feats since its opening in 1939 and has constructed this outsized display called "No-Hit Games" as befitting those pitchers who have thrown one—or more, as in the case of Bob Feller, Sandy Kofax, and Nolan Ryan—for their outsized achievement.

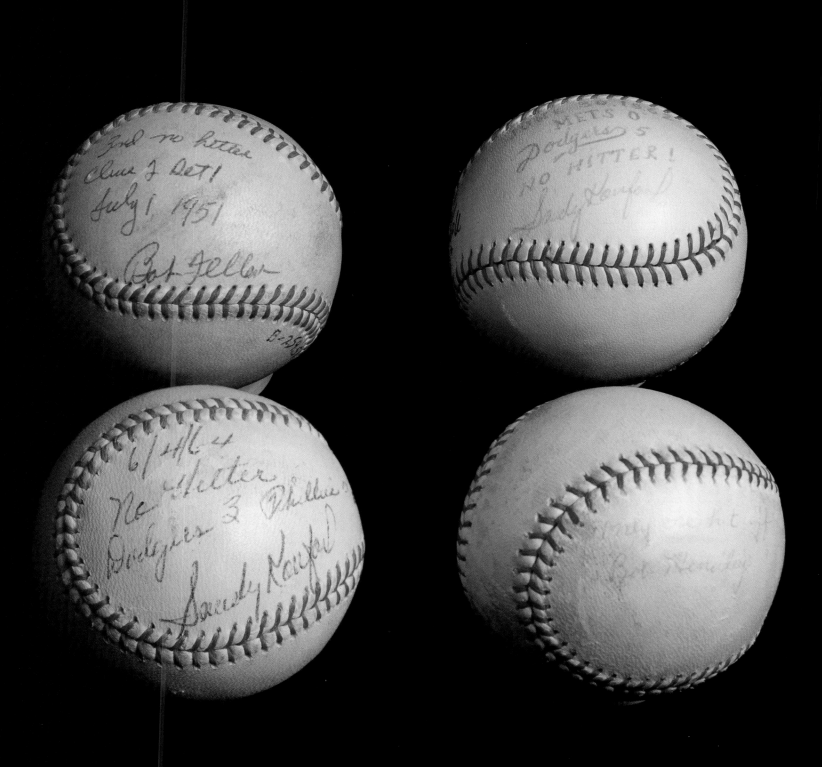

Four baseballs representing no-hitters thrown by Bob Feller and Sandy Koufax, two of only three modern pitchers (along with Nolan Ryan) to throw more than two no-hitters in their careers.

The very first no-hit game on record was thrown by Joseph McElroy Mann, pitching for Princeton in an intercollegiate game against Yale back on May 29, 1875. Two months later Joe Borden, pitching for Philadelphia in the old National Association against Chicago, threw professional baseball's first recorded no-hitter. Since that time there have been over 260 no-hitters thrown in Major League play, and 17 of those were 27-up-27-down perfect games. This visual honor roll of no-hitters, with a ball from every no-hitter thrown since the Hall of Fame's inception in 1939, celebrates those who have accomplished this outstanding feat of pitching excellence.

AUTUMN GLORY

Reggie Jackson

The World Series, called everything from "The World Serious" by writer Ring Lardner, "The Whirled Series" by cartoonist Walt Kelly, and "The Fall Classic" by millions of fans, is the most prestigious event on the American sports calendar. Some cynics might even say it is also the most pretentious, holding itself out to be a competition for the baseball championship of the world when it is, in reality, only for the championship of the northeastern quadrant of the Western Hemisphere. Although, when challenged on its geographic shortcomings, Yankee owner George Steinbrenner, whose team had just won the '78 Series, presciently said, "Well, we beat everybody who showed up."

Its beginnings are hidden somewhere in the dust of time, going all the way back to the 1880s when, as Al Spink, founder of *The Sporting News*, wrote at the time, "The World's Series in baseball was first played in 1884, fought out annually between the champions of the National League and the American Association." Then, after the American Association folded in 1891, the "Temple Cup" began in 1894 when, again according to Spink, "from 1894 until 1897 the Temple Cup games between the first and second teams in the National League were played for the trophy." Today all that remains of those Temple Cup games are a few write-ups in yellowing newspaper clips and the actual Cup itself, which is in the Hall of Fame.

Instead the World Series, as we have come to know it, began to take flight and form in 1903 when Barney Dreyfuss, owner of the

A well scuffed-up ball from the first modern Word Series, 1903, won by the Boston Americans over the Pittsburg Pirates, five games to three. ▶

Pittsburg (then spelled without an "h") Pirates, winners of three successive National League pennants, issued a challenge to Harry Killilea, owner of the American League pennant-winning Boston Americans, for the "world's championship." Boston surprised the heavily favored Pirates by winning five out of the eight games and the so-called championship of the world.

The next year Boston repeated in the American League and issued a challenge to the National League champion New York Giants. But John T. Brush, president of the Giants, branded the American League a "minor league" and issued a statement saying, "by winning the National League pennant, the Giants have already won the championship," thereby refusing the challenge.

However, Brush, prodded by strong public opinion, changed his mind after the 1904 season.

Working within the framework of the National Agreement, which he had helped draft, Major League Baseball established a best-of-seven series, won by the Giants over the Philadelphia Athletics in 1905.

Today, some 100 World Series later, the Series is still with us, the most enduring sports spectacle on the American—if not the world's—landscape. Over that stretch of time it has produced countless memorable moments, unlikely heroes, and great plays and players. More importantly, it has grown such that it no longer can be referred to in small letters; for the World Series is now writ large and everything about it is in caps.

Here, in this colorful display and timeline of the post-season are all those electrifying moments that have made the playoffs and the World Series what it is: the greatest sports spectacle of them all.

In what Los Angeles Dodgers manager Tommy Lasorda called "the greatest single performance I've ever seen," New York Yankee Reggie Jackson watches the third of his three home runs in the sixth game of the 1977 World Series, hit off three Dodger pitchers—Burt Hooten, Ellis Sosa, and Charlie Hough—on three consecutive pitches to clinch the Yankees' 21st World Championship.

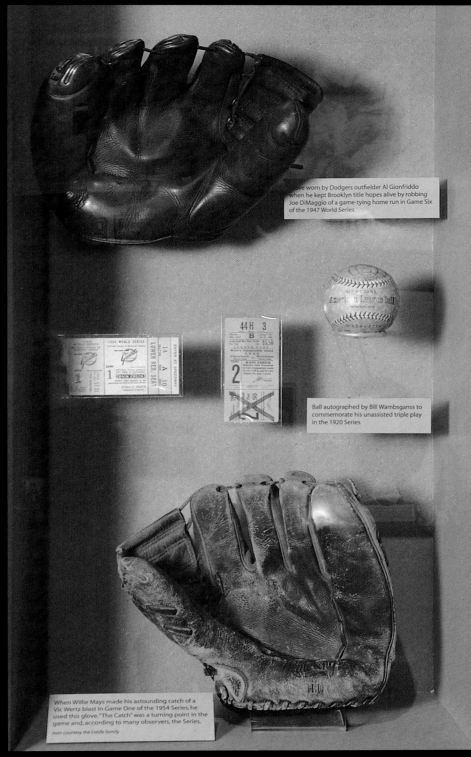

Glove worn by Dodgers outfielder Al Gionfriddo when he kept Brooklyn title hopes alive by robbing Joe DiMaggio of a game-tying home run in Game Six of the 1947 World Series

Ball autographed by Bill Wambsganss to commemorate his unassisted triple play in the 1920 Series

When Willie Mays made his astounding catch of a Vic Wertz blast in Game One of the 1954 Series, he used this glove. "The Catch" was a turning point in the game and, according to many observers, the Series.

loan courtesy the Liddle family

Not all of the great moments in World Series play are those made by the team at bat; sometimes they are made in the field. Here, in this post-season display are artifacts recall-ing three of the greatest: (top) Al Gionfriddo's catch of Joe DiMaggio's booming shot in Game 6 of the 1947 Series; (middle) Bill Wambsganss' unassisted triple play in Game 5 of the 1920 Series; and Willie Mays' unbelievable play—forever known simply as "The Catch"—in the 1954 World Series.

"The Catch," and equally amazing throw, by New York Giants' centerfielder Willie Mays of Vic Wertz's 425-foot drive in the 8th inning of the first game of the '54 Series, preserved a 2-2 tie and sent the game into extra innings where it was won in the 10th on a Dusty Rhodes home run as the Giants swept the Cleveland Indians in four games.

A jewelry case filled with the rings and press pins issued by World Series teams, along with prototypes of some of the pins and rings developed by "almost" teams in anticipation of their playing in the Series, and a medallion presented to Detroit first baseman Dan Brouthers by actress Helen Dauvray after the 1887 Series.

No sporting event captures the headlines or pulls at the heartstrings more than the World Series. It's where you can expect the unexpected, see the extraordinary, and be party to the dramatic. You can almost feel it in the exhilaration of a Yogi Berra as he leaps into the arms of a Don Larsen; hear it in the thwack of bat meeting ball, like surf hitting shore, as Bill Mazeroski swings; and see it in the hunched shoulders of a despairing Bill Buckner. This Hall of Fame display of some of those memorable moments captures the drama of the World Series—from the Mets jumping for joy after winning the '69 Series, Carlton Fisk waving his home run fair in the '75 Series, Sandy Koufax and John Roseboro celebrating a Dodger victory over the Yankees in the '63 Series, and Enos Slaughter's World Series-winning dash for home in the '46 Series. Great moments all in baseball's greatest showcase, the World Series.

The retro cap worn by Kent Tekulve of the victorious Pittsburgh Pirates' "We are Family" team, which defeated the Baltimore Orioles four-games-to-three in the 1979 World Series.

TICKETS:

(top) The ticket for the sixth and final game of the 1977 World Series between the New York Yankees and Los Angeles Dodgers—won by the Yankees 8-4 on three home runs on three consecutive pitches by Reggie Jackson off three Dodger pitchers. (middle) Ticket for the fourth game of the 1920 World Series between the Cleveland Indians and the Brooklyn Dodgers, won by the Indians, 5-1, behind Stan Coveleski's five-hitter, the second of his three wins in Cleveland's five-games-to-two World Series win. (bottom) Ticket for the opening game of the 1935 World Series between the Detroit Tigers and Chicago Cubs, won by the Cubs on Lon Warneke's four-hitter, 3-0. The Tigers would come back to win the Series in six games for their first-ever world championship.

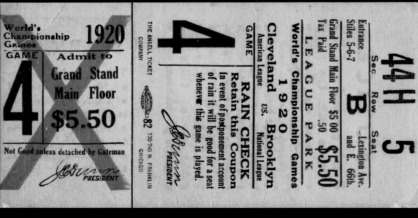

Three years before the modern World Series began in 1903, the *Pittsburg Chronicle-Telegraph* sponsored a title serie
between the first- and second-place teams in the 1900 National League pennant race, the Brooklyn Superbas and the
Pittsburg Pirates. Brooklyn won the Series and the trophy, which was given to Brooklyn's star pitcher, Joe McGinnity
along with a $100 bonus.

BASEBALL CARDS

Before the 1970s, baseball cards were hardly the business they are today. Remember how it was if you were a kid back in those days, after a baseball game, walking out of a drugstore across the street from the corner lot with a pack of newly purchased bubble gum in one hand and your baseball glove tucked under your arm, slowly unwrapping the packet to peek inside to see what baseball cards the packet contained? Whether you already had those cards or if they were new additions to your collection?

Back then collecting baseball cards was hardly as lucrative as it is today. We never analyzed it; it was simply "the thing to do." Every waking moment, or so it seemed, was devoted to our baseball card collection, memorizing those you already had and those you needed. Then, finding someone on the playground who had brought "dupes" (duplicates) with them—usually in a cigar box—rifling through their batch of cards, all the while chanting the young collector's litany, "got it; got it; got it; need it; got it; etc." before getting down to the business at hand: swapping. (And if you lived in, say, Washington, D.C., calculating the number of Washington Senator players' cards you needed to swap just to get one Joe DiMaggio or Ted Williams).

Back then, who ever thought that those pleasures of our youth would become the treasures of our older age?

Maybe it all started with a book called *The Sports Collectors Bible*, which came out in the early '70s and not only organized the until-then disorganized groupings of cards but gave them prices—the Honus Wagner card valued at the then unbelievable price of $17,500! Or maybe it was the first card trading show, held in Yorktown, New York, and attended by 23 collectors from all over the country.

Whatever it was, collecting baseball cards was now more than a mere hobby. As one youngster, his eyes barely able to see the top of the dealer's table, asked the dealer at one of those early card shows, "Is there money in these cards?" As it turns out, there was gold in them thar cards!

Cards have a looooong history, going all the way back to the 1860s when Goodwin & Company issued cards with pictures of various nineteenth-century American heroes—police captains, show girls, bicyclists, prizefighters, and Indian chiefs—all designed to sell their cigarettes. However, since baseball was the national obsession, they soon began turning out cards depicting heroes of the diamond with each pack of Old Judge and Gypsy Queen cigarettes. The cards were small, 1¾ x 2½ inches, and sepia colored with pictures of the players standing perfectly motionless, with hands or bats extended toward a ball hanging by a visible string from the ceiling.

The most famous and valuable sports collectible, the T-206 "White-bordered" Honus Wagner card, part of a series issued by the American Tobacco Company from 1909–11. A non-smoker, Wagner considered the card to be an implicit endorsement of smoking and demanded the company recall his card. Now considered to be sports collecting's "Holy Grail," the card commands over two million dollars in the marketplace.

WAGNER. PITTSBURG

Soon other cigarette companies, like Allen & Ginter and D. Buchner, issued beautifully colored cards and P. H. Mayo & Bros. Tobacco Company proffering black-and-white cards, all the better to increase sales of brands now long forgotten. When the American Tobacco Company eliminated all competition by acquiring the independent companies, the need for sales promotion gimmicks like baseball cards ended. So, too, did the issuance of the cards themselves.

In 1890 the Sherman Antitrust Act took effect and the tobacco trust was divided into separate entities. Competition was revived, and with it came a deluge of baseball cards promoting such exotically named brands as Fatima, Mecca, Sweet Caporals, El Principa de Wales and over 200 brands, all, as Jimmy Durante would say, "Trying to get into the act" by issuing their own cards.

By the first decade of the 20th century candy manufacturers, having discovered that the majority of those collecting baseball cards were youngsters, got into the act and soon such companies as Amer-

ican Caramel, C.A. Briggs, "E" Candy/Caramel, U.S. Caramel, Mello-Mint and Cracker Jack got a "sweet tooth" for the market, issuing cards of their own. In the '30s, chewing gum companies like Tattoo Orbit, Goudey Gum, and DeLong Gum brought out their own series of cards.

Just as World War I had, World War II brought an end to the production of cards because of wartime scarcities. With the end of hostilities bubble gum cards re-emerged, first the Leaf Confectionery Co., Bowman, and the Frank H. Fleer Corporation, and later by the company most identified with baseball cards, Topps Chewing Gum, Inc.

Today nostalgia is big business. And nothing is bigger than the baseball cards shown here in this exhibit memorializing a fabulous array of great players, some within our living memory, others portals to bygone eras. However, as baseball writer Bill Madden says, "It's nice to know nostalgia is worth something, even though it will never be for sale."

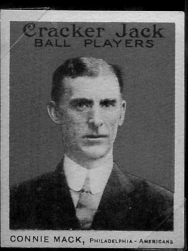

CONNIE MACK, Philadelphia - Americans

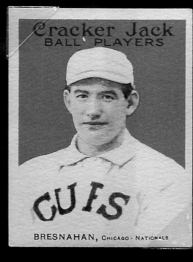

BRESNAHAN, Chicago - Nationals

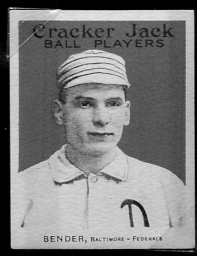

BENDER, Baltimore - Federals

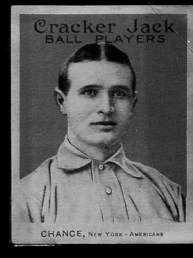

CHANCE, New York - Americans

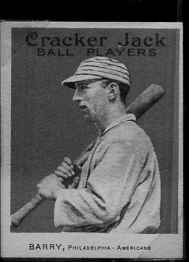

BARRY, Philadelphia - Americans

ALEXANDER, Philadelphia - Nationals

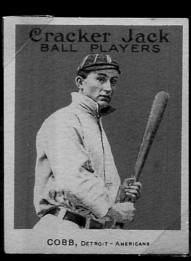

COBB, Detroit - Americans

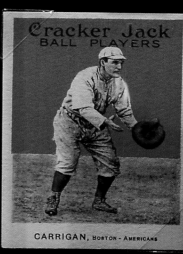

CARRIGAN, Boston - Americans

COLLINS, Chicago - Americans

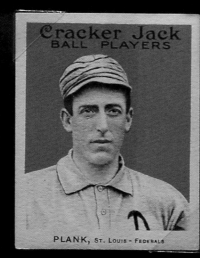

PLANK, St. Louis - Federals

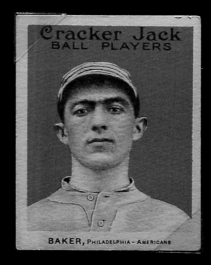

BAKER, Philadelphia - Americans

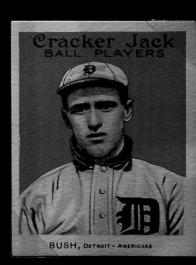

BUSH, Detroit - Americans

1914-15, Cracker Jack

Ted Williams: 1951 Bowman

Sandy Koufax: 1961 Topps

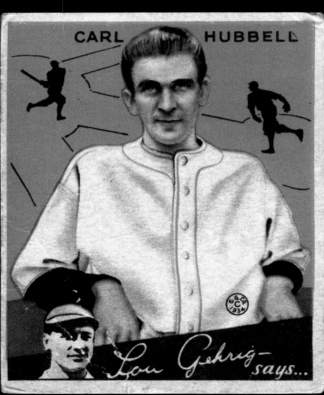

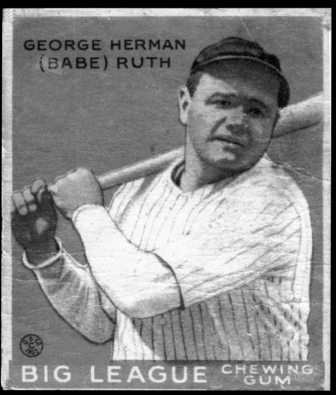

Carl Hubbell: 1934 "Big League" by Goudy Gum

Babe Ruth: 1933 "Big League" by Goudy Gum

Mickey Mantle: 1961 Topps

Robin Roberts: 1952 Topps

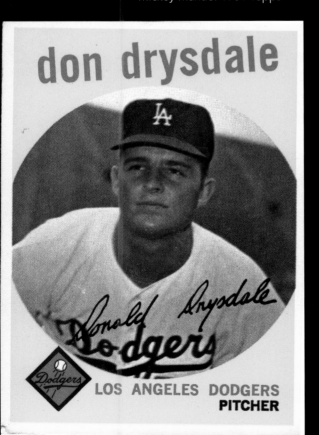

Roberto Clemente: 1956 Topps

Don Drysdale: 1959 Topps

ABBOTT & COSTELLO

From the moment they first uttered those famous words, "Who's on first?" to a national radio audience on Kate Smith's radio show back in 1938, Bud Abbott and Lou Costello's comedy routine has been part of classic Americana, combining sports, slang and wordplay. Repeating the same phrase back and forth, it had a completely different meaning when each one said it.

Introduced in a day and age when many players had fanciful nicknames—like "Pepper" or "Frenchy" or "Ducky"—the skit struck a chord with baseball fans as they chanted off the apparently misleading names of those on Abbott & Costello's team verbatim: "Who" on first; "What" on second; "I Don't Know" on third; "I Don't Give a Darn" at shortstop; "Tomorrow" pitching; "Today" catching; "Why" in left field; and "Because" in center.

The only position not mentioned in the routine was right field.

Performed on stage and radio over 10,000 times, and in movies like One Night in the Tropics and Naughty Nineties, the skit was named "Best Comedy Sketch of the 20th Century" by *Time* magazine in 1999.

Although one of the most frequently asked questions is, "Are Abbott and Costello in the Baseball Hall of Fame?" the answer is "No" as members, but "Yes" as the subjects of an entertaining exhibit. Lou Costello, dressed as a peanut vendor named Sebastian Dinwiddie, asks Bud Abbott, in the role of the Wolves' manager Dexter Broadhurst, "Who's on First?" And with that, you will begin to enjoy their verbal "pepper game" just as millions have over the years.

The gold-plated record of the famous "Who's On First" routine, donated to the Hall of Fame in 1956 by the duo who made it famous, Bud Abbott and Lou Costello.

"TAKE ME OUT TO THE BALL GAME"

The 1900s was an era when America sang its songs—on street corners, in barbershops, around campfires, in nickelodeons, anywhere and everywhere. Most of the publishers of those songs along Tin Pan Alley—named for a block along New York's 28th Street for the sound of pianos tinkling away all day—looked for any emotion, any subject matter to sell their songs, the favorite emotion being the art of pitching woo, whether pitched down by the old millstream or under a shining harvest moon.

By 1908 baseball was as popular a place to woo as any place—or, as Detroit manager Hughie Jennings said in an interview, "I believe that whenever a young fellow takes a lady to a ball game he has very serious intentions." The year 1908 was also the year when the most dominant pitcher in baseball was a pitcher for the New York Giants named Christy Mathewson. The winner of 140 games over the previous five seasons and on his way to a 37-win season in 1908, Mathewson was seen as being made of sunshine and blood-red tissue, as clean-cut as the then-idealized "Gibson Man," embodying everything that was seen to be honorable in those days, including promising his mother he would never pitch on Sundays. He had even gone to college, as opposed to most other players who were so described as "tobacco-chewing, beer-guzzling bums." Matty not only brought respectability to the game, but he brought women to the ballpark. His very presence on the field any given day would prompt a young pompadoured lady to say to her beau, "Let's go out to the Polo Grounds to watch the young collegian play." Which was just another way of saying, "Take Me Out to the Ball Game."

Those exact thoughts occurred to a tunesmith named Jack Norworth one spring afternoon in 1908 as he rode a subway and chanced to notice a poster advertising a ball game at the Polo Grounds. Inspired by the advertisement, Norworth, who knew how to write a story in song, having written, among other songs, "Shine On, Harvest Moon," hurriedly scribbled down on a piece of scrap paper the story of a young lady named Katie Casey, telling the tale (in the oft-forgotten verse) of how, when her beau had ideas of going "to see a show," instead asked him to "Take Me Out to the Ball Game."

Notes in hand, Norworth took them to a music publishing house run by Harry Von Tilzer, whose brother, Albert, had written over three thousand songs before his first big hit, "Only a Bird in a Gilded Cage," and later "Wait Till the Sun Shines, Nelly." Albert provided the music to Norworth's words and together they published what was called at the time, "The Sensational Base Ball Song."

But sensational it was not. At least not in the beginning, or until it began being played over and over again in those sing-a-longs accompanying lantern shows of the time while cameramen changed reels. It then became the hit Norworth and Von Tilzer had hoped for, selling millions of copies of sheet music.

Ironically, "Take Me Out to the Ball Game" was not played at a ballgame until Pepper Martin and his tub-thumping group of Gashouse Gang members played it before the fourth game of the 1934 Series to an appreciative St. Louis crowd. Since then it has been sung at ballparks everywhere, most famously by gravel-voiced Cubs announcer Harry Caray, heard in a display on the third floor singing more than a little off-key during the seventh-inning stretch at Wrigley Field.

Recorded hundreds of times by such artists as Frank Sinatra, Liberace, and even Harpo Marx, "Take Me Out to the Ball Game" has become America's third most frequently sung song—behind only "The Star-Spangled Banner" and "Happy Birthday." And, in 2008, on the occasion of the 100th anniversary of Jack Norworth's scribbled story of Katie Casey's plea to her beau to take her out to the ball game, the U.S. Post Office issued a stamp celebrating the song, putting the official stamp of approval on one of the best-known songs in the American treasury, baseball's anthem, "Take Me Out to the Ball Game."

The original lyrics of baseball's anthem, "Take Me Out to the Ball Game," written by Jack Norworth in 1908 on a subway train after seeing a sign advertising a New York Giants game—complete with crossed-out words, misspelled words and doodles.

SCRIBES

Baseball's early popularity wafted on two wings—word of mouth and word of the press—as the public's newfound fascination with the game coincided with the coming into existence of the modern newspaper.

Newspaper coverage of the game began as early as the 1850s and by 1887 the *Sunday Mercury* of New York printed telegraph reports of the National Club of Washington's tour through the Midwest. Soon baseball news became part of every newspaper and those while-you-get-your-hair-cut weeklies of the time, appearing in seas of type surrounding an island of lithography and giving it the appearance of a tombstone.

The writing of the time was quaint by modern standards. Take, for example, this story written in 1887: "Tiernan was lucky enough to get first base on balls. Just as he started to burglarize the second hassock, Ward smote the ball furiously to right center. Tiernan ran all the way home with New York's first run of the game. Then there was a cheer, and a gamin on the bleaching boards cried, 'Hooray! We ain't skunked.'"

By the turn of the century some writers were still calling a curve ball "a mackerel," the dugout "the dog kennel," a spectacular play "a la carte," and home plate "the pay station." *The Chicago Tribune's* report of a 1909 Cubs game contained the following head-scratchers: "The Cardinals were outbatted by many parsangs;" "Jeff Overall cut the cardiac region of the plate"; and "But for Brown's unfortunate decease, he could have scored standing up."

Sportswriting was to change in 1910 with the emergence of a new breed of writer when Grantland Rice came to New York and, along with fellow wordsmiths Damon Runyon, Ring Lardner, Westbrook Pegler, W.O. McMeehan, O.B. Keller and Fred Lieb, changed the style of sportswriting forever. Together they were to lift the craft, combining the poetry of baseball with the prose of literature. Their literary merit was such that one observer was prompted to write: "Sports pages popular only in barbershops and pool rooms found their way into more and more homes—by the front door."

World Series
In Press
Box
Oct. 19...

Members of the press (plus famous fan "Nuf Ced" McGreevey, with mustache) take their places in the press box before
the start of the 1911 World Series between the Philadelphia Athletics and the New York Giants, a Series in which the
scribes labeled Philadelphia third baseman Frank Baker "Home Run" for his two home runs as he led the Athletics to

A view from the broadcast booth, including the microphones used by (left to right) NBC's broadcast pioneer Graham McNamee, the voice of the first World Series to be broadcast; CBS's Ted Husing; and Wrigley Field PA announcer Pat Pieper. In the foreground are the typewriters used by (left to right) New York sportswriter Kenny Smith and sportswriting giant Grantland Rice.

Together, along with several other sports writers of the time, like Bugs Baer and John Drebinger, they gave us many of the most memorable lines of all time—like Lardner's "Although he was a poor hitter, he also was a poor fielder"; Baer's "He had the greatest day since Lizzie Borden got two for two in Fall River"; Runyon's "Mathewson pitched against Cincinnati yesterday. Another way of putting it is that Cincinnati lost a game of baseball. The first statement means the same as the second"; Keller's "How do we know what (Walter) Johnson's got? Nobody's seen it yet"; and Rice's classic, "For when the One Great Scorer comes To write against your name, He marks—not that you won or lost—But how you played the game."

In turn this first wave of great sportswriters was followed by others who stepped into their shoes and stood on their shoulders, like Red Smith, Jim Murray, Frank Graham, Shirley Povich, Jimmy Cannon and Dick Young, down to baseball writers of today, such as Dave Anderson, Peter Gammons, Bill Madden and so many others, all of whom have been members of the calling Red Smith labeled "The most pleasant way of making a living man has yet developed, sports writing."

Their many contributions to the sport and to baseball journalism are acknowledged by the fascinating display entitled "Scribes," honoring those who have served as baseball's storytellers down through the ages.

The microphones used by (left to right) Bob Elson of Milwaukee, Ernie Harwell of Detroit, and Wayne Hoyt of Cincinnati. The "coat of many colors" worn by national broadcaster Lindsey Nelson. And the score books of (left to right) Edgar Munzel of the *Chicago Sun-Times* and Allen Lewis of the *Philadelphia Inquirer*.

MIKEMEN

By the early 1920s a new phenomenon called "radio" had burst upon the scene transmitting an estimated 56 weekly hours of talk, 42 of classical music, and 259 of popular entertainment into the nation's living rooms over swan's-neck loud speakers. Beginning on the afternoon of August 5, 1921, part of that menu of popular entertainment became live baseball games, with the first broadcast beaming over the airwaves from station KDKA in Pittsburgh with announcer Harold Arlin broadcasting a game between the Pirates and the Phillies. That fall NBC's flagship station, WJZ in New York, carried the World Series between the Giants and the Yankees with a reporter from the *Newark Call* phoning in the play-by-play for rebroadcast over the airways by announcer Tommy Cowan. NBC's head, David Sarnoff, saw the mating of radio and baseball as a perfect wedding of two pastimes and continued broadcasting the World Series in 1922 with Grantland Rice manning the microphone. In 1923, he hired radio announcer Graham McNamee, an entertainer who had worked with

comedian Ed Wynn, to handle the broadcast. McNamee, possessing bell-shaped tones and a flair for words combined with a frenzied commentary, wove word pictures all game long, never letting the facts on the field interfere with his vibrant call. After the first game of the Series, sportswriter Ring Lardner, who had been seated next to McNamee all game long, got up and said to nobody in particular, "They must have been playing a doubleheader here this afternoon—the game I saw and the game McNamee announced."

Regardless of McNamee's histrionics, radio, with its sound of imagery, had proven it was made for the game of baseball. It became every fan's lifeline to their favorite team as the sounds of the game wafted into their living rooms on a leisurely summer afternoon with announcers painting word pictures that enabled them to see things with their ears.

To most of the fans the announcer was more closely identified with the team than many of its players. To them he was like a favorite uncle who told stories and occasionally wove his own catchphrases into their play-by-play, creating his own language. What Brooklyn fan will ever forget Red Barber's "They're tearin' up the pea patch" or "The bases are F.O.B." (full of Brooklyns), or his signature "Oh, Doctor . . ."? Or any Yankee fan Mel Allen's "How about that?" or "Going . . . going . . . gone!"? Or a Cubbie fan Bert Wilson's "We don't care who wins . . . as long as it's the Cubs"? Or a Boston Braves fan Frankie Frisch's "Oh, those base on balls"? Or a Pirate fan Rosey Rowswell's "Doozie Maroonie"? Or an Indian fan Jimmy Dudley's "Lotsa good luck, ya heah!"? Or a Reds fan Marty Brennaman's "And *this* one belongs to the Reds!"? Or a Mariners fan Dave Neihaus's "My, oh my. . . ."? Or a Yankee fan Phil Rizzuto's "Holy Cow!"? Or a Red Sox fan Ned Martin's "Long gone and hard to find."?

In their own inimitable style announcers have even sung songs; Dizzy Dean chirping away with his rendition of "The Wabash Cannonball" and Arch McDonald offering a chorus or two of "They Cut Down the Old Pine Tree." Some have localized the broadcast by tying in a regional sponsor, as when Mel Allen called every Yankee homer a "Ballantine Blast" and Curt Gowdy welcomed Red Sox listeners with a cheery "Hi, neighbor. Have a 'Gansett" (as in Narragansett beer). Then there were those announcers who identified fans in the stands, like Ernie Harwell who called out the home town of every Tiger fan who caught a foul ball, and Harry Caray who wished every fan from Illinois and nearby communities a happy birthday, or Phil Rizzutto who thanked every Italian restaurant east of the Hudson for sending him cannoli.

Quirky, funny, homey, and more, they were a far cry from the old days when every announcer merely said an obligatory, "And, if you're in the neighborhood, stop in . . . they're plenty of seats available."

These are the men—along with other great voices like Vin Scully, Herb Carneal, Harry Kalas and so many other Ford E. Frick Award Winners— who have shaped our baseball experience and are now honored by being part of the display of winners of the prestigious Ford E. Frick Award for Broadcasting Excellence.

The winners of the prestigious Ford E. Frick Award for Broadcasting Excellence.

BASEBALL AT THE MOVIES

By the turn of the 20th century thousands of stores across the country had converted their emporia into nickelodeons—small theatres offering "moving pictures" for a five-cent admission fee. It wasn't long before the first baseball movie, *"The Ball Game,"* a brief baseball film produced by Thomas Edison in 1898, took its place amongst the travelogues and westerns of the day.

Over the next two decades baseball movies were few and far between, with either shorts like *The Fate of the Rotten Umpire*; *How the Office Boy Saw the Ball Game*; *The Pinch Hitter*; *His Last Game*; and *The Busher*; or features wrapped around a current superstar, like Honus Wagner in *Spring Fever* (1919), Frank "Home Run"

Baker in *The Short Stop's Double* (1913), Ty Cobb in *Somewhere in Georgia* (1917), and John McGraw in *One Touch of Nature* (1917). The few made were so preposterously forced and devoid of plot that they were, to use a word of the times, "turkeys," and producers quickly returned to making their usual standard fare of car-chase comedies, shoot-'em-up westerns, and cast-of-thousands Civil War moving pictures.

If the public didn't care for baseball movies, baseball players didn't care much for "movies" either, Detroit Tiger manager Hughie Jennings admonishing his 1911 club that they were "bad for their eyesight" and advising them that they should stay away from "picture shows."

In 1920 the movies finally found the perfect vehicle for a baseball movie, Babe Ruth, whose 29 home runs the previous season had lit up baseball's skies and made him the first hero of what sportswriter Paul Gallico called "The Golden Age of Sports." The movie, *Headin' Home*, cast Ruth as a country bumpkin living with his widowed mother in a white-picket-fenced-in home with a cute little sister, "Pigtails," and her tag-along dog, "Herman." When Ruth wasn't saving the dog from the local dogcatcher he was out in the woods carving up trees for baseball bats which he used to hit home runs—one of which he hit through a church window five blocks away. Unaffected by the fame his home runs had gained for him, he returned to his hometown a hero. One critic wrote of Ruth's performance, "Babe Ruth and *Headin' Home* do not deal, except occasionally and briefly, in the regulation movie stuff. They try comedy, not heroics, and score not infrequently." Ruth, who made fifty thousand dollars for his movie debut, came back later in the decade to make an appearance in *The Babe Comes Home*, another successful effort.

With the success of Ruth's movies, baseball films were not rare during the Depression. There were over 30 baseball movies made between 1921 and 1941, and in 1942 Hollywood produced *The Pride of the Yankees*, the story of Lou Gehrig, who had died tragically the previous year. Starring Gary Cooper, the film was a three-hanky success culminating in Gehrig's famous "luckiest man on the face of the earth" farewell speech, and showcased former Yankee greats such as Ruth, Bill Dickey, Mark Koenig and Bob Meusel in cameo roles.

In 1948, Hollywood returned to the subject of baseball, this time a biopic of Babe Ruth, *The Babe Ruth Story*. Unfortunately, the picture was a disaster, both at the box office and with the critics, one writing of the star, William Bendix,

"Regardless of advertised coaching, Mr. Bendix still swings like a rusty gate." The review added, "The atmosphere of a big-league ball park is as remote from this picture as that of a church."

Although many thought baseball pictures were now "box-office poison," *The Babe Ruth Story* was merely the beginning as Hollywood turned to baseball as one of its favorite subjects, the next year producing *It Happens Every Spring* and *The Stratton Story*.

In 1950 Hollywood began turning out baseball picture after baseball picture, almost one a year, ranging from biopics to musicals to comedies, and re-introducing us to old stars portrayed in celluloid like Dizzy Dean (in *The Pride of St. Louis*) and Grover Cleveland Alexander (in *The Winning Team*) as well as new ones years later like "Moonlight" Graham (in *Field of Dreams*) and "Crash" Davis (in *Bull Durham*).

The line-up of baseball movies made over the last half century is almost as impressive as the line-up of the '27 Yankees, and includes such entertaining titles as: *The Jackie Robinson Story*, starring Jackie Robinson playing himself (1950); *Angels in the Outfield* (1951); *The Pride of St. Louis* (1952); *The Winning Team* (1952); *Damn Yankees* (1958); *Safe at Home* (1962); *Bang the Drum Slowly* (1973); *The Bingo Long Traveling All-Stars and Motor Kings* (1976); *The Bad News Bears* (1976); *The Natural* (1984); *Bull Durham* (1988); *Eight Men Out* (1988); *Major League* (1989); *Field of Dreams* (1989); *Mr. Baseball* (1992); *The Babe* (1992); *A League of Their Own* (1992); *The Scout* (1994); *Cobb* (1994); The Fan (1996); *For Love of the Game* (1999); *61** (2001); *The Rookie* (2002); *Fever Pitch* (2005); *Everyone's Hero* (2006) and *The Final Season* (2007).

Many of the placards for these movies can be found in the "Baseball at the Movies" display, a display dedicated to the mating of two national pastimes: baseball and the movies.

Some of the props used in baseball movies, from left to right: props and costumes used from *A League of Their Own*; the Durham Bulls uniform worn by Tim Robbins in *Bull Durham*; the White Sox uniform worn by Ray Liotta in *Field of Dreams*; the Cincinnati Reds uniform from *Eight Men Out*; and the Owls Big Lake uniform worn by Dennis Quaid in *The Rookie*; along with various props, bats and balls from *Eight Men Out*.

The "Baseball at the Movies" display with artifacts and pictures from various baseball movies, including (far left window) the uniform worn by Robert Redford in *The Natural*; (right of the door window) uniforms from *The Bingo Long Traveling All-Stars and Motor Kings*; and (far right) uniforms from the movies *The Babe Ruth Story*, *Damn Yankees*, and *The Pete Gray Story*. Along the walls are photos from movies such as (left to right) *The Bad News Bears*, *The Bingo Long Traveling All-Stars and Motor Kings*, *Bang the Drum Slowly*, *Damn Yankees*, *The Jackie Robinson Story*, *Angels in the Outfield*, *Kill the Umpire*, *The Stratton Story*, and *Pride of the Yankees*. All surround a television monitor displaying movie trailers of many of the great baseball movies on a loop.

Between the Baseball at the Movies and Sandlot Kids' Clubhouse exhibits stands this impressive statue of the fictional Mighty Casey from Ernest Lawrence Thayer's famous poem, "Casey at the Bat."

SANDLOT KIDS' CLUBHOUSE

The Hall of Fame brochure describes the "Sandlot Kids' Clubhouse" as "A uniquely designed experience for young, aspiring Hall of Famers. The clubhouse features a host of activities for children ages 4-10, with games, film clips, reading and creative artifact presentations."

But the Sandlot Kids' Clubhouse is more. Much more. It is all about connecting generations and passing on the older generation's love affair with baseball to the younger ones. For no sport is as family-oriented as the game of baseball, second and third-generation players following in their father and grandfather's footsteps onto the diamond, and off, youngsters remembering learning about the game from their fathers and grandfathers or playing catch with them—just as Kevin Costner, in his role of Ray Kinsella in *Field of Dreams*, asks the spectre of his father, "Wanna have a catch?"

One of the most heartwarming stories of this bonding of father and son in their mutual love of the game is the one that begins with a photo found under a World War II display case during the Hall of Fame's 1994 renovation. The photo was turned over to the Chief Curator of the Museum, who found this loving inscription on the back: "You were never [too] tired to play catch. On your days off you helped build the Little League field. You always came to watch me play. You were a Hall of Fame dad. I wish I could share this moment with you. Your son, Pat." Unable to identify the photo, Spencer spent months in his search until finally, with the help of others, it was identified as being that of Joe O'Donnell from nearby Wellsville, New York, whose son Pat had placed the photo in a small opening between the bottom of the display case and the floor seven years before as a symbolic way of lighting a candle in honor of his deceased father for having shared his love of baseball with him.

It is this love affair for the ages, both young and old, that can be seen at the Sandlot Kids' Clubhouse as fathers and grandfathers share films and books with their youngsters, ensuring that shared memories are memories for life. These memories make the older generation "Hall of Famers" in the mind's eye of their kids, as Joe O'Donnell was to his son, Pat.

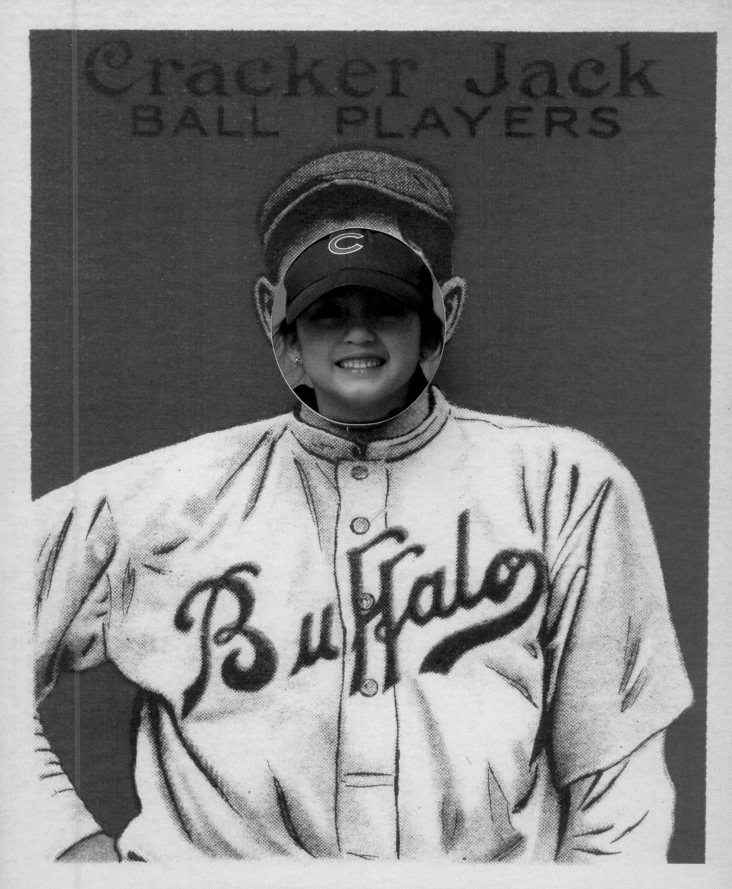

FUTURE HALL OF FAMER

THE ART OF BASEBALL

For decades artists and sculptors have devoted their attention to the American experience. No experience is more American than the game of baseball. Here, in The Art of Baseball exhibit on the first floor, can be found ample testimony to the influence the National Pastime has had on these artists.

This extraordinary exhibit provides the viewer a wonderful panorama of their richly varied talents, each, in their own medium, seeing the game through their own eyes, their works speaking for themselves.

This remarkable variety of artwork fea-tures representations of every era of the game from J. G. Brown's enduring vision of early baseball, an 1860 oil on canvas entitled "The Little Baseball Player," to Norman Rockwell's famed cover art in "Game Called Because of Rain," to LeRoy Neiman's acrylic "The Hall of Famer," and to Rhoda Sherbell's oil on white gypsum cement sculpture "Casey Stengel," along with several other pieces on everything from the beginnings of the game up to the present.

It's an exhibit no baseball fan can afford to miss, one worthy of a major museum of art.

"The Mighty Babe" by artist Robert Thom celebrates Babe Ruth's legendary "called shot" against the Chicago Cubs in Game 3 of the 1932 World Series.

Sincerely
Norman
Rockwell

THE MUSEUM SHOP

There is no better way to wind up your magical tour of the Hall of Fame than to visit the Hall of Fame Museum Store where you'll find an extensive selection of baseball gifts of Hall of Fame proportions—from caps, jackets, jerseys and shirts to gifts, collectibles, books and more. Whether the item you're looking for is that of your favorite team or as a remembrance of your visit to Cooperstown, the Museum Shop is the perfect exclamation point for your visit.

◀ A study of Norman Rockwell's "Game Called Because of Rain".

THE A. BARTLETT GIAMATTI RESEARCH CENTER

In a voice sounding as if he had just gargled with ground glass, Casey Stengel once famously said, "You could look it up." So it was only natural that an oil painting of "The Old Professor" would be hung in a prominent place on the wall of the A. Bartlett Giamatti Research Center to serve as constant reminder of Casey's words of wisdom to the Library's dedicated staff of researchers. Approximately 60,000 times a year, they look up the answers to questions posed by writers, historians, archivists, and fans, culled from the millions of documents and artifacts, newspaper, magazine, and scrapbook clippings, and thousands of player files housed in the largest repository of information possessed by any sports library in the world.

Part of the Hall of Fame since it first opened in 1939, the library quickly outgrew its cramped quarters as it acquired more and more historic documents—including the donated scrapbooks of Hall of Famers John McGraw, Frankie Frisch and George Weiss. Efforts to provide the library with expanded space culminated in the construction of its own building, facing Cooper Park and its classic statue of James Fenimore Cooper, in 1968.

At the dedication of the new facility, former Baseball Commissioner Ford Frick, after acknowledging the contributions of local philanthropist and civic leader Stephen Clark for "starting the whole thing," went on to praise those who had a hand in the building of the new library, saying, "We are here after years of work to dedicate the only library that has been built by sports people for sports people."

In 1993 the Library was completely renovated and in 1997 the public reading room was renamed the A. Bartlett Giamatti Research Center in honor of the former Commissioner for his efforts in making it the leading sports library in the world.

The A. Bartlett Giamatti Research Center, part of the new wing conjoined with the main building of the Hall of Fame, boasts more than two-and-a-half million documents and items in its growing collection, including thousands of files, over 500,000 photographs, untold numbers of scorecards, magazines, scrapbooks and books, and hundreds of hours of original recorded oral history and filmed interviews. Recently the Library has added its catalog to the website. Called ABNER, an anagram standing for "American Baseball Network for Electronic Research" (http://abner.baseballhalloffame.org/search), the catalog permits author, title, and subject access to the archives.

All of which has made the library the go-to resource for information, books and materials for millions of baseball researchers the world over.

BASEBALL HALL OF FAME OUTREACH PROGRAMS

The Hall of Fame's address might be 25 Main Street, Cooperstown, but it really is The World, for over and above welcoming thousands of visitors every year from around the world at its Cooperstown address, the Hall of Fame has taken its programs far beyond the village of Cooperstown to a global audience.

With a dedication to their guiding principles of "Preserving History, Honoring Excellence, and Connecting Generations," the Hall of Fame has instituted a wide variety of programs to carry out their stated mission, both at home and worldwide. In the process it has become a cultural and educational designation for millions of baseball fans-hyphen-students.

Placing a premium on what is considered the *real* National Pastime, education, the Hall of Fame uses baseball as a teaching tool to convey important concepts to students in the area of science, math, geography, communications arts, history and other subjects. Their home-away-from-home program is held in the Hall of Fame's Education Gallery with the lesson often conducted by legendary Hall of Famers and the Hall of Fame's professional staff who blend baseball stories and the priceless artifacts together with the subject at hand, ensuring the experience is rich and rewarding for the students.

Other on-site programs include Artifact Spotlights, relating the historic legacy of the items in the Hall of Fame's collection; the Discovery Tour, which takes young fans and their families through the Museum; and any one of hundreds of other programs scheduled annually.

For those unable to make the pilgrimage to Cooperstown, the Hall of Fame comes to them, collaborating with the AT&T Foundation to deliver web-based workshops and interactive instruction, combining baseball and technology for classroom fans and school-aged learners. The Hall has also reached out in their EBBETS Field Trip series—an anagram meaning "Electronically Bringing Baseball Education to Students"—with live videoconferences featuring primary source material from the Hall of Fame to an estimated million viewers in 500 classrooms across the country each year. Another of their acclaimed programs is their "America Grows Inning by Inning," a program providing education with instructional resources combining technology and hands-on experience of baseball's place in America's social history. In 2002, the Hall hosted their first Electronic Field Trip, "Untold Stories: Baseball and the Multicultural Experience," reaching more than 12 million students around the country, making the Hall of Fame the University of Baseball.

The Hall of Fame's trove of baseball treasures was also taken on the road in its much-heralded *Baseball As America* national exhibition tour. Beginning with its opening at the American Museum of Natural History, *Baseball As America* has visited other Major League cities such as Los Angeles, Chicago, Washington, D.C. St. Louis, Detroit, Dallas and Boston, exhibiting more than 500 artifacts and 200 graphics mined from its vast quarry of artifacts—including items of local interest, such as the bat wielded by Phillies' three-time MVP third baseman Mike Schmidt when he hit his 536th home run exhibited in Philadelphia; Curt Schilling's bloody sock shown in Boston; the ball and ticket from Nolan Ryan's record seventh no-hitter displayed in Dallas; et cetera—bringing baseball home to the more than two-and-a-half million visitors to the exhibition.

The Hall of Fame continues to "build" its programs, extending them to Membership Drives, a semi-monthly magazine, *Memories and Dreams*, Fantasy Camps and a new online website for those who wish to stay connected to Cooperstown, "baseballhall.org."

Just as the language of baseball is spoken around the world, so too is the name of Cooperstown, the "home" of baseball. And its home *is* The World.

INDUCTION WEEKEND

One weekend every year Cooperstown turns into July 4th, New Year's Eve, and Halloween all rolled into one, as it celebrates a golden weekend of golden memories. On that last weekend in July—called "Hall of Fame Weekend"—all roads lead to Cooperstown as it becomes baseball's version of Brigadoon for four days. New inductees, their achievements to be forever immortalized in bronze, join the ranks of baseball's legends. Previous inductees, a little aged and hardly looking like their old baseball cards, return to relive bygone days with their fellow Hall of Famers. And fans, emotionally connected to the game and players they love, descend upon the town to take a stroll down Main Street's memory lane.

Hall of Fame Weekend is a tradition that started back in 1939 with the dedication of the Hall of Fame itself as a part of the "Centennial of Baseball" celebration. In a pageant worthy of the name, the main street of Cooperstown festooned with bunting, the first 25 members of the Hall of Fame— including the original 1936 class of Ty Cobb, Babe Ruth, Honus Wagner, Christy Mathewson, and Walter Johnson—were honored. Giving his acceptance speech Babe Ruth acknowledged the honor, saying, "I'm very glad that in my day I was able to earn my place." Then went on to say, "And I hope youngsters of today have the same opportunity to experience such feelings."

It wasn't until two of those so-called "youngsters," Jimmie Foxx and Mel Ott were inducted in 1951 that the tradition of honoring all Hall of Fame inductees was renewed, with Connie Mack the only previously inducted Hall of Famer in attendance. By 1955 some of the previous members began to return, with five on hand to witness the induction of Joe DiMaggio. Ten years later 22 returned to see Frankie Frisch inducted. Today, most of the Hall of Fame members attend Hall of Fame Weekend to welcome the new members into their exclusive club.

As the number of returning former inductees grew, so too did the number of fans who came to the induction ceremonies. By 1968 the induction ceremonies had been moved to the steps of the Library to accommodate their growing number. Still, the number of visitors kept growing and again the ceremonies were moved to the more spacious grounds of the Clark Sports Center to provide adequate room for the more than 20,000 visitors who annually made the pilgrimage to Cooperstown to bear witness to the presentation of what has been called "the greatest individual achievement award bestowed upon an athlete."

Over the years those thousands in attendance have heard many a memorable Hall of Fame acceptance speech, from Yogi Berra's humorous one thanking everyone in the audience, "for making this day necessary," to Ted Williams's stirring, "I hope that someday the names of Satchel Paige and Josh Gibson in some way can be added as a symbol of the great Negro players that are not here only because they were not given a chance."

But the one speech that captures the feelings of every baseball fan is the one Babe Ruth gave at the first induction ceremony that ended with: "I hope it goes another hundred years, and the next hundred years will be the greatest." For those attending the Hall of Fame Weekend, each year continues to be just that: "the greatest."

Hall of Fame Induction Weekend, 2008, welcomed Cal Ripken Jr. and Tony Gwynn into baseball immortality.

THE HALL OF FAME PLAQUE GALLERY

Located directly behind the entryway on the first floor is a large hall called "The Plaque Gallery," a modest name for baseball's version of Mt. Olympus. For here, in this pantheon of baseball's greatest, can be found the likenesses of nearly 300 lower-cased gods enshrined in bronze, their achievements as permanent as the red bricks that make up the building itself.

Entering the hall and seeing the high-vaulted ceilings, the marble columns, and the beam of light streaming through the window illuminating the five original inductees—Ty Cobb, Babe Ruth, Honus Wagner, Christy Mathewson, and Walter Johnson—the visitor can be excused for believing they have entered a cathedral. Fittingly, one then goes slowly from plaque-to-plaque, almost in cathedral-like silence, reverentially reading the brief biographies underneath each likeness, some as short as the 27 words underneath Ruth's image to the more than 100 under latter-day greats, each an ode to that inductee's greatness.

As the visitor studies each plaque with a combination of nostalgia and discovery, it almost seems as if the plaque comes alive, the player's bronze face ready to break into new wrinkles, like a glove donned for the first time, with an appreciative smile for the attention they've received. Don Sutton, inducted into the Hall of Fame in 1998, sensed their presence when, on the night before his induction, he was standing in an alcove containing plaques of the previous inductees, talking to well-wishers, when he thought he felt his coattails being tugged. Turning around, he found nothing but the plaques on the wall which he believes were "welcoming me into the Hall of Fame."

It's the same with many of the visitors to the Plaque Gallery who come away with the feeling that these plaques take on a life of their own, the players' achievements speaking volumes and their plaques speaking for themselves and to their viewers. For each plaque is living proof that history never relinquishes its hold over man or monument, and these Hall of Fame honorees were both.

HONUS WAGNER
LOUISVILLE, N.L., 1897–1899.
PITTSBURGH, N.L., 1900–1917.
THE GREATEST SHORTSTOP IN BASEBALL
HISTORY. BORN CARNEGIE, PA., FEB. 24, 1874
KNOWN TO FAME AS "HONUS", "HANS" AND
"THE FLYING DUTCHMAN." RETIRED IN 1917,
HAVING SCORED MORE RUNS, MADE MORE
HITS AND STOLEN MORE BASES THAN
ANY OTHER PLAYER IN THE HISTORY
OF HIS LEAGUE

In front of the window looking into baseball's most hallowed ground, the Hall of Fame Plaque Gallery, stands a small plaque reading: "In the Hall of Fame Gallery are plaques dedicated to baseball's greatest heroes, upon whose shoulders the game has been built."

Inside the beautiful marble and oak room are almost 300 images of greatness, those legends who have made baseball the game that it is. Fittingly, the plaques of the first five elected to the Hall of Fame in 1936—Ty Cobb, Babe Ruth, Honus Wagner, Christy Mathewson, and Walter Johnson—are in the rotunda, surrounded by those who came after them. All others are arranged according to the year of their inductions, beginning on the right side.

Presented here is every plaque found in the gallery, placed in alphabetical order for ease of reference. Also included under each plaque is the year in which the player was inducted into the fraternity of "baseball's greatest heroes."

HENRY "HANK" L. AARON
MILWAUKEE N.L., ATLANTA N.L.,
MILWAUKEE A.L. 1954-1976
HIT 755 HOME RUNS IN 23-YEAR CAREER TO
BECOME MAJORS' ALL-TIME HOMER KING. HAD
20 OR MORE FOR 20 CONSECUTIVE YEARS. AT
LEAST 30 IN 15 SEASONS AND 40 OR BETTER
EIGHT TIMES. ALSO SET RECORDS FOR GAMES
PLAYED (3,298), AT-BATS (12,364), LONG HITS
(1,477), TOTAL BASES (6,856), RUNS BATTED
IN (2,297). PACED N.L. IN BATTING TWICE
AND HOMERS, RUNS BATTED IN AND SLUGGING
PCT. FOUR TIMES EACH. WON MOST VALUABLE
PLAYER AWARD IN N.L. IN 1957.

1982

GROVER CLEVELAND ALEXANDER
GREAT NATIONAL LEAGUE PITCHER
FOR TWO DECADES WITH PHILLIES,
CUBS AND CARDINALS STARTING
IN 1911. WON 1926 WORLD CHAMPIONSHIP
FOR CARDINALS BY STRIKING OUT
LAZZERI WITH BASES FULL IN
FINAL CRISIS AT YANKEE STADIUM.

1938

WALTER EMMONS ALSTON
SOFT-SPOKEN, LOW-PROFILE ORGANIZATION MAN
WHO MANAGED THE DODGERS FOR 23 YEARS,
LEADING TEAM TO ITS ONLY WORLD CHAMPIONSHIP
IN BROOKLYN IN 1955 AND TO PENNANT IN 1956
BEFORE TEAM MOVED TO WEST COAST. IN LOS
ANGELES HIS CLUBS WON WORLD TITLES IN
1959, 1963 AND 1965 AND PENNANTS IN 1966 AND
1974, AND ONLY JOHN MCGRAW, WITH 10, TOPPED
ALSTON'S SEVEN N.L. PENNANTS. TEAMS FINISHED
IN FIRST DIVISION 18 TIMES, WINNING 2,040 GAMES.

1983

GEORGE LEE ANDERSON
"SPARKY"
CINCINNATI, N.L. 1970-1978
DETROIT, A.L. 1979-1995
ONE OF THE GAME'S MOST SUCCESSFUL AND COLORFUL MANAGERS,
HIS 2,194 WINS RANK THIRD IN HISTORY BEHIND CONNIE MACK AND
JOHN MCGRAW. THE CRANK THAT TURNED THE BIG RED MACHINE, HIS
SKILLFUL LEADERSHIP HELPED THOSE CINCINNATI TEAMS DOMINATE
IN THE 1970s. REVERED AND TREASURED BY HIS PLAYERS FOR HIS
HUMILITY, HUMANITY, ETERNAL OPTIMISM AND KNOWLEDGE OF THE
GAME. BASEBALL'S ONLY MANAGER TO WIN A WORLD SERIES IN BOTH
LEAGUES AND LEAD TWO FRANCHISES IN VICTORIES. HIS TEAMS WON
THREE WORLD SERIES, SEVEN DIVISION TITLES AND FIVE PENNANTS,
COMPILING A .619 POST-SEASON WINNING PERCENTAGE.

2000

ADRIAN CONSTANTINE ANSON
"CAP"
GREATEST HITTER AND GREATEST
NATIONAL LEAGUE PLAYER-MANAGER
OF 19TH CENTURY. STARTED WITH
CHICAGO'S IN NATIONAL LEAGUE'S
FIRST YEAR 1876. CHICAGO MANAGER
FROM 1879 TO 1897, WINNING 5 PENNANTS.
WAS .300 CLASS HITTER 20 YEARS,
BATTING CHAMPION 4 TIMES.

1939

LUIS ERNESTO APARICIO
CHICAGO A.L. 1956-1962; 1968-1970
BALTIMORE A.L. 1963-1967
BOSTON A.L. 1971-1973
REGULAR SHORTSTOP FOR ALL OF HIS 18 SEASONS.
SET MAJOR LEAGUE CAREER RECORDS FOR MOST
GAMES (2,581), ASSISTS (8,016), CHANCES ACCEPTED
(12,564) AND DOUBLE PLAYS (1,553) BY A SHORTSTOP;
AND HAS MOST A.L. PUTOUTS (4,548). LED A.L. IN
FIELDING 8 TIMES. TOPPED LEAGUE IN STEALS
HIS FIRST 9 SEASONS, BEGINNING STOLEN BASE
RENAISSANCE. A.L. ROOKIE OF THE YEAR IN 1956.

1984

LUCIUS BENJAMIN APPLING
CHICAGO A.L. 1930-1950
A.L. BATTING CHAMPION IN 1936 AND 1943.
PLAYED 2,218 GAMES AT SHORTSTOP
FOR MAJOR LEAGUE MARK.
HAD 2,749 HITS.
LIFETIME BATTING AVERAGE OF .310.
LED A.L. IN ASSIST 7 YEARS.
HOLDS A.L. RECORD FOR CHANCES
ACCEPTED BY SHORTSTOP 11,569.

1964

DON RICHARD ASHBURN
(RICHIE)
PHILADELPHIA, N.L. 1948-1959
CHICAGO, N.L. 1960-1961
NEW YORK, N.L. 1962
DURABLE, HUSTLING LEAD-OFF HITTER AND CLUTCH
PERFORMER WITH SUPERB KNOWLEDGE OF STRIKE ZONE.
BATTED .308 LIFETIME WITH NINE .300 SEASONS AND
2,574 HITS IN 2,189 GAMES. WINNING BATTING
CHAMPIONSHIPS IN 1955 AND 1958. AS A CENTER
FIELDER, ESTABLISHED MAJOR LEAGUE RECORDS FOR
MOST YEARS LEADING LEAGUE IN CHANCES (9), MOST
YEARS 500 OR MORE PUTOUTS (4) AND MOST SEASONS
400 OR MORE PUTOUTS (9).

1995

HOWARD EARL AVERILL
"ROCK"
CLEVELAND A.L.   DETROIT A.L.
BOSTON N.L. 1929-1941
COMPILED .318 CAREER BATTING AVERAGE
AND HIT 238 HOME RUNS. TWICE MADE
MORE THAN 200 HITS IN SEASON, PACING
LEAGUE WITH 232 IN 1936. DROVE IN
100 OR MORE RUNS FIVE TIMES. RAPPED
FOUR HOMERS, THREE CONSECUTIVELY
IN FIRST GAME AND BATTED IN 11 RUNS
IN 1930 TWIN-BILL.

1975

JOHN FRANKLIN BAKER
PHILADELPHIA A.L. 1908-1914
NEW YORK A.L. 1916-1922
MEMBER OF CONNIE MACK'S FAMOUS
$100,000 INFIELD. LED AMERICAN LEAGUE
IN HOME-RUNS 1911-12-13, TIED IN 1914.
WON TWO WORLD SERIES GAMES FROM
GIANTS IN 1911 WITH HOME-RUNS THUS
GETTING NAME "HOME RUN" BAKER. PLAYED
IN SIX WORLD SERIES 1910-11-13-14-21-22.

1955

DAVID JAMES BANCROFT
"BEAUTY"
PHILADELPHIA N.L., NEW YORK N.L.,
BOSTON N.L., BROOKLYN N.L.
1915-1930
SET MAJOR LEAGUE RECORD FOR CHANCES
HANDLED BY A SHORTSTOP IN A SEASON-984
IN 1922. LED LEAGUE IN PUTOUTS FOR SHORT-
STOPS IN 1918-1920-1921-1922. HIT .319 IN 1921,
.321 IN 1922 AND .304 IN 1923 WITH
NEW YORK GIANTS. HIT .319 IN 1925 AND
.311 IN 1926 WITH BOSTON.
PLAYER-MANAGER OF BRAVES, 1924-1927.

1971

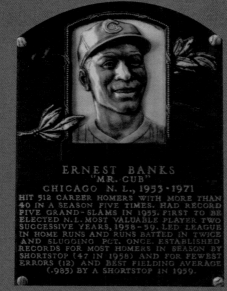

ERNEST BANKS
"MR. CUB"
CHICAGO N.L., 1953-1971
HIT 512 CAREER HOMERS WITH MORE THAN
40 IN A SEASON FIVE TIMES. HAD RECORD
FIVE GRAND-SLAMS IN 1955. FIRST TO BE
ELECTED N.L. MOST VALUABLE PLAYER TWO
SUCCESSIVE YEARS, 1958-59. LED LEAGUE
IN HOME RUNS AND RUNS BATTED IN TWICE
AND SLUGGING PCT. ONCE. ESTABLISHED
RECORDS FOR MOST HOMERS IN SEASON BY
SHORTSTOP (47 IN 1958) AND FOR FEWEST
ERRORS (12) AND BEST FIELDING AVERAGE
(.985) BY A SHORTSTOP IN 1959.

1977

ALBERT JOSEPH BARLICK
UMPIRE
NATIONAL LEAGUE 1940-1971
EARNED RESPECT OF PEERS AND PLAYERS ALIKE WITH
BOOMING, BASSO CALLS, CLEAR AND DECISIVE HAND
SIGNALS, KNOWLEDGE OF RULES, PROFICIENCY ON
BALLS AND STRIKES, ABILITY TO ANTICIPATE AND
THEN HANDLE ROUGH SITUATIONS AND UNCEASING
HUSTLE. PROFESSIONAL UMPIRE FOR FIVE DECADES,
AND AT AGE 25, ONE OF YOUNGEST TO REACH MAJORS,
WHERE HE WORKED 27 FULL SEASONS.

1989

EDWARD GRANT BARROW
CLUB EXECUTIVE, MANAGER, LEAGUE
PRESIDENT IN MINORS AND MAJORS FROM
1894 TO 1945. CONVERTED BABE RUTH FROM
PITCHER TO OUTFIELDER AS MANAGER BOSTON
A.L. IN 1918. DISCOVERED HONUS WAGNER
AND MANY OTHER GREAT STARS. WON WORLD
SERIES IN 1918. BUILT NEW YORK YANKEES INTO
OUTSTANDING ORGANIZATION IN BASEBALL
AS BUSINESS MANAGER FROM 1920 TO 1945,
WINNING 14 PENNANTS, 10 WORLD SERIES.

1953

JACOB PETER BECKLEY
"OLD EAGLE EYE"
1888-1907
FAMED NATIONAL LEAGUE SLUGGER
MADE 2,930 HITS FOR LIFETIME .309 BATTING
AVERAGE. HOLDS RECORD IN MAJORS FOR
FIRST BASE: FOR CHANCES ACCEPTED 25,000
MOST PUTOUTS 23,696, MOST GAMES 2,368.
PLAYED 20 SEASONS WITH PITTSBURGH,
NEW YORK, CINCINNATI AND ST. LOUIS.

1971

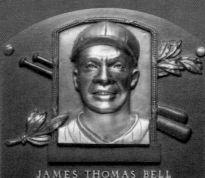

JAMES THOMAS BELL
"COOL PAPA"
NEGRO LEAGUES 1922-1950
COMBINED SPEED, DARING AND BATTING
SKILL TO RANK AMONG BEST PLAYERS
IN NEGRO LEAGUES. CONTEMPORARIES
RATED HIM FASTEST MAN ON BASE
PATHS. HIT OVER .300 REGULARLY,
TOPPING .400 ON OCCASION. PLAYED
29 SUMMERS AND 21 WINTERS
OF PROFESSIONAL BASEBALL.

1974

JOHNNY LEE BENCH
CINCINNATI, N.L., 1967-1983
REDEFINED STANDARDS BY WHICH CATCHERS ARE
MEASURED DURING 17 SEASONS WITH "BIG RED MACHINE";
CONTROLLED GAME ON BOTH SIDES OF PLATE WITH
HIS HITTING (389 HOMERS-RECORD 327 AS A CATCHER,
1,376 RBI'S), THROWING OUT OPPOSING BASE RUNNERS,
CALLING PITCHES AND BLOCKING HOME PLATE. N.L.
MVP, 1970 AND 1972. WON 10 GOLD GLOVES. LAST GAME,
9TH INNING HOMER LED TO 1972 PENNANT.

1989

CHARLES ALBERT BENDER
"CHIEF"
PHILADELPHIA A.L. 1903-1914
PHILADELPHIA A.L. 1916-1917
CHICAGO A.L. 1925
FAMOUS CHIPPEWA INDIAN. WON OVER 200
GAMES. PITCHED FOR ATHLETICS IN 1905-
1910-1911-1913-1914 WORLD SERIES.
DEFEATED N.Y. GIANTS 3-0 FOR A'S ONLY
VICTORY IN 1905. FIRST PITCHER IN
WORLD SERIES OF 6 GAMES (1911) TO PITCH
3 COMPLETE GAMES. PITCHED NO-HIT GAME
AGAINST CLEVELAND IN 1910.
HIGHEST A.L. PERCENTAGES IN
1910-1911-1914.

1953

LAWRENCE PETER BERRA
"YOGI"
NEW YORK, A.L. 1946 - 1963
NEW YORK, N.L. 1965

PLAYED ON MORE PENNANT-WINNERS (14) AND
WORLD CHAMPIONS (10) THAN ANY PLAYER IN
HISTORY. HAD 358 HOME RUNS AND LIFETIME
.285 BATTING AVERAGE. SET MANY RECORDS
FOR CATCHERS, INCLUDING 148 CONSECUTIVE
GAMES WITHOUT AN ERROR. VOTED A.L. MOST
VALUABLE PLAYER 1951-54-55. MANAGED
YANKEES TO PENNANT IN 1964.

1972

WADE ANTHONY BOGGS
BOSTON, A.L., 1982-1992
NEW YORK, A.L., 1993-1997
TAMPA BAY, A.L., 1998-1999

A DISCIPLINED HITTER WHOSE COMMANDING KNOWLEDGE OF THE STRIKE ZONE
MADE HIM ONE OF BASEBALL'S TOUGHEST OUTS. ONLY 20TH CENTURY PLAYER
WITH SEVEN STRAIGHT 200-HIT SEASONS. REACHED BASE SAFELY IN 80 PERCENT
OF GAMES PLAYED. BEGAN CAREER WITH 10 CONSECUTIVE SEASONS HITTING
ABOVE .300. A FIVE-TIME BATTING CHAMPION WHO ALSO LED THE LEAGUE IN ON-
BASE PERCENTAGE AND INTENTIONAL WALKS SIX TIMES EACH. A 12-TIME ALL-
STAR. HIT .328 WITH 3,010 HITS AND 1,412 WALKS. MEMBER OF THE 1996 WORLD
SERIES CHAMPION YANKEES AND WON TWO GOLD GLOVES. LEGENDARY FOR HIS
SUPERSTITIONS.

2005

JAMES LE ROY BOTTOMLEY
"SUNNY JIM"
ST. LOUIS N.L., CINCINNATI N.L.,
ST. LOUIS A.L. 1922 - 1937

SUPERB CLUTCH HITTER. DROVE IN
100 OR MORE RUNS SIX YEARS IN ROW,
1924 - 1929. LEADING LEAGUE TWICE.
ESTABLISHED RECORD BY BATTING IN
12 RUNS IN ONE GAME. MOST VALUABLE
PLAYER 1928. HIT SEVEN HOMERS
IN SPAN OF FIVE GAMES IN 1929. HAD
LIFETIME .310 BATTING AVERAGE.

1974

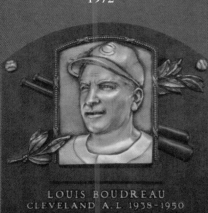

LOUIS BOUDREAU
CLEVELAND A.L. 1938 - 1950
BOSTON A.L. 1951 - 1952

LED A.L. SHORTSTOPS IN FIELDING EIGHT
SEASONS. SET MAJOR LOOP MARK FOR DOUBLE
PLAYS BY SHORTSTOP (134) AND WON BATTING
TITLE, 1944. PACED A.L. IN DOUBLES THREE
TIMES. MOST VALUABLE PLAYER, 1948, WHEN
HE BATTED .355 TO LEAD INDIANS TO PENNANT
AS PLAYER-PILOT. LIFETIME BATTING
AVERAGE .295

1970

ROGER BRESNAHAN
BATTERY MATE OF CHRISTY MATHEWSON
WITH THE NEW YORK GIANTS, HE WAS
ONE OF THE GAME'S MOST NATURAL
PLAYERS AND MIGHT HAVE STARRED
AT ANY POSITION. THE "DUKE OF TRALEE"
WAS ONE OF THE FEW MAJOR LEAGUE
CATCHERS FAST ENOUGH TO BE USED
AS A LEADOFF MAN.

1945

GEORGE HOWARD BRETT
KANSAS CITY, A.L., 1973 - 1993

PLAYED EACH GAME WITH CEASELESS INTENSITY AND UNBRIDLED
PASSION. LIFETIME MARKS INCLUDE .305 BA, 317 HR, 1,595 RBI AND
3,154 HITS. ELEVEN .300 SEASONS. A 13-TIME ALL-STAR AND THE
FIRST PLAYER TO WIN BATTING TITLES IN THREE DECADES (1976,
'80, '90). HIT .390 IN 1980 MVP SEASON AND LED ROYALS TO FIRST
WORLD SERIES TITLE IN 1985. RANKS AMONG ALL-TIME LEADERS IN
HITS, DOUBLES, LONG HITS AND TOTAL BASES. A.L. CAREER RECORD,
MOST INTENTIONAL WALKS. A CLUTCH HITTER WHOSE PROFOUND
RESPECT FOR THE GAME LED TO UNIVERSAL REVERENCE.

1999

LOUIS CLARK BROCK
CHICAGO N.L., 1961-1964
ST. LOUIS N.L., 1964-1979

BASEBALL'S ALL-TIME LEADER IN STOLEN BASES WITH
938. SET MAJOR LEAGUE RECORD BY STEALING OVER
50 BASES 12 TIMES AND N.L. RECORD WITH 118 STEALS
IN 1974. LED N.L. IN STOLEN BASES 8 TIMES. COLLECTED
3,023 HITS DURING 19 YEAR CAREER AND HOLDS
WORLD SERIES RECORD WITH .391 BATTING AVERAGE
IN 21 POST-SEASON GAMES.

1985

DAN BROUTHERS
HARD-HITTING FIRST BASEMAN OF
EIGHT MAJOR LEAGUE CLUBS, HE WAS
PART OF ORIGINAL "BIG FOUR" OF BUFFALO
TRADED WITH OTHER MEMBERS OF
THAT COMBINATION TO DETROIT, HE HIT
.419 AS CITY WON ITS ONLY NATIONAL
LEAGUE CHAMPIONSHIP IN 1887.

1945

MORDECAI PETER BROWN
(THREE-FINGERED AND MINER)
MEMBER OF CHICAGO N.L. CHAMPIONSHIP
TEAM OF 1906,'07,'08,'10. A RIGHT HANDED
PITCHER, WON 239 GAMES DURING MAJOR
LEAGUE CAREER THAT ALSO INCLUDED
ST. LOUIS AND CINCINNATI N.L. AND CLUBS
IN F.L. FIRST MAJOR LEAGUER TO PITCH
FOUR CONSECUTIVE SHUTOUTS, ACHIEVING
THIS FEAT ON JUNE 13, JUNE 25, JULY 2
AND JULY 4 IN 1908.

1999

RAYMOND BROWN
"RAY"
NEGRO LEAGUES, 1930-1948

A MAINSTAY OF THE HOMESTEAD GRAYS PITCHING STAFF FOR 14 SEASONS, UTILIZING A VARIETY OF BREAKING BALLS, INCLUDING A DEVASTATING CURVEBALL, TO HELP LEAD THEM TO EIGHT PENNANTS IN NINE YEARS FROM 1937-1945. RANKS AMONG ALL-TIME NEGRO LEAGUES LEADERS IN WINS, WINNING PERCENTAGE AND SHUTOUTS. SELECTED TO THREE EAST-WEST ALL-STAR GAMES. TOSSED ONE-HITTER AGAINST BIRMINGHAM BLACK BARONS IN 1944 NEGRO LEAGUES WORLD SERIES. SPENT SEVERAL STANDOUT SEASONS PITCHING IN CUBA, PUERTO RICO AND MEXICO.

2006

WILLARD JESSE BROWN
"ESE HOMBRE" "HOME RUN"
NEGRO LEAGUES, 1935-1952, 1958
ST. LOUIS A.L., 1947

A POWER-HITTING CENTER FIELDER WHO HELPED LEAD THE KANSAS CITY MONARCHS TO SIX PENNANTS IN 10 SEASONS FROM 1937-1946, INCLUDING A NEGRO LEAGUES CHAMPIONSHIP IN 1942. A FREE-SWINGER WHOSE AVERAGE REGULARLY TOPPED .300. PLAYED IN EIGHT EAST-WEST ALL-STAR GAMES. FIRST BLACK PLAYER TO BELT A HOME RUN IN THE AMERICAN LEAGUE, DURING A BRIEF STINT WITH THE ST. LOUIS BROWNS IN 1947. TWO-TIME TRIPLE CROWN WINNER IN PUERTO RICAN WINTER LEAGUE.

2006

HON. MORGAN G. BULKELEY

FIRST PRESIDENT OF THE NATIONAL LEAGUE AND A LEADER IN ITS ORGANIZATION IN 1876 WHICH LAID THE FOUNDATION OF THE NATIONAL GAME FOR POSTERITY.

1937

JAMES PAUL DAVID BUNNING
DETROIT, A.L. 1955-1963
PHILADELPHIA, N.L. 1964-1967, 1970-1971
PITTSBURGH, N.L. 1968-1969
LOS ANGELES, N.L. 1969

MAINTAINED DEDICATION AND CONSISTENCY THROUGHOUT 17 SEASONS WHILE POSTING CAREER RECORD OF 224-184 WITH 3.27 ERA. INTIMIDATING RIGHT-HANDED SIDEARMER WON 100 GAMES, PITCHED NO-HITTER AND STRUCK OUT 1,000 IN BOTH LEAGUES. 1964 PERFECT GAME WAS FIRST IN N.L. IN 20TH CENTURY. SECOND ALL-TIME IN STRIKEOUTS (2,855) UPON RETIREMENT IN 1971. ENJOYED SECOND CAREER AS MULTI-TERM U.S. CONGRESSMAN

1996

JESSE C. BURKETT
BATTING STAR WHO PLAYED OUTFIELD FOR THE NEW YORK, CLEVELAND AND ST. LOUIS N.L. TEAMS AND THE ST. LOUIS AND BOSTON A.L. TEAMS. SHARES WITH ROGERS HORNSBY AND TY COBB THE RECORD OF HITTING .400 OR BETTER THE MOST TIMES. ACCOMPLISHED THIS ON THREE OCCASIONS. TOPPED THE N.L. IN HITTING THREE TIMES, BATTING OVER .400 TO GAIN THE CHAMPIONSHIP IN 1895 AND 1896.

1946

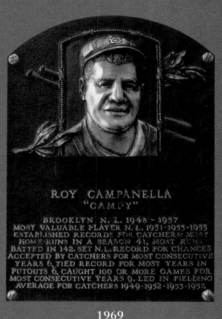

ROY CAMPANELLA
"CAMPY"

BROOKLYN N.L. 1948-1957
MOST VALUABLE PLAYER N.L. 1951-1953-1955 ESTABLISHED RECORDS FOR CATCHERS: MOST HOME-RUNS IN A SEASON 41, MOST RUNS BATTED IN 142. SET N.L. RECORD FOR CHANCES ACCEPTED BY CATCHERS FOR MOST CONSECUTIVE YEARS 6, TIED RECORD FOR MOST YEARS IN PUTOUTS 6, CAUGHT 100 OR MORE GAMES FOR MOST CONSECUTIVE YEARS 9. LED IN FIELDING AVERAGE FOR CATCHERS 1949-1952-1953-1957.

1969

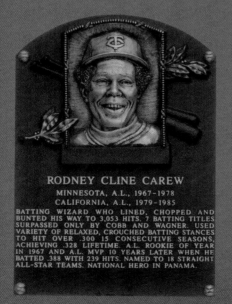

RODNEY CLINE CAREW
MINNESOTA, A.L., 1967-1978
CALIFORNIA, A.L., 1979-1985

BATTING WIZARD WHO LINED, CHOPPED AND BUNTED HIS WAY TO 3,053 HITS. 7 BATTING TITLES SURPASSED ONLY BY COBB AND WAGNER. USED VARIETY OF RELAXED, CROUCHED BATTING STANCES TO HIT OVER .300 15 CONSECUTIVE SEASONS. ACHIEVING .328 LIFETIME. A.L. ROOKIE OF YEAR IN 1967 AND A.L. MVP 10 YEARS LATER WHEN HE BATTED .388 WITH 239 HITS. NAMED TO 18 STRAIGHT ALL-STAR TEAMS. NATIONAL HERO IN PANAMA.

2003

MAX GEORGE CAREY
PITTSBURGH N.L. 1910-1926, 1930
BROOKLYN N.L. 1926-1929, 1932-1933

HOLDS NATIONAL LEAGUE RECORDS FOR OUT-FIELDERS: GAMES PLAYED, 2421; PUT OUTS, 6363; ASSISTS, 339; TOTAL CHANCES, 6702. MODERN LEAGUE RECORD FOR MOST STOLEN BASES,738. MAJOR LEAGUE RECORD MOST YEARS LEADING LEAGUE IN STOLEN BASES,10. BATTING AVERAGE .285 FOR 20 SEASONS. IN 1922 51 STOLEN BASES IN 53 ATTEMPTS.

1938

STEVEN NORMAN CARLTON
"LEFTY"
ST. LOUIS, N.L., 1965-1971
PHILADELPHIA, N.L., 1972-1986
SAN FRANCISCO, N.L., 1986
CHICAGO, A.L., 1986
CLEVELAND, A.L., 1987
MINNESOTA, A.L., 1987-1988

EXTREMELY FOCUSED COMPETITOR WITH COMPLETE DEDICATION TO EXCELLENCE. THRIVED ON MOUND BY PHYSICALLY AND MENTALLY CHALLENGING HIMSELF OFF THE FIELD. OUT PITCH WAS HARD, BITING SLIDER. 329 VICTORIES SECOND ONLY TO SPAHN AMONG LEFTIES AND 4,136 STRIKEOUTS EXCEEDED ONLY BY RYAN. SHARES N.L. RECORD WITH 19 STRIKEOUTS IN GAME. SIX 20 WIN SEASONS. ONLY HURLER TO WIN 4 CY YOUNG AWARDS.

1999

GARY EDMUND CARTER
"KID"
MONTREAL, N.L., 1974-1984, 1992
NEW YORK, N.L., 1985-1989
SAN FRANCISCO, N.L., 1990
LOS ANGELES, N.L., 1991
AN EXUBERANT ON-FIELD GENERAL WITH A SIGNATURE SMILE WHO WAS KNOWN FOR CLUTCH HITTING AND ROCK-SOLID DEFENSE OVER 19 SEASONS. HIS TIRELESS WORK ETHIC AND DURABILITY LED TO THE ALL-TIME RECORD FOR TOTAL CHANCES BY A CATCHER, AND NATIONAL LEAGUE RECORDS FOR GAMES CAUGHT, PUTOUTS, AND YEARS LEADING THE LEAGUE IN PUTOUTS. AN 11-TIME ALL-STAR, TWICE THE GAME MVP EARNED THREE GOLD GLOVE AWARDS AND CLUBBED 324 HOME RUNS. A CATALYST FOR THE EXPOS FIRST POSTSEASON BERTH IN 1981 AND A KEY TO THE METS 1986 WORLD CHAMPIONSHIP.

2003

ALEXANDER JOY CARTWRIGHT, Jr.
"FATHER OF MODERN BASE BALL."
SET BASES 90 FEET APART.
ESTABLISHED 9 INNINGS AS GAME
AND 9 PLAYERS AS TEAM. ORGANIZED
THE KNICKERBOCKER BASEBALL CLUB
OF N.Y. IN 1845. CARRIED BASEBALL
TO PACIFIC COAST AND HAWAII
IN PIONEER DAYS.

1938

ORLANDO MANUEL CEPEDA PENNES
"BABY BULL" "CHA-CHA"
SAN FRANCISCO, N.L., 1958 – 1966, ST. LOUIS, N.L., 1966 – 1968
ATLANTA, N.L., 1969 – 1972, OAKLAND, A.L., 1972
BOSTON, A.L., 1973, KANSAS CITY, A.L., 1974
A POWERFUL FIRST BASEMAN AND CONSISTENT RUN PRODUCER FOR 17 MAJOR LEAGUE SEASONS. NOTWITHSTANDING CHRONIC KNEE PROBLEMS, HIS ABILITY TO DRIVE THE BALL WITH AUTHORITY WAS RESPECTED AND FEARED BY THE OPPOSITION. UNANIMOUS SELECTION FOR BOTH THE 1958 N.L. ROOKIE OF THE YEAR AWARD AND 1967 MVP HONORS. THE 11-TIME ALL-STAR LED THE N.L. IN HOME RUNS (46) AND RBI (142) IN 1961. BATTED .300 NINE TIMES AND SLUGGED 379 HOME RUNS. HIS STALWART LEADERSHIP PROPELLED HIS CLUBS TO THREE WORLD SERIES.

1999

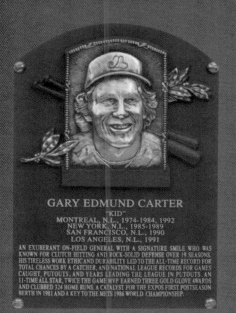

HENRY CHADWICK
BASEBALL'S PREEMINENT PIONEER
WRITER FOR HALF A CENTURY.
INVENTOR OF THE BOX SCORE.
AUTHOR OF THE FIRST RULE-BOOK
IN 1858. CHAIRMAN OF RULES
COMMITTEE IN FIRST NATION-WIDE
BASEBALL ORGANIZATION.

1938

FRANK LEROY CHANCE
FAMOUS LEADER OF CHICAGO CUBS. WON PENNANT WITH CUBS IN FIRST FULL SEASON AS MANAGER IN 1906-THAT TEAM COMPILED 116 VICTORIES UNEQUALLED IN MAJOR LEAGUE HISTORY-ALSO WON PENNANTS IN 1907, 08 AND 1910 AND WORLD SERIES WINNER IN 07 AND 08. STARTED WITH CHICAGO IN 1898. ALSO MANAGER NEW YORK A.L. AND BOSTON A.L.

1946

ALBERT BENJAMIN CHANDLER
"HAPPY"
BASEBALL'S SECOND COMMISSIONER, 1945-1951. UNITED STATES SENATOR (1939-1945). GOVERNOR OF KENTUCKY (1935-39, 1955-59). IRON-WILLED AND HONEST, HE WAS KNOWN AS A "PLAYERS' COMMISSIONER" BECAUSE OF HIS BROAD CONCERN FOR ALL PHASES OF THE GAME.

1982

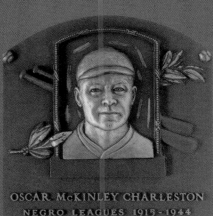

OSCAR McKINLEY CHARLESTON
NEGRO LEAGUES 1915-1944
RATED AMONG ALL-TIME GREATS OF NEGRO LEAGUES. VERSATILE STAR BATTED WELL OVER .300 MOST YEARS. SPEED, STRONG ARM AND FIELDING INSTINCTS MADE HIM STANDOUT CENTER FIELDER. LATER MOVED TO FIRST BASE. ALSO MANAGED SEVERAL TEAMS DURING 40 YEARS IN NEGRO BASEBALL.

1976

JOHN DWIGHT CHESBRO
"HAPPY JACK"
FAMED PITCHER WHO LED BOTH LEAGUES IN PERCENTAGE-NATIONAL LEAGUE IN 1902; AMERICAN LEAGUE IN 1904. SERVED WITH PITTSBURGH N.L. AND THE NEW YORK AND BOSTON A.L. WON 41 GAMES, TOPS IN MAJORS, IN 1904 AND DURING BIG LEAGUE CAREER COMPILED 192 VICTORIES WHILE LOSING ONLY 128.

1946

NESTOR CHYLAK JR.
UMPIRE
AMERICAN LEAGUE, 1954 – 1978
CONSIDERED BY MANY TO BE THE NONPAREIL UMPIRE OF THE POST-WAR ERA. A MODEL OF CONSISTENCY WITH INVARIABLE ACCURACY BOTH BEHIND THE PLATE AND ON THE BASES. RESPECTED BY PLAYERS AND MANAGERS ALIKE, EFFECTIVELY COMBINING AUTHORITARIANISM, TACT AND A SENSE OF HUMOR. LAUDED FOR HIS WILLINGNESS TO LEND AN EAR TO OBJECTIONS. HIS ILLUSTRIOUS 25-YEAR CAREER INCLUDED SIX ALL-STAR GAMES AND FIVE WORLD SERIES ASSIGNMENTS. SERVED MANY YEARS AS A CREW CHIEF AND THEN AS ASSISTANT SUPERVISOR OF AMERICAN LEAGUE UMPIRES FROM 1979 – 1982.

1999

FRED CLARKE

THE FIRST OF THE SUCCESSFUL "BOY MANAGERS" AT TWENTY-FOUR HE PILOTED LOUISVILLE'S COLONELS IN THE NATIONAL LEAGUE. WON 4 PENNANTS FOR PITTSBURGH AND A WORLD CHAMPIONSHIP IN 1909. STARRED AS AN OUTFIELDER FOR 22 SEASONS.

1945

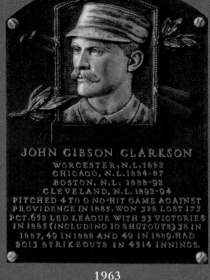

JOHN GIBSON CLARKSON

WORCESTER, N.L. 1882
CHICAGO, N.L. 1884-87
BOSTON, N.L. 1888-92
CLEVELAND, N.L. 1892-94
PITCHED 4 TO 0 NO-HIT GAME AGAINST PROVIDENCE IN 1885. WON 328 LOST 173 PCT. .652 LED LEAGUE WITH 53 VICTORIES IN 1885 (INCLUDING 10 SHUTOUTS) 38 IN 1887, 49 IN 1888 AND 49 IN 1889. HAD 2013 STRIKEOUTS IN 4514 INNINGS.

1963

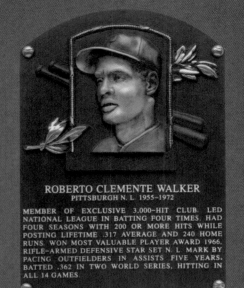

ROBERTO CLEMENTE WALKER

PITTSBURGH N. L. 1955-1972

MEMBER OF EXCLUSIVE 3,000-HIT CLUB. LED NATIONAL LEAGUE IN BATTING FOUR TIMES. HAD FOUR SEASONS WITH 200 OR MORE HITS WHILE POSTING LIFETIME .317 AVERAGE AND 240 HOME RUNS. WON MOST VALUABLE PLAYER AWARD 1966. RIFLE-ARMED DEFENSIVE STAR SET N. L. MARK BY PACING OUTFIELDERS IN ASSISTS FIVE YEARS. BATTED .362 IN TWO WORLD SERIES, HITTING IN ALL 14 GAMES.

1973

TYRUS RAYMOND COBB

DETROIT-PHILADELPHIA, A.L. 1905-1928
LED AMERICAN LEAGUE IN BATTING TWELVE TIMES AND CREATED OR EQUALLED MORE MAJOR LEAGUE RECORDS THAN ANY OTHER PLAYER. RETIRED WITH 4191 MAJOR LEAGUE HITS.

1936

GORDON "MICKEY" COCHRANE

PHILADELPHIA A.L. 1925-1933
DETROIT A.L. 1934-1937
FIERY CATCHER COMPILED A NOTABLE RECORD BOTH AS A PLAYER AND MANAGER THE SPARK OF THE ATHLETICS' CHAMPIONSHIP TEAMS OF 1929-30-31, HAD AN AVERAGE BATTING MARK OF .346 FOR THOSE THREE YEARS. LED DETROIT TO TWO LEAGUE CHAMPIONSHIPS AND A WORLD SERIES TITLE IN 1935.

1947

EDWARD TROWBRIDGE COLLINS

PHILADELPHIA-CHICAGO
PHILADELPHIA, A.L. -1906-1930
FAMED AS BATSMAN, BASE RUNNER AND SECOND BASEMAN AND ALSO AS FIELD CAPTAIN. BATTED .333 DURING MAJOR LEAGUE CAREER, SECOND ONLY TO TY COBB IN MODERN BASE STEALING. MADE 3313 HITS IN 2826 GAMES.

1939

JAMES COLLINS

CONSIDERED BY MANY THE GAME'S GREATEST THIRD BASEMAN. HE REVOLUTIONIZED STYLE OF PLAY AT THAT BAG. LED BOSTON RED SOX TO FIRST WORLD CHAMPIONSHIP IN 1903. A CONSISTENT BATTER, HIS DEFENSIVE PLAY THRILLED FANS OF BOTH MAJOR LEAGUES.

1945

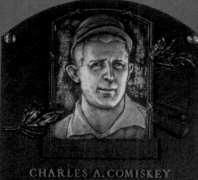

EARLE BRYAN COMBS

NEW YORK YANKEES 1924-1935

LEAD-OFF HITTER AND CENTER FIELDER OF YANKEE CHAMPIONS OF 1926-27-28-32. LIFETIME BATTING AVERAGE .329, 200 OR MORE HITS THREE SEASONS. LED LEAGUE WITH 231 HITS IN 1927 WHILE BATTING .356. PACED A.L. IN TRIPLES THREE TIMES AND TWICE LED OUTFIELDERS IN PUTOUTS. BATTED .350 IN FOUR WORLD SERIES

1970

CHARLES A. COMISKEY
"THE OLD ROMAN"

STARTED 50 YEARS OF BASEBALL AS ST. LOUIS BROWNS FIRST-BASEMAN IN 1882 AND WAS FIRST MAN AT THIS POSITION TO PLAY AWAY FROM THE BAG FOR BATTERS. AS BROWNS' MANAGER-CAPTAIN-PLAYER WON 4 STRAIGHT AMERICAN ASSOCIATION PENNANTS STARTING 1885. WORLD CHAMPIONS FIRST 2 YEARS. OWNER AND PRESIDENT CHICAGO WHITE SOX 1900 TO 1931.

1939

JOHN BERTRAND CONLAN
"JOCKO"
UMPIRE
NATIONAL LEAGUE 1941-1965
SUNNY DISPOSITION, ACCURACY AND
HUSTLE EARNED HIM RATING AS STANDOUT
UMPIRE AND HE WON RESPECT OF
PLAYERS AND MANAGERS WITH HIS
FAIRNESS. ONLY ARBITER TO WORK IN
EACH OF FIRST FOUR N.L. PENNANT
PLAYOFFS. CHOSEN FOR SIX WORLD SERIES
AND SIX ALL-STAR GAMES.

1974

THOMAS HENRY CONNOLLY
UMPIRE
NATIONAL LEAGUE - 1898-1899
AMERICAN LEAGUE - 1901-1953
OFFICIATED IN FIRST A.L. GAME IN
CHICAGO, 1901. UMPIRED IN EIGHT
WORLD SERIES, INCLUDING THE FIRST
ONE IN 1903 AND IN GAMES WHEN BOSTON
NEW YORK AND PHILADELPHIA PARKS
WERE DEDICATED. NAMED CHIEF OF A.L.
STAFF IN 1931. BORN IN ENGLAND, HE
BECAME A PROFESSIONAL UMPIRE IN 1894

1953

ROGER CONNOR
TROY N.L., NEW YORK N.L.,
NEW YORK P.L., PHILADELPHIA N.L.,
ST. LOUIS N.L. 1880-1897
POWER-HITTING STAR OF DEAD-BALL ERA.
SET CAREER HOME RUN RECORD FOR 19TH
CENTURY PLAYERS. WON LEAGUE BATTING
CHAMPIONSHIP IN 1885 AND HIT .300 OR
BETTER 12 TIMES. HIT THREE HOMERS
IN A GAME IN 1888 AND MADE SIX HITS IN
SIX AT-BATS IN A GAME IN 1895.

1976

ANDREW LEWIS COOPER
"ANDY" "LEFTY"
NEGRO LEAGUES, 1920-1941

A SUPERB LEFT-HANDED CONTROL PITCHER WHOSE REPERTOIRE INCLUDED
A WIDE ARRAY OF PITCHES AND SPEEDS WHICH CONFUSED HITTERS FOR
TWO DECADES. EXCELLED WITH DETROIT STARS FROM 1920-1927, BEFORE
TRADE TO KANSAS CITY MONARCHS FOR FIVE PLAYERS. PITCHED
MONARCHS TO A NATIONAL LEAGUE CHAMPIONSHIP IN 1929; AS
PLAYER-MANAGER, ADDED THREE MORE TITLES IN 1937, 1939 AND 1940.
OFTEN PITCHED IN RELIEF BETWEEN STARTING ASSIGNMENTS. RANKS
AMONG NEGRO LEAGUES LEADERS IN VIRTUALLY EVERY CAREER PITCHING
CATEGORY AND WON MORE THAN TWO-THIRDS OF HIS DECISIONS.

2006

STANLEY ANTHONY COVELESKI
PHILADELPHIA A.L.   1912
CLEVELAND A.L. 1916-1924
WASHINGTON A.L. 1925-1927
NEW YORK A.L.   1928
STAR PITCHER WITH A RECORD OF 214 WINS,
141 LOSSES, AVERAGE .603, E.R.A. 2.88.
WON 20 OR MORE GAMES IN 5 SEASONS. WON
13 STRAIGHT GAMES IN 1925. PITCHED AND
WON 3 GAMES FOR CLEVELAND IN 1920
WORLD SERIES WITH E.R.A. 0.67.

1969

SAMUEL EARL CRAWFORD
"WAHOO SAM"
CINCINNATI N.L. 1899-1902
DETROIT A.L. 1903-1917
HAD LIFETIME RECORD OF 2964 HITS,
BATTING AVERAGE OF .309. PLAYED 2505
GAMES. HOLDS MAJOR LEAGUE RECORD
FOR MOST TRIPLES, 312. LEAGUE LEADER
ONE OR MORE SEASONS IN DOUBLES, TRIPLES,
RUNS BATTED IN, RUNS SCORED, CHANCES
ACCEPTED, HOME RUNS (N.L. 1901 - A.L. 1908)
AND TOTAL BASES (N.L. 1902 - A.L. 1913).

1957

JOSEPH EDWARD CRONIN
PITTSBURGH N.L. 1926-1927
WASHINGTON A.L. 1928-1934
BOSTON A.L. 1935-1945
NAMED ALL-STAR SHORTSTOP SEVEN
SEASONS. MOST VALUABLE PLAYER A.L.
1930. LED A.L. SHORTSTOPS IN FIELDING
1931-1932. MOST PUTOUTS AND DOUBLE
PLAYS 1930-31-32. LIFETIME BATTING
AVERAGE .302. WON PENNANT IN 1933 IN
FIRST SEASON AS MANAGER WASHINGTON
A.L. AT AGE 26. TRADED TO BOSTON 1934 FOR
REPORTED RECORD PRICE OF $250,000.

1956

W. A. "CANDY" CUMMINGS
PITCHED FIRST CURVE BALL IN BASEBALL
HISTORY. INVENTED CURVE AS AMATEUR
ACE OF BROOKLYN STARS IN 1867. ENDED
LONG CAREER AS HARTFORD PITCHER IN
NATIONAL LEAGUE'S FIRST YEAR 1876.

1939

HAZEN SHIRLEY CUYLER
"KIKI"
PITTSBURGH N.L. 1921 TO 1927
CHICAGO N.L. 1928 TO 1935
CINCINNATI N.L. 1935 TO 1937
BROOKLYN N.L. 1938
LED N.L. IN STOLEN BASES 1926, 1928,
1929, 1930. BATTED .354 IN 1924,
.357 IN 1925, .360 IN 1929, .355 IN 1930.
LIFETIME TOTAL 2299 HITS,
BATTING AVERAGE .321.
NAMED TO ALL STAR TEAM IN 1925.

1968

RAYMOND EMMETT DANDRIDGE
NEGRO AND MEXICAN LEAGUES
1933 - 1948

FLASHY BUT SMOOTH THIRD BASEMAN. DEFENSIVELY, A BRILLIANT FIELDER WITH POWERFUL ARM. OFFENSIVELY, A SPRAY HITTER WITH OUTSTANDING BAT CONTROL. PLAYED FOR DETROIT STARS, NEWARK DODGERS, NEWARK EAGLES AND NEW YORK CUBANS IN NEGRO LEAGUES AND FOR VERACRUZ AND MEXICO CITY IN MEXICAN LEAGUES. AMERICAN ASSOCIATION MVP IN 1950 WITH .311, 11 HOME RUNS AND 80 RBI'S PLAYING FOR MINNEAPOLIS MILLERS.

1987

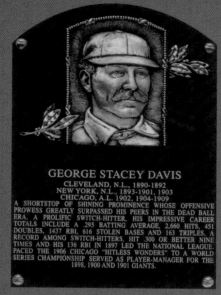

GEORGE STACEY DAVIS
CLEVELAND, N.L., 1890-1892
NEW YORK, N.L., 1893-1901, 1903
CHICAGO, A.L. 1902, 1904-1909

A SHORTSTOP OF SHINING PROMINENCE WHOSE OFFENSIVE PROWESS GREATLY SURPASSED HIS PEERS IN THE DEAD BALL ERA. A PROLIFIC SWITCH-HITTER, HIS IMPRESSIVE CAREER TOTALS INCLUDE A .295 BATTING AVERAGE, 2,660 HITS, 451 DOUBLES, 1437 RBI, 616 STOLEN BASES AND 163 TRIPLES, A RECORD AMONG SWITCH-HITTERS. HIT .300 OR BETTER NINE TIMES AND HIS 136 RBI IN 1897 LED THE NATIONAL LEAGUE. PACED THE 1906 CHICAGO "HITLESS WONDERS" TO A WORLD SERIES CHAMPIONSHIP. SERVED AS PLAYER-MANAGER FOR THE 1898, 1900 AND 1901 GIANTS.

1998

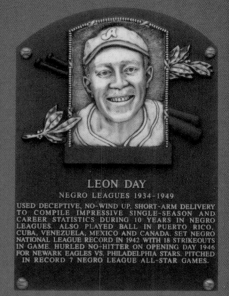

LEON DAY
NEGRO LEAGUES 1934-1949

USED DECEPTIVE, NO-WIND UP, SHORT-ARM DELIVERY TO COMPILE IMPRESSIVE SINGLE-SEASON AND CAREER STATISTICS DURING 10 YEARS IN NEGRO LEAGUES. ALSO PLAYED BALL IN PUERTO RICO, CUBA, VENEZUELA, MEXICO AND CANADA. SET NEGRO NATIONAL LEAGUE RECORD IN 1942 WITH 18 STRIKEOUTS IN GAME. HURLED NO-HITTER ON OPENING DAY 1946 FOR NEWARK EAGLES VS. PHILADELPHIA STARS. PITCHED IN RECORD 7 NEGRO LEAGUE ALL-STAR GAMES.

1995

JAY HANNA (DIZZY) DEAN
ST. LOUIS (N.L.) 1932-1937
CHICAGO (N.L.) 1938-1941

ONE OF FOUR N.L. PITCHERS TO WIN 30 OR MORE GAMES UNDER MODERN REGULATIONS. PITCHED IN 1934 (ST. L.) 1938 (CHICAGO) WORLD SERIES. LED LEAGUE IN STRIKEOUTS 1932-33-34-35. SINGLE GAME RECORD WITH 17, JULY 30, 1933. FIRST PITCHER TO MAKE TWO HITS IN ONE INNING IN WORLD SERIES. MOST VALUABLE N.L. PLAYER IN 1934.

1953

ED DELAHANTY

ONE OF THE GAME'S GREATEST SLUGGERS. LED NATIONAL LEAGUE HITTERS IN 1899 WITH AN AVERAGE OF .408 FOR PHILADELPHIA; AMERICAN LEAGUE BATTERS IN 1902 WITH A MARK OF .376 FOR WASHINGTON. MADE 6 HITS IN 6 TIMES AT BAT TWICE DURING CAREER AND ONCE HIT 4 HOME RUNS IN A GAME.

1945

WILLIAM MALCOLM DICKEY
NEW YORK A.L. 1928-1946

SET RECORD BY CATCHING 100 OR MORE GAMES 13 SUCCESSIVE SEASONS. PLAYED WITH YANKEES, CHAMPIONS OF 1932-36-37-38-39-41-42-43, WHEN CLUB WON 7 WORLD SERIES TITLES. HOLDS NUMEROUS WORLD SERIES RECORDS FOR CATCHERS, INCLUDING MOST GAMES, 38. PLAYED ON 8 ALL-STAR TEAMS FROM 1932 TO 1946. LIFETIME BATTING AVERAGE OF .313 IN 1789 GAMES.

1954

MARTIN DIHIGO
"EL MAESTRO"
NEGRO LEAGUES 1923-1947

MOST VERSATILE OF NEGRO LEAGUE STARS. PLAYED IN BOTH SUMMER AND WINTER BALL MOST OF CAREER. REGISTERED MORE THAN 260 VICTORIES AS PITCHER. WHEN NOT ON MOUND HE PLAYED OUTFIELD OR INFIELD, USUALLY BATTING WELL OVER .300. ALSO MANAGED DURING AND AFTER PLAYING DAYS.

1977

JOSEPH PAUL DI MAGGIO
NEW YORK A.L. 1936 TO 1951

HIT SAFELY IN 56 CONSECUTIVE GAMES FOR MAJOR LEAGUE RECORD 1941. HIT 2 HOME-RUNS IN ONE INNING 1936. HIT 3 HOME-RUNS IN ONE GAME (3 TIMES). HOLDS NUMEROUS BATTING RECORDS. PLAYED IN 10 WORLD SERIES (51 GAMES) AND 11 ALL STAR GAMES. MOST VALUABLE PLAYER A.L. 1939, 1941, 1947.

1955

LAWRENCE EUGENE DOBY
CLEVELAND, A.L. 1947-55, 1958
CHICAGO, A.L. 1956-57, 1959
DETROIT, A.L., 1959

EXCEPTIONAL ATHLETIC PROWESS AND A STAUNCH CONSTITUTION LED TO A SUCCESSFUL PLAYING CAREER AFTER INTEGRATING THE AMERICAN LEAGUE IN 1947. A SEVEN-TIME ALL-STAR WHO BATTED .283 WITH 253 HOME RUNS AND 970 RBI IN 13 MAJOR LEAGUE SEASONS. THE POWER-HITTING CENTER FIELDER PACED THE A.L. IN HOME RUNS TWICE AND COLLECTED 100 RBI FIVE TIMES, WHILE LEADING THE INDIANS TO PENNANTS IN 1948 AND 1954. APPOINTED MANAGER OF THE WHITE SOX IN 1978, THE SECOND AFRICAN-AMERICAN TO LEAD A MAJOR LEAGUE CLUB. PLAYED FOUR SEASONS WITH NEWARK IN THE NEGRO NATIONAL LEAGUE. FOLLOWING PLAYER CAREER WORKED AS A SCOUT AND MAJOR LEAGUE BASEBALL EXECUTIVE.

1998

ROBERT PERSHING DOERR

BOSTON, A.L., 1937-1951

QUIET LEADER OF RED SOX DURING 1940'S. CONSISTENT SECOND BASEMAN, TOP DOUBLE PLAY MAN AND FINE CLUTCH HITTER. LIFETIME BATTING AVERAGE OF .288 WITH SIX SEASONS OF OVER 100 RBI'S. HELD A.L. RECORD FOR 2B BY HANDLING 414 CONSECUTIVE CHANCES WITHOUT ERROR. LED A.L. 2B IN DOUBLE PLAYS FIVE TIMES, PUTOUTS FOUR TIMES AND ASSISTS ON THREE OCCASIONS. BATTED .409 IN 1946 WORLD SERIES.

1986

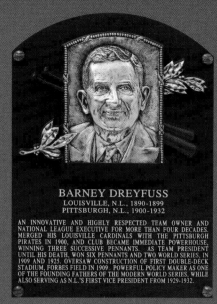

BARNEY DREYFUSS

LOUISVILLE, N.L., 1890-1899
PITTSBURGH, N.L., 1900-1932

AN INNOVATIVE AND HIGHLY RESPECTED TEAM OWNER AND NATIONAL LEAGUE EXECUTIVE FOR MORE THAN FOUR DECADES. MERGED HIS LOUISVILLE CARDINALS WITH THE PITTSBURGH PIRATES IN 1900, AND CLUB BECAME IMMEDIATE POWERHOUSE, WINNING THREE SUCCESSIVE PENNANTS. AS TEAM PRESIDENT UNTIL HIS DEATH, WON SIX PENNANTS AND TWO WORLD SERIES, IN 1909 AND 1925. OVERSAW CONSTRUCTION OF FIRST DOUBLE-DECK STADIUM, FORBES FIELD IN 1909. POWERFUL POLICY MAKER AS ONE OF THE FOUNDING FATHERS OF THE MODERN WORLD SERIES, WHILE ALSO SERVING AS N.L.'S FIRST VICE PRESIDENT FROM 1929-1932.

2008

DONALD SCOTT DRYSDALE

BROOKLYN N.L. 1956-1957
LOS ANGELES N.L. 1958-1969

HARD-THROWING SIDE-ARMER NOTED FOR INTIMIDATING STYLE AND DURABILITY. HAD 209-166 RECORD WITH 2.95 ERA AND 2,486 STRIKEOUTS. LED N.L. IN STRIKEOUTS 3 TIMES AND HURLED 49 SHUTOUTS. WAS 25-9 IN 1962 AND WON CY YOUNG AWARD. THREW 6 SHUTOUTS IN A ROW IN 1968, SETTING RECORD WITH 58 CONSECUTIVE SCORELESS INNINGS. PITCHED IN RECORD 8 ALL-STAR GAMES.

1984

HUGH DUFFY

BRILLIANT AS A DEFENSIVE OUTFIELDER FOR THE BOSTON NATIONALS, HE COMPILED A BATTING AVERAGE IN 1894 WHICH WAS NOT TO BE CHALLENGED IN HIS LIFETIME - .438.

1945

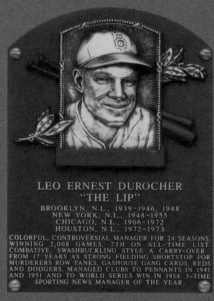

LEO ERNEST DUROCHER
"THE LIP"

BROOKLYN, N.L., 1939-1946, 1948
NEW YORK, N.L., 1948-1955
CHICAGO, N.L., 1966-1972
HOUSTON, 1972-1973

COLORFUL, CONTROVERSIAL MANAGER FOR 24 SEASONS, WINNING 2,008 GAMES, 7TH ON ALL-TIME LIST. COMBATIVE, SWASHBUCKLING STYLE A CARRY-OVER FROM 17 YEARS AS STRONG FIELDING SHORTSTOP FOR MURDERERS ROW YANKS, GASHOUSE GANG CARDS, REDS AND DODGERS. MANAGED CLUBS TO PENNANTS IN 1941 AND 1951 AND TO WORLD SERIES WIN IN 1954. 3-TIME SPORTING NEWS MANAGER OF THE YEAR.

1994

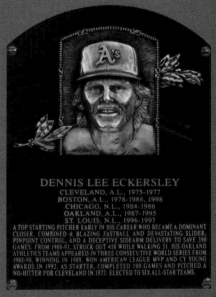

DENNIS LEE ECKERSLEY

CLEVELAND, A.L., 1975-1977
BOSTON, A.L., 1978-1984, 1998
CHICAGO, N.L., 1984-1986
OAKLAND, A.L., 1987-1995
ST. LOUIS, N.L., 1996-1997

A TOP STARTING PITCHER EARLY IN HIS CAREER WHO BECAME A DOMINANT CLOSER. COMBINED A BLAZING FASTBALL AND DEVASTATING SLIDER, PINPOINT CONTROL, AND A DECEPTIVE SIDEARM DELIVERY TO SAVE 390 GAMES. FROM 1988-93, STRUCK OUT 458 WHILE WALKING 51. HIS OAKLAND ATHLETICS TEAMS APPEARED IN THREE CONSECUTIVE WORLD SERIES FROM 1988-90, WINNING IN 1989. WON AMERICAN LEAGUE MVP AND CY YOUNG AWARDS IN 1992. AS STARTER, COMPLETED 100 GAMES AND PITCHED A NO-HITTER FOR CLEVELAND IN 1977. ELECTED TO SIX ALL-STAR TEAMS.

2004

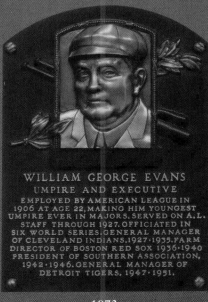

WILLIAM GEORGE EVANS
UMPIRE AND EXECUTIVE

EMPLOYED BY AMERICAN LEAGUE IN 1906 AT AGE 22, MAKING HIM YOUNGEST UMPIRE EVER IN MAJORS. SERVED ON A.L. STAFF THROUGH 1927. OFFICIATED IN SIX WORLD SERIES. GENERAL MANAGER OF CLEVELAND INDIANS,1927-1935. FARM DIRECTOR OF BOSTON RED SOX 1936-1940. PRESIDENT OF SOUTHERN ASSOCIATION, 1942-1946. GENERAL MANAGER OF DETROIT TIGERS, 1947-1951.

1973

JOHN JOSEPH EVERS
"THE TROJAN"

MIDDLE-MAN OF THE FAMOUS DOUBLE PLAY COMBINATION OF TINKER TO EVERS TO CHANCE. WITH THE PENNANT WINNING CHICAGO CUBS OF 1906, 07-08-10 AND WITH THE BOSTON BRAVES' MIRACLE TEAM OF 1914, VOTED MOST VALUABLE PLAYER IN N.L. IN 1914. SERVED AS PLAYER, COACH AND MANAGER IN BIG LEAGUES AND AS A SCOUT FROM 1902 THROUGH 1934. SHARES RECORD FOR MAKING MOST SINGLES IN FOUR GAME WORLD SERIES.

1946

WM. B. "BUCK" EWING

GREATEST 19TH CENTURY CATCHER. GIANT IN STATURE AND GIANT CAPTAIN OF NEW YORK'S FIRST NATIONAL LEAGUE CHAMPIONS 1888 AND 1889. WAS GENIUS AS FIELD LEADER, UNSURPASSED IN THROWING TO BASES, GREAT LONG-RANGE HITTER. NATIONAL LEAGUE CAREER 1881 TO 1899 TROY, N.Y. GIANTS AND CLEVELAND; CINCINNATI MANAGER.

1939

URBAN CLARENCE FABER
CHICAGO A. L. 1914-1933
DURABLE RIGHTHANDER WHO WON 253,
LOST 211, E.R.A. 3.13 GAMES IN TWO DECADES
WITH WHITE SOX. VICTOR IN 3 GAMES
OF 1917 WORLD'S SERIES AGAINST GIANTS.
WON 20 OR MORE GAMES IN SEASON
FOUR TIMES, THREE IN SUCCESSION.

1964

ROBERT WILLIAM ANDREW FELLER
CLEVELAND A. L. 1936 TO 1941
1945 TO 1956
PITCHED 3 NO-HIT GAMES IN A.L., 12 ONE HIT GAMES.
SET MODERN STRIKEOUT RECORD WITH 18 IN GAME,
348 FOR SEASON. LED A.L. IN VICTORIES 6 (ONE TIE)
SEASONS. LIFETIME RECORD: WON 266, LOST 162, P.C.
.621, E.R. AVERAGE 3.25, STRUCKOUT 2581.

1962

RICHARD BENJAMIN FERRELL
ST. LOUIS A.L. 1929-1933, 1941-1943
BOSTON A.L. 1933-1937
WASHINGTON A.L. 1937-1941, 1944-1947
CAUGHT MORE GAMES (1,806) THAN ANY OTHER
AMERICAN LEAGUER. DURABLE DEFENSIVE STAND-OUT
WITH FINE ARM. EXPERT AT HANDLING PITCHERS.
MET CHALLENGE OF 4 KNUCKLE-BALLERS IN SENATORS'
STARTING ROTATION. OFTEN FORMED BATTERY WITH
BROTHER, WES. HIT OVER .300 4 TIMES. SECOND
ONLY TO DICKEY IN A.L. CAREER PUTOUTS AT
RETIREMENT.

1984

ROLAND GLEN FINGERS
OAKLAND, A.L., 1968-1976
SAN DIEGO, N.L., 1977-1980
MILWAUKEE, A.L., 1981-1985
CAREER EPITOMIZED EMERGENCE OF MODERN-DAY
RELIEF ACE AS HE APPROACHED LEGENDARY STATUS
WITH CONSISTENT EXCELLENCE COMING OUT OF
BULLPEN. RELIED UPON SINKING FAST BALL TO
BECOME ALL-TIME MAJOR LEAGUE LEADER WITH
341 CAREER SAVES. APPEARED IN 16 WORLD SERIES
GAMES FOR OAKLAND, WINNING 2 AND SAVING 6.
A.L. MVP AND CY YOUNG AWARDEE IN 1981.

1992

CARLTON ERNEST FISK
"PUDGE"
BOSTON, A.L., 1969, 1971-80
CHICAGO, A.L., 1981-93
A COMMANDING FIGURE BEHIND THE PLATE FOR A RECORD 24
SEASONS, HE CAUGHT MORE GAMES (2,226) AND HIT MORE HOME RUNS
(351) THAN ANY CATCHER BEFORE HIM. HIS GRITTY RESOLVE AND
COMPETITIVE FIRE EARNED HIM THE RESPECT OF TEAMMATES AND
OPPOSING PLAYERS ALIKE. A STAUNCH TRAINING REGIMEN EXTENDED
HIS DURABILITY AND ENHANCED HIS PRODUCTIVITY—AS EVIDENCED
BY A RECORD 72 HOME RUNS AFTER AGE 40. HIS DRAMATIC HOME RUN
TO WIN GAME SIX OF THE 1975 WORLD SERIES IS ONE OF BASEBALL'S
UNFORGETTABLE MOMENTS. WAS THE 1972 AMERICAN LEAGUE ROOKIE
OF THE YEAR AND AN 11-TIME ALL-STAR.

2000

ELMER HARRISON FLICK
PHILADELPHIA, N.L. 1898-1902
CLEVELAND, A.L. 1902-1910
OUTFIELDER WHO BATTED .378 FOR
1900 PHILLIES. LEFT LIFETIME MARK
OF .315 FOR 13 SEASONS. A.L. BATTING
CHAMPION IN 1905. LED A.L. IN TRIPLES,
1905-06-07, AND IN STEALS, 1904, TYING
FOR LEADERSHIP AGAIN IN 1906.

1963

EDWARD CHARLES FORD
"WHITEY"
NEW YORK, A.L., 1950-1967
POSTED BEST WINNING PERCENTAGE (.690)
AMONG TWENTIETH CENTURY PITCHERS
WITH 200 OR MORE DECISIONS. HAD 236
VICTORIES AND 106 LOSSES LIFETIME. EARNED
RUN AVERAGE 2.75 PACED A.L. IN VICTORIES
AND WINNING P.C. THREE TIMES AND IN
EARNED RUN AVERAGE AND SHUTOUTS
TWICE. WON CY YOUNG AWARD IN 1961. SET
WORLD SERIES STANDARDS FOR GAMES
PITCHED 22, INNINGS 146, WINS 10, AND
STRIKEOUTS 94, AND WITH 33 2/3 CONSECUTIVE
SCORELESS INNINGS.

1974

ANDREW (RUBE) FOSTER
RATED FOREMOST MANAGER AND EXECUTIVE IN
HISTORY OF NEGRO LEAGUES. ACCLAIMED TOP
PITCHER IN BLACK BASEBALL FOR NEARLY A
DECADE IN EARLY 1900s. FORMED CHICAGO
AMERICAN GIANTS IN 1911 AND BUILT THEM
INTO MIDWEST'S DOMINANT BLACK TEAM. IN
1920 HE ORGANIZED NEGRO NATIONAL LEAGUE
HEADED LEAGUE AND MANAGED CHICAGO TEAM
UNTIL RETIREMENT FOLLOWING 1926 SEASON.

1981

WILLIAM HENDRICK FOSTER
NEGRO LEAGUES, 1923-1937
REGARDED AS ONE OF THE BEST LEFT-HANDED
PITCHERS IN NEGRO LEAGUE HISTORY AND ALSO
MANAGED SEVERAL CLUBS. DEVASTATING SIDEARM
DELIVERY MADE HIM CONSISTENT WINNER
INSTRUMENTAL IN CHICAGO AMERICAN GIANTS' NEGRO
LEAGUE PENNANT AND WORLD SERIES SUCCESS IN
1926, 1927, 1928 AND 1933. WON 26 STRAIGHT IN
1926 AND HAD 32-3 MARK IN 1927. COACHED
BASEBALL AT ALMA MATER, ALCORN A & M COLLEGE
IN MISSISSIPPI, 1960-1978

1996

JACOB NELSON FOX
"NELLIE"
PHILADELPHIA, A.L., 1947-1949
CHICAGO, A.L., 1950-1963
HOUSTON, N.L., 1964-1965
SURE-HANDED SECOND BASEMAN AND SKILLFUL BATSMAN WAS
A CATALYST FOR THE "GO-GO" WHITE SOX OF THE 1950s. A
12-TIME AMERICAN LEAGUE ALL-STAR WHO NEVER STRUCK OUT
MORE THAN 18 TIMES IN A SEASON. HIS STRIKEOUT TO AT BAT
RATIO BEING THIRD BEST ALL-TIME. ONCE WENT RECORD 98
GAMES WITHOUT A STRIKEOUT. PLAYED RECORD 798 CONSECUTIVE
GAMES AT SECOND. LED LEAGUE IN HITS FOUR TIMES, PUTOUTS
10 TIMES, FIELD PCT. SIX TIMES. WON 1959 A.L. MVP HONORS
BY HELPING CHICAGO TO FIRST FLAG IN 40 YEARS.

1997

JAMES E. (JIMMY) FOXX
PHILADELPHIA (A.L.) 1926-35
BOSTON (A.L.) 1936-42; CHICAGO (N.L.) 1942-44
PHILADELPHIA (N.L.) 1945
NOTED FOR HIS BATTING, PARTICULARLY AS A
HOME RUN HITTER. COLLECTED 534 HOME RUNS
IN 2,317 GAMES. HAD A LIFETIME BATTING
AVERAGE OF .325 AND, IN THREE WORLD
SERIES, COMPILED A MARK OF .344. APPEARED
IN SEVEN ALL STAR GAMES IN WHICH HE
BATTED .316. PLAYED FIRST AND THIRD BASES
AND ALSO WAS A CATCHER.

1951

FORD CHRISTOPHER FRICK
SPORTSWRITER – SPORTSCASTER

FOUNDER OF BASEBALL HALL OF FAME.
PRESIDENT OF NATIONAL LEAGUE 1934-1951.
COMMISSIONER OF BASEBALL 1951-1965.

1970

FRANK FRISCH
NEW YORK N.L. 1919-1926
ST. LOUIS N.L. 1927-1938
PITTSBURGH N.L. 1940-1946
JUMPED FROM COLLEGE TO THE MAJORS,
THE "FORDHAM FLASH" WAS AN OUTSTANDING
INFIELDER, BASE-RUNNER AND BATTER.
HAD A LIFETIME BATTING MARK OF .316.
HOLDS MANY RECORDS. PLAYED IN 50
WORLD SERIES GAMES. MANAGED ST. LOUIS
FROM 1933 THROUGH 1938 AND WON WORLD
SERIES IN 1934. MANAGED PITTSBURGH
FROM 1940 THROUGH 1946.

1947

JAMES F. (PUD) GALVIN
ST. LOUIS N.A. 1875
BUFFALO N.L. 1879-1885
PITTSBURGH A.A. 1885-1886
PITTSBURGH N.L. 1887-1889 1891-1892
PITTSBURGH P.L. 1890
ST. LOUIS N.L. 1892
WON 365 GAMES. LOST 311.
WHEN ELECTED ONLY FOUR PITCHERS
HAD WON MORE GAMES.
PITCHED NO-HIT GAMES IN 1880 AND 1884.
PITCHED 649 COMPLETE GAMES.

1965

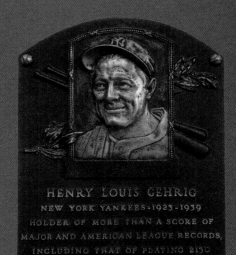

HENRY LOUIS GEHRIG
NEW YORK YANKEES 1923-1939
HOLDER OF MORE THAN A SCORE OF
MAJOR AND AMERICAN LEAGUE RECORDS,
INCLUDING THAT OF PLAYING 2130
CONSECUTIVE GAMES. WHEN HE RETIRED
IN 1939, HE HAD A LIFE TIME BATTING
AVERAGE OF 340.

1939

CHARLES L. GEHRINGER
SECOND BASEMAN WITH DETROIT A.L. FROM
1925 THROUGH 1941 AND COACH IN 1942.
COMPILED LIFETIME BATTING AVERAGE
OF .321. IN 2323 GAMES, COLLECTED 2839
HITS. NAMED MOST VALUABLE PLAYER IN
A.L. IN 1937. BATTED .321 IN WORLD SERIES
COMPETITION AND HAD A .500 AVERAGE
FOR SIX ALL-STAR GAMES.

1949

RICHARD MICHAEL GOSSAGE
"RICH" "GOOSE"
CHICAGO, A.L., 1972-1976, PITTSBURGH, N.L., 1977
NEW YORK, A.L., 1978-1983, 1989, SAN DIEGO, N.L., 1984-1987
CHICAGO, N.L., 1988, SAN FRANCISCO, N.L., 1989
TEXAS, A.L., 1991, OAKLAND, A.L., 1992-1993, SEATTLE, A.L., 1994
A DOMINANT RELIEF PITCHER WITH A TRADEMARK MOUSTACHE,
WHOSE MENACING GLARE AND EXPLODING FASTBALL INTIMIDATED
BATTERS FOR MORE THAN TWO DECADES. POSTED A 124-107 RECORD
WITH 310 SAVES, 1,502 STRIKEOUTS AND A 3.01 ERA IN 1,002 GAMES,
CLOSING OUT VICTORIES CONVINCINGLY. INCREDIBLY DURABLE,
POSTED 52 SAVES OF AT LEAST SEVEN OUTS. A NINE-TIME ALL-STAR
WHO LED THE A.L. IN SAVES THREE TIMES. PITCHED IN THREE WORLD
SERIES, CLINCHING VICTORY FOR NEW YORK IN 1978.

2008

JOSHUA (JOSH) GIBSON
NEGRO LEAGUES 1930-1946
CONSIDERED GREATEST SLUGGER IN NEGRO
BASEBALL LEAGUES. POWER-HITTING CATCHER
WHO HIT ALMOST 800 HOME RUNS IN LEAGUE
AND INDEPENDENT BASEBALL DURING HIS
17-YEAR CAREER. CREDITED WITH HAVING
BEEN NEGRO NATIONAL LEAGUE BATTING
CHAMPION IN 1936-38-42-45.

1972

ROBERT GIBSON
ST. LOUIS N. L. 1959-1975
FIVE-TIME 20-GAME WINNER. HIS 3,117
STRIKEOUTS MADE HIM ONLY 2ND PITCHER TO
REACH 3,000. FIRST TO FAN 200 OR MORE IN
A SEASON 9 TIMES. SET N. L. MARK WITH 1.12
ERA IN 1968, HURLING 13 SHUTOUTS. TWICE
WORLD SERIES MVP, SETTING RECORDS FOR
CONSECUTIVE VICTORIES (7), CONSECUTIVE
COMPLETE GAMES (8), AND STRIKEOUTS IN A
GAME (17) AND A SERIES (35). VOTED N. L.
MVP IN 1968 AND CY YOUNG AWARD WINNER IN
1968 AND 1970. WON NINE GOLD GLOVE AWARDS.

1981

WARREN CRANDALL GILES
DEVOTED 50 YEARS TO BASEBALL AS CLUB
AND LEAGUE EXECUTIVE, INCLUDING 33 IN
MAJOR LEAGUES. HEADED CINCINNATI REDS
FROM 1937 TO 1951, CAPTURING PENNANTS
IN 1939-40. NATIONAL LEAGUE PRESIDENT
LONGER THAN ANY OTHER MAN - 18 YEARS
FROM 1951 THROUGH 1969. PRESIDED OVER
FRANCHISE SHIFTS TO PACIFIC COAST AND
EXPANSION TO 12 CLUBS AND INTO CANADA
AS N. L. ENJOYED UNPRECEDENTED
PROSPERITY.

1979

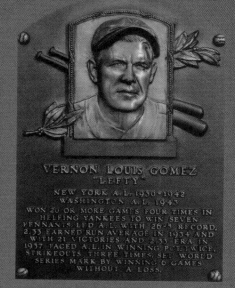

VERNON LOUIS GOMEZ
"LEFTY"
NEW YORK A. L. 1930-1942
WASHINGTON A. L. 1943
WON 20 OR MORE GAMES FOUR TIMES IN
HELPING YANKEES TO WIN SEVEN
PENNANTS. LED A. L. WITH 26-5 RECORD,
2.33 EARNED RUN AVERAGE IN 1934 AND
WITH 21 VICTORIES AND 2.33 ERA IN
1937. FACED A. L. IN WINNING PCT. TWICE,
STRIKEOUTS, THREE TIMES. SET WORLD
SERIES MARK BY WINNING 6 GAMES
WITHOUT A LOSS.

1972

LEON ALLEN GOSLIN
"GOOSE"
WASHINGTON A. L. 1921 TO 1930, 1933, 1938
ST. LOUIS A. L. 1930 TO 1932
DETROIT A. L. 1934 TO 1937
BATTED .344 IN 1924, .334 IN 1925,
.354 IN 1926, .334 IN 1927. LED A. L.
IN BATTING IN 1928 WITH .379 AVERAGE.
RUNS BATTED IN FOR 1924-129.
HIT .300 OR BETTER 11 YEARS.
LIFETIME TOTAL OF 2735 HITS,
BATTING AVERAGE .316.
MADE 37 HITS IN 5 WORLD SERIES.

1968

ULYSSES F. GRANT
"FRANK"
PRE-NEGRO LEAGUES, 1886-1903
ONE OF BASEBALL'S EARLY STARS WHO BECAME AN INSPIRATION
FOR FUTURE GENERATIONS OF AFRICAN-AMERICAN
BALLPLAYERS. BEGAN CAREER AS SECOND BASEMAN IN
INTEGRATED MINOR LEAGUES FROM 1886-1891. A SLICK FIELDER
WITH A STRONG ARM, WHO HIT FOR AVERAGE AND HAD
SURPRISING POWER DESPITE SLIGHT 5'7" FRAME. SEGREGATION
EVENTUALLY FORCED HIM TO PLAY FOR TOP TOURING BLACK
TEAMS, MOST NOTABLY THE CUBAN GIANTS, WHERE HE SERVED AS
TEAM CAPTAIN AND OFTEN MENTORED YOUNGER PLAYERS.

2006

HENRY BENJAMIN GREENBERG
DETROIT A. L. 1933 TO 1946
PITTSBURGH N. L. 1947
ONE OF BASEBALL'S GREATEST RIGHT-HANDED
BATTERS. TIED FOR MOST HOME RUNS BY
RIGHT-HANDED BATTER IN 1938-58. MOST
RUNS-BATTED-IN 1935-37-40-46, AND HOME
RUNS 1938-40-46. WON 1945 PENNANT ON
LAST DAY OF SEASON WITH GRAND SLAM
HOME RUN IN 9TH INNING. PLAYED IN 4
WORLD SERIES, 2 ALL-STAR GAMES. MOST
VALUABLE A. L. PLAYER TWICE-1935-1940.
LIFETIME BATTING AVERAGE .313.

1956

CLARK C. GRIFFITH
ASSOCIATED WITH MAJOR LEAGUE BASEBALL
FOR MORE THAN 50 YEARS AS A PITCHER,
MANAGER AND EXECUTIVE. SERVED AS A
MEMBER OF THE CHICAGO AND CINCINNATI
TEAMS IN THE N. L. AND THE CHICAGO,
NEW YORK AND WASHINGTON CLUBS
IN THE A. L. COMPILED MORE THAN 200
VICTORIES AS A PITCHER. MANAGER OF THE
CINCINNATI N. L. AND CHICAGO, NEW YORK
AND WASHINGTON A. L. TEAMS FOR 20 YEARS.

1946

BURLEIGH ARLAND GRIMES
1916-1934
ONE OF THE GREAT SPITBALL PITCHERS.
WON 270 GAMES, LOST 212 FOR 7 MAJOR
LEAGUE CLUBS. FIVE 20 VICTORY SEASONS.
WON 13 IN ROW FOR GIANTS IN 1927.
MANAGED DODGERS IN 1937 AND 1938.
LIFETIME E. R. A. 3.52.

1964

ROBERT MOSES GROVE
PHILADELPHIA A. L. 1925-1933
BOSTON A. L. 1934-1941
WINNER OF 300 GAMES IN THE MAJORS
OVER A SPAN OF 17 YEARS. LED A. L. IN
STRIKEOUTS SEVEN CONSECUTIVE SEASONS.
WON 20 OR MORE GAMES EIGHT SEASONS.
IN 1931, WHILE WINNING 31 GAMES AND
LOSING FOUR, COMPILED A WINNING STREAK
OF 16 STRAIGHT. WON 79 GAMES FOR THE
THREE TIME PENNANT WINNING
ATHLETICS TEAM OF 1929-30-31.

1947

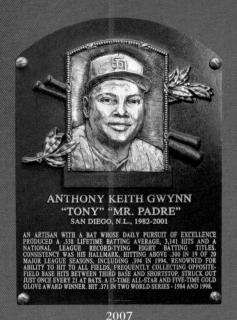

ANTHONY KEITH GWYNN
"TONY" "MR. PADRE"
SAN DIEGO, N.L., 1982-2001

AN ARTISAN WITH A BAT WHOSE DAILY PURSUIT OF EXCELLENCE
PRODUCED A .338 LIFETIME BATTING AVERAGE, 3,141 HITS AND A
NATIONAL LEAGUE RECORD-TYING EIGHT BATTING TITLES.
CONSISTENCY WAS HIS HALLMARK, HITTING ABOVE .300 IN 19 OF 20
MAJOR LEAGUE SEASONS, INCLUDING .394 IN 1994. RENOWNED FOR
ABILITY TO HIT TO ALL FIELDS, FREQUENTLY COLLECTING OPPOSITE-
FIELD BASE HITS BETWEEN THIRD BASE AND SHORTSTOP. STRUCK OUT
JUST ONCE EVERY 21 AT BATS. A 15-TIME ALL-STAR AND FIVE-TIME GOLD
GLOVE AWARD WINNER. HIT .371 IN TWO WORLD SERIES - 1984 AND 1998.

2007

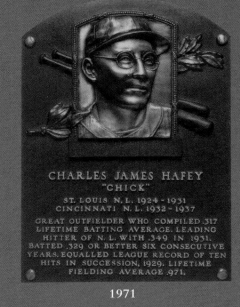

CHARLES JAMES HAFEY
"CHICK"

ST. LOUIS N. L. 1924 - 1931
CINCINNATI N. L. 1932 - 1937

GREAT OUTFIELDER WHO COMPILED .317
LIFETIME BATTING AVERAGE. LEADING
HITTER OF N. L. WITH .349 IN 1931.
BATTED .329 OR BETTER SIX CONSECUTIVE
YEARS. EQUALLED LEAGUE RECORD OF TEN
HITS IN SUCCESSION, 1929. LIFETIME
FIELDING AVERAGE .971.

1971

JESSE JOSEPH (POP) HAINES
CINCINNATI N. L. 1918
ST. LOUIS N. L. 1920-1937

DURABLE RIGHT-HANDER WON 210 GAMES,
LOST 158--ALL IN HIS 18 YEARS WITH
CARDINALS. GAINED 20-VICTORY CLASS
THREE TIMES. TOSSED 5-0 NO-HITTER
VS. BOSTON, 1924. DEFEATED YANKEES
TWICE IN 1926 WORLD SERIES. LED N. L.
IN COMPLETE GAMES (25), SHUTOUTS (6)
WHILE POSTING 24-10 RECORD, 1927.

1970

WILLIAM R. HAMILTON
PHILADELPHIA N.L. 1890-1895
BOSTON N.L. 1896-1901

HOLDS RECORDS FOR SINGLE SEASON:
RUNS SCORED, 196 IN 1894; STOLEN
BASES, 115 IN 1891. LIFETIME TOTAL
STOLEN BASES, 937. BATTED .595 IN
1893, .399 IN 1894, .393 IN 1895.
LED NATIONAL LEAGUE IN 1891 WITH
.338 AVERAGE. LIFETIME BATTING
AVERAGE OF .344. SCORED 100 OR
MORE RUNS DURING 10 SEASONS.

1961

EDWARD HUGH HANLON
(NED)

PITTSBURGH, N.L. 1889, 1891
PITTSBURGH, P.L. 1890
BALTIMORE, N.L. 1892-1898
BROOKLYN, N.L. 1899-1905
CINCINNATI, N.L. 1906-1907

MANAGER OF FIVE PENNANT WINNING TEAMS WITH BALTIMORE
AND BROOKLYN. EMPLOYING INNOVATIVE TACTICS SUCH AS
HIT AND RUN, SQUEEZE AND 'BALTIMORE CHOP'. FOUR OF
HIS PLAYERS--McGRAW, ROBINSON, JENNINGS AND HUGGINS
THEMSELVES BECAME HALL OF FAME MANAGERS. ALSO HEADED
BASEBALL'S RULES COMMITTEE. A SPEEDY OUTFIELDER WITH
DETROIT DURING HIS PLAYING DAYS

1996

WILLIAM HARRIDGE
PRESIDENT OF AMERICAN LEAGUE 1931-1958
AFTER SERVING AS SECRETARY OF
LEAGUE 1927-1931 AND SECRETARY TO
A. L. PRESIDENT 1911-1927.
CHAIRMAN OF AMERICAN LEAGUE
BOARD OF DIRECTORS 1958-1971.

1972

STANLEY RAYMOND HARRIS
"BUCKY"

SERVED 40 YEARS IN MAJORS AS PLAYER,
MANAGER AND EXECUTIVE, INCLUDING 29 AS
PILOT. SLICK SECOND SACKER EARNED TAG
OF "BOY WONDER" BY GUIDING WASHINGTON
TO 1924 WORLD TITLE AS 27-YEAR-OLD IN
DEBUT AS PLAYER - PILOT. WON A.L. FLAG
AGAIN IN 1925. LED 1947 YANKEES TO
WORLD TITLE. MANAGED DETROIT, BOSTON
RED SOX AND PHILADELPHIA PHILLIES.

1975

CHARLES LEO (GABBY) HARTNETT
CHICAGO N.L. 1922 TO 1940
NEW YORK N.L. 1941

CAUGHT 100 OR MORE GAMES PER SEASON
FOR 12 YEARS, EIGHT IN SUCCESSION, 1930
TO 1937 FOR LEAGUE RECORD. SET MARK
FOR CONSECUTIVE CHANCES FOR CATCHER
WITHOUT ERROR, 452 IN 1933-34. HIGHEST
FIELDING AVERAGE FOR CATCHER IN 100 OR
MORE GAMES IN 7 SEASONS. MOST PUTOUTS
N.L. 7292; MOST CHANCES ACCEPTED N.L.
8546. LIFETIME BATTING AVERAGE .297.

1955

HARRY EDWIN HEILMANN
DETROIT, A.L.-CINCINNATI, N.L.
1916 -1932

RIGHT HANDED HITTING OUTFIELDER AND
FIRST BASEMAN, WON AMERICAN LEAGUE
BATTING CHAMPIONSHIP FOUR TIMES
1921, '23, '25 AND '27. IN 1923, BATTED .403.
COLLECTED 2660 HITS AND 183 HOME RUNS
IN 2,146 MAJOR LEAGUE GAMES. HAD
LIFETIME BATTING AVERAGE OF .342 AND
FIELDING MARK OF .975.

1952

WILLIAM JENNINGS HERMAN
CHICAGO, N.L.   BROOKLYN, N.L.
BOSTON, N.L.   PITTSBURGH, N.L.
1931 – 1947
MASTER OF HIT-AND-RUN PLAY. OWNED .304
LIFETIME BATTING AVERAGE. MADE 200 OR
MORE HITS IN SEASON THREE TIMES. LED
LEAGUE IN HITS (227) AND DOUBLES (57)
IN 1935. SET MAJOR LEAGUE RECORD FOR
SECOND BASEMEN WITH FIVE SEASONS OF
HANDLING 900 OR MORE CHANCES AND N.L.
MARK OF 466 PUTOUTS IN 1933. LED LOOP
KEYSTONERS IN PUTOUTS SEVEN TIMES.

1975

JOSEPH PRESTON HILL
"PETE"
PRE-NEGRO LEAGUES, 1899-1919
NEGRO LEAGUES, 1920-1921, 1923-1925
THE CATALYST AND CAPTAIN OF THE GREAT CHICAGO AMERICAN
GIANTS CLUBS OF THE 1910s. LEFT-HANDED LINE DRIVE HITTER WITH
EXCEPTIONAL BAT CONTROL WHO HIT TO ALL FIELDS. GRACEFULLY
ROAMED CENTER FIELD WITH COMBINATION OF SPEED, RANGE AND A
RIFLE ARM. RATTLED OPPOSING PITCHERS, CATCHERS AND INFIELDERS
WITH HIS CONSTANT MOTION ON THE BASE PATHS. RESPECTED LEADER
WHO SERVED AS PLAYER-MANAGER OF THE DETROIT STARS (1919-1921)
AND BALTIMORE BLACK SOX (1924-1925). ALSO STARRED IN CUBAN
WINTER LEAGUE.

2006

HARRY BARTHOLOMEW HOOPER
BOSTON A.L. 1909-1920
CHICAGO A.L. 1921-1925
LEADOFF HITTER AND RIGHT FIELDER OF
1912-15-16-18 WORLD CHAMPION RED SOX.
NOTED FOR SPEED AND STRONG ARM.
COLLECTED 2,466 HITS FOR .281 CAREER
AVERAGE. HAD 3,981 PUTOUTS AND 344
ASSISTS. LIFETIME FIELDING AVERAGE .966.

1971

ROGERS HORNSBY
NATIONAL LEAGUE BATTING CHAMPION
7 YEARS -1920 TO 1925; 1928. LIFETIME
BATTING AVERAGE .358 HIGHEST IN
NATIONAL LEAGUE HISTORY. HIT .424 IN
1924, 20TH CENTURY MAJOR LEAGUE RECORD.
MANAGER 1926 WORLD CHAMPION ST. LOUIS
CARDINALS. MOST-VALUABLE-PLAYER
1925 AND 1929.

1942

WAITE CHARLES HOYT
"SCHOOLBOY"
NEW YORK YANKEE PITCHER 1921-1930.
LIFETIME RECORD: 237 GAMES WON, 182
GAMES LOST, .566 AVERAGE, EARNED RUN
AVERAGE 3.59. PITCHED 3 GAMES IN 1921
WORLD SERIES AND GAVE NO EARNED RUNS.
ALSO PITCHED FOR BOSTON, DETROIT AND
PHILADELPHIA A.L. AND BROOKLYN,
NEW YORK AND PITTSBURGH N.L.

1969

ROBERT CAL HUBBARD
UMPIRE
AMERICAN LEAGUE 1936-1951
ONE OF MOST RESPECTED, EFFICIENT AND
AUTHORITATIVE UMPIRES IN HISTORY OF
MAJORS. GENTLE GIANT BOASTED SPECIAL
KNACK FOR DEALING WITH SITUATIONS ON
FIELD. WORKED FOUR WORLD SERIES AND
THREE ALL-STAR GAMES. SERVED AS LEAGUE'S
ASSISTANT UMPIRE SUPERVISOR IN 1952 AND AS
UMPIRE SUPERVISOR FROM 1953 TO 1969.

1976

CARL HUBBELL
NEW YORK N.L. 1928-1943
HAILED FOR IMPRESSIVE PERFORMANCE IN
1934 ALL-STAR GAME WHEN HE STRUCK OUT
RUTH, GEHRIG, FOXX, SIMMONS AND CRONIN
IN SUCCESSION. NICKNAMED GIANTS'
MEAL TICKET. WON 253 GAMES IN MAJORS,
SCORING 16 STRAIGHT IN 1936. COMPILED
STREAK OF 46⅓ SCORELESS INNINGS IN
1933. HOLDER OF MANY RECORDS.

1947

MILLER JAMES HUGGINS
1904—1929
MANAGER OF ST. LOUIS CARDINALS
AND NEW YORK YANKEES.
LED YANKEES TO 6 PENNANTS
IN 1921, 1922, 1923, 1926, 1927 AND 1928 AND
3 WORLD SERIES VICTORIES 1923, 1927 AND 1928.
SECOND BASEMAN IN PLAYING DAYS
WITH REDS AND CARDINALS, 1904-1916.

1964

WILLIAM AMBROSE HULBERT
WAVY-HAIRED, SILVER TONGUED EXECUTIVE AND
ENERGETIC, INFLUENTIAL LEADER. WHILE PART-
OWNER OF CHICAGO NATIONAL ASSOCIATION TEAM,
WAS INSTRUMENTAL IN FOUNDING NATIONAL LEAGUE
IN 1876. ELECTED N.L. PRESIDENT LATER THAT
YEAR AND IS CREDITED WITH ESTABLISHING
RESPECTABILITY, INTEGRITY AND SOUND
FOUNDATION FOR NEW LEAGUE WITH HIS
RELENTLESS OPPOSITION TO BETTING, ROWDINESS,
AND OTHER PREVALENT ABUSES WHICH WERE
THREATENING THE SPORT

1995

JAMES AUGUSTUS HUNTER
"CATFISH"
KANSAS CITY, A.L., 1965 – 1967
OAKLAND, A.L., 1968 – 1974
NEW YORK, A.L., 1975 – 1979
THE BIGGER THE GAME, THE BETTER HE PITCHED.
ONE OF BASEBALL'S MOST DOMINANT PITCHERS FROM
1970-76, WINNING OVER 20 FIVE STRAIGHT TIMES. COMPILED
224-166 MARK WITH 3.26 ERA BEFORE ARM TROUBLE
ENDED CAREER AT AGE 33. HURLED PERFECT GAME
VS. TWINS IN 1968. 1974 A.L. CY YOUNG AWARD WINNER.
5-3 IN 12 WORLD SERIES GAMES.

1987

MONFORD (MONTE) IRVIN
NEGRO LEAGUES 1937-1948
NEW YORK N.L., CHICAGO N.L.,
1949 – 1956
REGARDED AS ONE OF NEGRO LEAGUES' BEST
HITTERS. STAR SLUGGER OF NEWARK EAGLES
WON 1946 NEGRO LEAGUE BATTING TITLE.
LED N.L. IN RUNS BATTED IN AND PACED
"MIRACLE" GIANTS IN HITTING IN 1951
DRIVE TO PENNANT. BATTED .458 AND
STOLE HOME IN 1951 WORLD SERIES.

1973

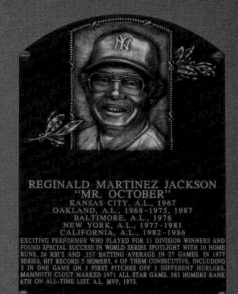

REGINALD MARTINEZ JACKSON
"MR. OCTOBER"
KANSAS CITY, A.L., 1967
OAKLAND, A.L., 1968-1975, 1987
BALTIMORE, A.L., 1976
NEW YORK, A.L., 1977-1981
CALIFORNIA, A.L., 1982-1986
EXCITING PERFORMER WHO PLAYED FOR 11 DIVISION WINNERS AND
FOUND SPECIAL SUCCESS IN WORLD SERIES SPOTLIGHT WITH 10 HOME
RUNS, 24 RBI'S AND .357 BATTING AVERAGE IN 27 GAMES. IN 1977
SERIES, HIT RECORD 5 HOMERS, 4 OF THEM CONSECUTIVE, INCLUDING
3 IN ONE GAME ON 3 FIRST PITCHES OFF 3 DIFFERENT HURLERS.
MAMMOTH CLOUT MARKED 1971 ALL STAR GAME. 563 HOMERS RANK
6TH ON ALL-TIME LIST. A.L. MVP, 1973.

1993

TRAVIS CALVIN JACKSON
NEW YORK N.L., 1922-1936
PREMIER DEFENSIVE SHORTSTOP WHO SWUNG
PRODUCTIVE BAT. KNOWN FOR OUTSTANDING
ARM AND EXCEPTIONAL RANGE AFIELD. LED
N.L. SHORTSTOPS IN ASSISTS FOUR TIMES,
TOTAL CHANCES THREE YEARS AND FIELDING
PCT. AND DOUBLE PLAYS TWICE. ADEPT AS
BUNTER, HE BATTED OVER .300 SIX YEARS
WHILE COMPILING .291 LIFETIME AVERAGE.
DROVE IN MORE THAN 90 RUNS 5 – TIMES,
REACHING 101 ON .268 AVERAGE IN 1934.

1982

FERGUSON ARTHUR JENKINS
PHILADELPHIA, N.L., 1965-1966
CHICAGO, N.L., 1966-1973, 1982-1983
TEXAS, A.L., 1974-1975, 1978-1981
BOSTON, A.L., 1976-1977
CANADA'S FIRST HALL-OF-FAMER. 284-226
LIFETIME WITH 3,192 STRIKEOUTS AND 3.34 ERA
DESPITE PLAYING 12 OF HIS 19 YEAR CAREER IN
HITTERS' BALLPARKS-WRIGLEY FIELD AND FENWAY
PARK. WON 20 GAMES 7 SEASONS, INCLUDING 6
CONSECUTIVE, 1967 – 1972. CY YOUNG AWARD
WINNER, 1971. TRADEMARKS WERE PINPOINT CONTROL
AND CHANGING SPEEDS.

1991

HUGHIE JENNINGS
OF BALTIMORE'S FAMOUS OLD ORIOLES,
HE WAS ONE OF THE GAME'S MIGHTY
MITES. A STAR SHORTSTOP HE WAS A
CONSTANT THREAT AT THE PLATE.
ONCE HIT .397. PILOTED DETROIT
TO THREE CHAMPIONSHIPS.

1945

BYRON BANCROFT JOHNSON
ORGANIZER OF THE AMERICAN
LEAGUE AND ITS PRESIDENT FROM
ITS ORGANIZATION IN 1900 UNTIL
HIS RESIGNATION BECAUSE OF
ILL HEALTH IN 1927.
A GREAT EXECUTIVE.

1937

WALTER PERRY JOHNSON
WASHINGTON 1907-1927
CONCEDED TO BE FASTEST BALL PITCHER
IN HISTORY OF GAME. WON 414 GAMES
WITH LOSING TEAM BEHIND HIM MANY YEARS
HOLDER OF STRIKE OUT AND SHUT OUT RECORDS

1936

WILLIAM JULIUS JOHNSON
"JUDY"
NEGRO LEAGUES 1923-1937
CONSIDERED BEST THIRD BASEMAN OF HIS
DAY IN NEGRO LEAGUES. OUTSTANDING AS
FIELDER AND EXCELLENT CLUTCH HITTER
WHO BATTED OVER .300 MOST OF CAREER.
HELPED HILLDALE TEAM WIN THREE FLAGS
IN ROW, 1923-24-25. ALSO PLAYED FOR
1935 CHAMPION PITTSBURGH CRAWFORDS.

1975

ADRIAN (ADDIE) JOSS
CLEVELAND A.L., 1902-1910
ONE OF PREMIER PITCHERS OF AMERICAN
LEAGUE'S FIRST DECADE. SPEED, SHARP
CONTROL HELPED HIM TO WIN 20 OR MORE
GAMES FOUR SEASONS IN A ROW. POSTED
LEAGUE-LEADING 27 VICTORIES AND THREE
ONE-HITTERS IN 1907. HURLED PERFECT
GAME IN 1908. HAD ANOTHER NO-HITTER
IN 1910. CREDITED WITH 45 SHUTOUTS
AMONG HIS 160 CAREER VICTORIES.

1978

ALBERT WILLIAM KALINE
DETROIT A.L., 1953-1974
TWELFTH PLAYER TO REACH ELITE 3,000-HIT
PLATEAU. SOCKED 399 HOMERS AND ATTAINED
.297 CAREER AVERAGE, WITH NINE YEARS IN
.300 CLASS. FINISHED IN ALL-TIME TOP 15
WITH 2,834 GAMES, 3,007 HITS, 1,583 RUNS
BATTED IN AND 4,852 TOTAL BASES. PLAYED
100 OR MORE GAMES 20 YEARS AND HAD 242
CONSECUTIVE ERRORLESS GAMES IN OUTFIELD,
1970-1972, FOR A.L. RECORDS. LED IN HITS
AND WON BATTING TITLE IN 1955 AT AGE 20.

1980

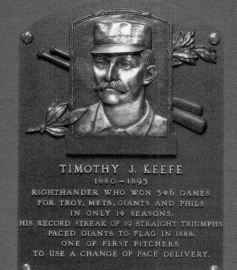

TIMOTHY J. KEEFE
1880 - 1893
RIGHTHANDER WHO WON 346 GAMES
FOR TROY, METS, GIANTS AND PHILS
IN ONLY 14 SEASONS.
HIS RECORD STREAK OF 19 STRAIGHT TRIUMPHS
PACED GIANTS TO FLAG IN 1888.
ONE OF FIRST PITCHERS
TO USE A CHANGE OF PACE DELIVERY.

1964

WILLIE KEELER
"HIT 'EM WHERE THEY AIN'T!"
BASEBALL'S GREATEST PLACE-HITTER;
BEST BUNTER. BIG LEAGUE CAREER
1892 TO 1910 WITH N.Y. GIANTS.
BALTIMORE ORIOLES, BROOKLYN SUPERBAS,
N.Y. HIGHLANDERS. NATIONAL LEAGUE
BATTING CHAMPION '97-'98.

1900

GEORGE CLYDE KELL
PHILADELPHIA A.L. 1943-1946
DETROIT A.L. 1946-1952
BOSTON A.L. 1952-1954
CHICAGO A.L. 1954-1956
BALTIMORE A.L. 1956-1957
PREMIER A.L. THIRD BASEMAN OF 1940'S AND
1950'S. SOLID HITTER AND SURE-HANDED FIELDER
WITH STRONG, ACCURATE ARM. BATTED OVER
.300 9 TIMES, LEADING LEAGUE WITH .343 IN
1949. LED A.L. THIRD BASEMEN IN FIELDING
PCT. 7 TIMES, ASSISTS 4 TIMES AND PUTOUTS
AND DOUBLE PLAYS TWICE.

1900

JOSEPH JAMES KELLEY
1891 - 1908
STANDOUT HITTER AND LEFT FIELDER OF
CHAMPION 1894-95-96 BALTIMORE ORIOLES
AND 1899-1900 BROOKLYN SUPERBAS. BATTED
OVER .300 FOR 11 CONSECUTIVE YEARS WITH
HIGH OF .391 IN 1894. EQUALLED RECORD
WITH 9 HITS IN 9 AT-BATS IN DOUBLEHEADER.
ALSO PLAYED FOR BOSTON, PITTSBURGH AND
CINCINNATI OF N.L. AND BALTIMORE OF A.L.
MANAGED CINCINNATI 1902 TO 1905 AND
BOSTON N.L. IN 1908.

1900

GEORGE LANGE KELLY
"HIGHPOCKETS"
NEW YORK N.L., PITTSBURGH N.L.
CINCINNATI N.L., CHICAGO N.L.
BROOKLYN, N.L., 1915-1930 AND 1932
ESTABLISHED MAJOR LEAGUE RECORD BY
HITTING SEVEN HOME RUNS IN SIX CONSECUTIVE
GAMES (1924). RAPPED HOMERS IN THREE
SUCCESSIVE INNINGS (1923). DROVE IN MORE THAN
100 RUNS FOUR CONSECUTIVE YEARS, 1921-24.
SET LEAGUE RECORDS FOR CHANCES ACCEPTED
(1,862) AND PUTOUTS (1,759) BY FIRST BASEMAN
IN 1920. ALSO LED IN CHANCES ACCEPTED
1921-22-23.

1939

MIKE J. (KING) KELLY
COLORFUL PLAYER AND AUDACIOUS
BASE-RUNNER. IN 1887 FOR BOSTON
HE HIT .394 AND STOLE 84 BASES.
HIS SALE FOR $10,000 WAS ONE OF
THE BIGGEST DEALS OF BASEBALL'S
EARLY HISTORY.

1983

HARMON CLAYTON KILLEBREW
WASHINGTON A.L. 1954-1960
MINNESOTA A.L. 1961-1974
KANSAS CITY A.L. 1975
MUSCULAR SLUGGER WITH MONUMENTAL HOME
RUN AND RBI SUCCESS. HIS 573 HOMERS OVER
22 YEARS RANK FIFTH ALL-TIME AND SECOND
ONLY TO RUTH AMONG A.L. HITTERS. TIED OR
LED A.L. IN HOME RUNS 6 TIMES, BELTED OVER
40 ON 8 OCCASIONS AND IS THIRD IN HOME RUN
FREQUENCY. DROVE IN OVER 100 RUNS 9 TIMES.
A.L. MVP IN 1969.

1971

RALPH McPHERRAN KINER
PITTSBURGH, N.L. CHICAGO, N.L.
CLEVELAND, A.L. 1946-1955
HIT 369 HOME RUNS AND AVERAGED BETTER
THAN 100 RUNS BATTED IN PER SEASON IN
TEN-YEAR CAREER. ONLY PLAYER TO LEAD HIS
LEAGUE OR SHARE LEAD IN HOMERS SEVEN
YEARS IN A ROW, 1946-1952. TWICE HAD
MORE THAN 50 IN SEASON. SET N.L. MARK
OF 101 FOUR-BAGGERS IN TWO SUCCESSIVE
YEARS WITH 54 IN 1949 AND 47 IN 1950.
LED N.L. IN SLUGGING PCT. THREE TIMES.

1975

CHARLES HERBERT KLEIN
"CHUCK"
PHILADELPHIA N.L., CHICAGO N.L.,
PITTSBURGH N.L., 1928-1944
ONLY PLAYER IN 20TH CENTURY TO COLLECT
200 OR MORE HITS IN EACH OF FIRST FIVE
FULL MAJOR LEAGUE SEASONS ATTAINED
.320 CAREER AVERAGE AND 300 HOME RUNS.
LED N.L. IN HOMERS AND TOTAL BASES FOUR
TIMES AND IN RUNS SCORED AND SLUGGING
PCT. THREE EACH. SET LEAGUE RECORD FOR
MOST EXTRA BASE HITS IN SEASON—107 IN 1930.
VOTED MOST VALUABLE PLAYER IN 1932.

1980

WILLIAM J. KLEM
UMPIRE
NATIONAL LEAGUE-1905-1951
KNOWN AS "THE OLD ARBITRATOR" UMPIRED
IN 18 WORLD SERIES. CREDITED WITH
INTRODUCING ARM-SIGNALS INDICATING
STRIKES AND FAIR OR FOUL BALLS. FAMOUS
QUOTE: "BASEBALL IS MORE THAN A GAME
TO ME-IT'S A RELIGION." RETIRED AS ACTIVE
UMPIRE IN 1940. NAMED CHIEF OF N.L.
STAFF IN 1941.

1953

SANFORD KOUFAX
"SANDY"
BROOKLYN N.L. 1955-1957
LOS ANGELES N.L. 1958-1966
SET ALL-TIME RECORDS WITH 4 NO-HITTERS
IN 4 YEARS, CAPPED BY 1965 PERFECT GAME,
AND BY CAPTURING EARNED-RUN TITLE FIVE
SEASONS IN A ROW, 1962-1966. WON 25 OR
MORE GAMES THREE TIMES. HAD 11 SHUTOUTS
IN 1963. STRIKEOUT LEADER FOUR TIMES.
WITH RECORD 382 IN 1965. FANNED 18 IN A
GAME TWICE. MOST VALUABLE PLAYER 1963.
CY YOUNG AWARD WINNER 1963-65-66.

1972

BOWIE KENT KUHN
COMMISSIONER, 1969-1984
BASEBALL'S FIFTH COMMISSIONER WHO PRESIDED OVER ASTOUNDING
GROWTH IN THE GAME'S POPULARITY, WITH A PROACTIVE AND
INVENTIVE ADMINISTRATION. UNDER HIS LEADERSHIP, TRIPLED
MAJOR LEAGUE ATTENDANCE, EXTENDED POSTSEASON WITH
CREATION OF THE LEAGUE CHAMPIONSHIP SERIES AND
INTRODUCED NIGHT-TIME BASEBALL TO THE WORLD SERIES.
EXPANDED TELEVISION COVERAGE WITH DUAL NETWORK
BROADCASTS AND A VARIETY OF BASEBALL PROGRAMMING. KNOWN
AS A TOUGH DISCIPLINARIAN, ALSO AS A STRONG SUPPORTER OF
AMATEUR BASEBALL. INSTRUMENTAL IN THE HALL OF FAME'S 1971
DECISION TO INDUCT NEGRO LEAGUES PLAYERS.

2008

NAPOLEON (LARRY) LAJOIE
PHILADELPHIA (N) 1896-1900
PHILADELPHIA (A) 1901
CLEVELAND (A) 1902-14
PHILADELPHIA (A) 1915-16
GREAT HITTER AND MOST GRACEFUL
AND EFFECTIVE SECOND-BASEMAN
OF HIS ERA. MANAGED CLEVELAND 4
YEARS. LEAGUE BATTING CHAMPION
1901-03-04.

1937

KENESAW MOUNTAIN LANDIS
BASEBALL'S FIRST COMMISSIONER
ELECTED, 1920 — DIED IN OFFICE, 1944
HIS INTEGRITY AND LEADERSHIP
ESTABLISHED BASEBALL IN THE
RESPECT, ESTEEM AND AFFECTION
OF THE AMERICAN PEOPLE.

1944

THOMAS CHARLES LASORDA
LOS ANGELES, N.L., 1977-1996
ONE OF BASEBALL'S MOST ENGAGING PERSONALITIES
AND A GREAT AMBASSADOR FOR HIS SPORT. MANAGED
DODGERS WITH AN IMPENETRABLE PASSION, CLAIMING
TO "BLEED DODGER BLUE." IN HIS 47TH SEASON
WITH THE DODGERS ORGANIZATION WHEN HE RETIRED
AS MANAGER. FOURTH MANAGER IN HISTORY TO
GUIDE SAME FRANCHISE FOR 20 YEARS, DURING
WHICH HE WON EIGHT DIVISION TITLES, FOUR N.L.
PENNANTS AND WORLD CHAMPIONSHIPS IN 1981 AND
1988. 61 POST-SEASON GAMES MANAGED RANKS THIRD
MOST IN HISTORY.

1997

ANTHONY MICHAEL LAZZERI
"POOSH 'EM UP TONY"
NEW YORK, A.L. 1926-1937
CHICAGO, N.L. 1938
BROOKLYN, N.L. 1939
NEW YORK, N.L. 1939
FEARED CLUTCH HITTER WITH LONG BALL POWER.
PLAYED SECOND BASE WITH QUIET PROFICIENCY
ON FAMED "MURDERER'S ROW" YANKEE TEAMS WITH
RUTH AND GEHRIG. A .300 HITTER FIVE TIMES WITH
CAREER .292 MARK. DROVE IN OVER 100 RUNS
SEVEN TIMES. SET A.L. SINGLE GAME RECORD WITH
2 GRAND SLAMS AND 11 RBIS, 5/24/36. BELTED 60
HOMERS FOR SALT LAKE CITY (PCL) IN 1925.

1991

ROBERT GRANVILLE LEMON
CLEVELAND A.L.,
1941 – 1958
GAINED COVETED 20-VICTORY CLASS SEVEN
TIMES IN NINE-YEAR SPAN. BECAME ONLY
SIXTH PITCHER IN 20TH CENTURY TO POST
20 OR MORE WINS IN SEVEN SEASONS. HAD
207-128 RECORD FOR CAREER. PACED A.L.
OR TIED FOR LEAD IN VICTORIES THREE
TIMES. SHUTOUTS ONCE. INNINGS PITCHED
FOUR SEASONS AND COMPLETE GAMES FIVE
YEARS. HURLED NO-HITTER IN 1946.

1976

WALTER FENNER LEONARD
"BUCK"
NEGRO LEAGUES 1933 – 1950
FIRST BASEMAN OF HOMESTEAD GRAYS WHEN
TEAM WON NEGRO NATIONAL LEAGUE PENNANT
NINE YEARS IN A ROW, 1937 – 1945. TEAMED
WITH JOSH GIBSON TO FORM MOST FEARED
BATTING TWOSOME IN NEGRO BASEBALL FROM
1937 TO 1946. RANKED AMONG NEGRO HOME
RUN LEADERS. WON NEGRO NATIONAL LEAGUE
BATTING TITLE WITH 391 AVERAGE IN 1948.

1972

FREDERICK CHARLES LINDSTROM
NEW YORK N.L., PITTSBURGH N.L.,
CHICAGO N.L., BROOKLYN N.L.,
1924 - 1936
COMPILED LIFETIME .311 BATTING MARK,
INCLUDING SEVEN SEASONS OF .300 OR
BETTER. ONE OF ONLY THREE PLAYERS TO
AMASS 230 OR MORE HITS A YEAR TWICE.
AS YOUNGEST PLAYER (AGE 18) IN WORLD
SERIES HISTORY, HE TIED RECORD WITH
FOUR HITS IN GAME IN 1924. EQUALLED
MAJOR LEAGUE RECORD BY COLLECTING
NINE HITS IN 1928 DOUBLEHEADER.

1976

JOHN HENRY LLOYD
"POP"
NEGRO LEAGUES 1906-1932
REGARDED AS FINEST SHORTSTOP TO PLAY
IN NEGRO BASEBALL. SCIENTIFIC HITTER
BATTED OVER .400 SEVERAL TIMES DURING
HIS 27-YEAR CAREER. PERSONIFIED BEST
QUALITIES OF ATHLETE BOTH ON AND OFF
FIELD. INSTRUMENTAL IN HELPING OPEN
YANKEE STADIUM TO NEGRO BASEBALL IN
1930. MANAGED MORE THAN TEN SEASONS.

1977

ERNEST NATALI LOMBARDI
BROOKLYN, N.L., 1931
CINCINNATI, N.L., 1932 - 1941
BOSTON, N.L., 1942
NEW YORK, N.L., 1943 - 1947
HIT .306 OVER 17 SEASONS DESPITE SLOWNESS AFOOT.
TEN TIMES BATTING OVER .300. WON N.L. BATTING
TITLE WITH .342 IN 1938 AND AGAIN IN 1942 WITH
.330. HELD HANDS LOW, WITH INTERLOCKING GOLF
GRIP AND QUICK STROKE. N.L. MVP IN 1938. SKILLED
RECEIVER AND HANDLER OF PITCHERS. OUTSTANDING
ARM FROM CROUCH POSITION, RIFLING THROWS
WITH SIDE-ARM RELEASE.

1986

ALFONSO RAMON LOPEZ
RENOWNED FOR SHREWD LEADERSHIP DURING
36 - YEAR BIG LEAGUE CAREER AS CATCHER
AND MANAGER. WON TWO PENNANTS AND HAD
TEN SECOND-PLACE FINISHES WITH WINNING
PCT. OF .581 IN 17 SEASONS AT HELM OF
CLEVELAND AND CHICAGO WHITE SOX. ONLY
MANAGER TO INTERRUPT YANKEES' PENNANT
DYNASTY OF 1949 - 1964. GUIDING INDIANS
TO '54 FLAG WITH A.L. RECORD 111 WINS
AND PILOTING WHITE SOX TO 1959 TITLE.

1977

THEODORE AMAR LYONS
CHICAGO A.L., 1923 TO 1946
ENTIRE ACTIVE PITCHING CAREER OF 21
SEASONS WITH CHICAGO A.L. WON 260
GAMES, LOST 230. TIED FOR LEAGUE'S MOST
VICTORIES 1925 AND 1927. BEST EARNED RUN
AVERAGE, 2.10 IN 1942 WHEN HE STARTED
AND FINISHED ALL 20 GAMES. PITCHED
NO-HIT GAME, AUG. 21, 1926 AGAINST BOSTON.
PITCHED 21-INNING GAME MAY 24, 1929.

1955

CONNIE MACK
A STAR CATCHER BUT FAMED MORE
AS MANAGER OF THE PHILADELPHIA
ATHLETICS SINCE 1901.
WINNER OF 9 PENNANTS AND 5
WORLD CHAMPIONSHIPS.
RECEIVED THE BOK AWARD
IN PHILADELPHIA FOR 1929.

1937

JAMES RALEIGH MACKEY
"BIZ"
NEGRO LEAGUES, 1920-1947
A SUPERB DEFENSIVE CATCHER AND NATURAL LEADER WHO COULD
PLAY ALL POSITIONS. STARRED IN 1920s WITH HILLDALES OF
PHILADELPHIA, LEADING THEM TO 1925 NEGRO LEAGUES WORLD
SERIES TITLE. A LINE DRIVE SWITCH-HITTER WHOSE AVERAGE TOPPED
.300 MOST SEASONS. PLAYED IN FIVE EAST-WEST ALL-STAR GAMES. AS
PLAYER-MANAGER OF BALTIMORE ELITE GIANTS, MENTORED TEENAGE
CATCHER ROY CAMPANELLA. MANAGED FIVE OTHER FUTURE HALL OF
FAMERS DURING TENURE WITH NEWARK, LEADING EAGLES TO ONLY
CHAMPIONSHIP IN 1946.

2006

LELAND STANFORD MACPHAIL
"LARRY"
DYNAMIC, INNOVATIVE EXECUTIVE MADE HIS
MARK AS PROGRESSIVE HEAD OF THREE CLUBS,
CINCINNATI REDS, BROOKLYN DODGERS AND
NEW YORK YANKEES FROM 1933 TO 1947. WON
CHAMPIONSHIPS IN BOTH LEAGUES, WITH
DODGERS IN 1941 AND YANKEES IN 1947.
PIONEERED NIGHT BALL AT CINCINNATI IN
1935. ALSO INSTALLED LIGHTS AT EBBETS FIELD
AND YANKEE STADIUM. ORIGINATED PLANE
TRAVEL BY PLAYING PERSONNEL AND IDEA
OF STADIUM CLUB. HELPED SET UP EMPLOYEE
AND PLAYER PENSION PLANS.

1978

LELAND STANFORD MACPHAIL JR.
ONE OF THE LEADING EXECUTIVES IN BASEBALL HISTORY, HIS
NAME IS SYNONYMOUS WITH INTEGRITY AND SPORTSMANSHIP.
AS FARM DIRECTOR AND PLAYER PERSONNEL DIRECTOR OF
THE YANKEES (1949-58), HELPED BUILD A SYSTEM WHICH
YIELDED SEVEN WORLD CHAMPIONSHIPS. AS ORIOLES
GENERAL MANAGER (1959-65), HELPED LAY THE GROUNDWORK
FOR ONE OF THE GAME'S MOST CONSISTENTLY SUCCESSFUL
FRANCHISES, AND HE LATER REJOINED THE YANKEES IN THE
SAME CAPACITY. SERVED ADMIRABLY AS AMERICAN LEAGUE
PRESIDENT (1974-1983) BEFORE CONCLUDING HIS 45-YEAR
CAREER AS PRESIDENT OF THE PLAYER RELATIONS
COMMITTEE. HE AND HIS FATHER LARRY FORM THE FIRST
FATHER SON TANDEM IN THE HALL OF FAME.

1998

EFFA L. MANLEY
BROOKLYN EAGLES, 1935
NEWARK EAGLES, 1936-1948

A TRAILBLAZING OWNER AND TIRELESS CRUSADER IN THE CIVIL RIGHTS MOVEMENT
WHO EARNED THE RESPECT OF HER PLAYERS AND FELLOW OWNERS. AS BUSINESS
MANAGER AND CO-OWNER OF THE EAGLES, ENSURED TEAM'S FINANCIAL SUCCESS
WITH CREATIVE PROMOTIONS AND ADVERTISING. BELOVED BY FANS BECAUSE SHE
INTEGRATED HER PLAYERS INTO THE COMMUNITY AND FIELDED CONSISTENTLY
COMPETITIVE TEAMS, HIGHLIGHTED BY A 1946 NEGRO LEAGUES WORLD SERIES
CHAMPIONSHIP. REPRESENTED TEAM AT LEAGUE MEETINGS AND ESTABLISHED A
PRECEDENT OF NEGRO LEAGUES CLUBS RECEIVING FAIR COMPENSATION FOR
PLAYERS SIGNED TO MAJOR LEAGUE CONTRACTS.

2006

MICKEY CHARLES MANTLE
NEW YORK A.L. 1951-1968
HIT 536 HOME RUNS. WON LEAGUE HOMER TITLE
AND SLUGGING CROWN FOUR TIMES. MADE
2415 HITS. BATTED .300 OR OVER IN EACH
OF TEN YEARS WITH TOP OF .365 IN 1957.
TOPPED A.L. IN WALKS FIVE YEARS AND
IN RUNS SCORED SIX SEASONS. VOTED
MOST VALUABLE PLAYER 1956-57-62. NAMED
ON 20 A.L. ALL-STAR TEAMS. SET WORLD
SERIES RECORDS FOR HOMERS, 18; RUNS, 42;
RUNS BATTED IN, 40; TOTAL BASES, 123;
AND BASES ON BALLS, 43.

1974

HENRY EMMET MANUSH
1923—1939
SLUGGING OUTFIELDER
FOR 6 MAJOR LEAGUE CLUBS. BATTING
CHAMPION OF A.L. AT .378 WITH 1926 TIGERS.
LIFETIME AVERAGE OF .330 IN 2,009
MAJOR LEAGUE GAMES. HAD 2,524 HITS.

1964

WALTER J. V. MARANVILLE
"RABBIT"
BOSTON, PITTSBURGH, CHICAGO,
BROOKLYN AND ST. LOUIS,
NATIONAL LEAGUE, 1912-1935
PLAYED MORE GAMES, 2153, AT SHORTSTOP
THAN ANY OTHER NATIONAL LEAGUE PLAYER
AT BAT TOTAL, 10078, SURPASSED BY ONLY
ONE NATIONAL LEAGUER, HONUS WAGNER.
MADE 2605 HITS IN 23 SEASONS. MEMBER
OF 1914 BOSTON BRAVES "MIRACLE TEAM"
THAT WON PENNANT, THEN WORLD SERIES
FROM ATHLETICS IN 4 GAMES.

1954

JUAN ANTONIO
MARICHAL SANCHEZ
SAN FRANCISCO N.L. 1960-1973 BOSTON A.L. 1974
LOS ANGELES N.L. 1975
HIGH-KICKING RIGHT-HANDER FROM DOMINICAN
REPUBLIC WON 243 GAMES AND LOST ONLY 142
OVER 16 SEASONS. WON 20 GAMES SIX TIMES AND
NO-HIT HOUSTON IN 1963. LED N.L. IN COMPLETE
GAMES AND SHUTOUTS TWICE AND IN ERA WITH
2.10 IN 1969. COMPLETED 244 GAMES DURING
CAREER, STRIKING OUT 2,303 AND FINISHING
WITH 2.89 ERA.

1983

RICHARD WILLIAM MARQUARD
"RUBE"
NEW YORK N.L., BROOKLYN N.L.,
CINCINNATI N.L., BOSTON N.L.
1908-1925
THREE-TIME 20-GAME WINNER WITH
GIANT CHAMPIONS OF 1911-12-13. TIED ALL-TIME
RECORD WITH 19 VICTORIES IN A ROW WHILE
WINNING 26 AND LOSING 11 IN 1912. LED
N.L. IN WINNING PERCENTAGE AND
STRIKEOUTS IN 1911. TIED FOR MOST
VICTORIES, 1912. HURLED NO-HIT GAME
AGAINST DODGERS IN 1915.

1971

EDWIN LEE MATHEWS
BOSTON N.L., MILWAUKEE N.L.,
ATLANTA N.L., HOUSTON N.L.,
DETROIT A.L. 1952-1968
BECAME SEVENTH PLAYER IN MAJOR LEAGUE
HISTORY TO HIT 500 HOME RUNS. FINISHED
CAREER WITH 512. HIT 30 OR MORE HOMERS
NINE YEARS IN ROW 1953-1961. REACHING
40 MARK FOUR TIMES. ESTABLISHED RECORD
FOR HOMERS IN SEASON BY THIRD BASEMAN
WITH 47 IN 1953. LED N.L. IN HOME RUNS
TWICE AND IN WALKS FOUR TIMES. HAD
SEASONS OF 100 OR MORE RUNS BATTED IN.

1978

CHRISTY MATHEWSON
NEW YORK, N.L., 1900-1916.
CINCINNATI, N.L., 1916.
BORN FACTORYVILLE, PA., AUGUST 12, 1880.
GREATEST OF ALL THE GREAT PITCHERS
IN THE 20TH CENTURY'S FIRST QUARTER.
PITCHED 3 SHUTOUTS IN 1905 WORLD SERIES.
FIRST PITCHER OF THE CENTURY EVER TO
WIN 30 GAMES IN 3 SUCCESSIVE YEARS.
WON 37 GAMES IN 1908.
"MATTY WAS MASTER OF THEM ALL"

1936

WILLIE HOWARD MAYS, JR.
"THE SAY HEY KID"
NEW YORK N.L., SAN FRANCISCO N.L.,
NEW YORK N.L., 1951-1973
ONE OF BASEBALL'S MOST COLORFUL AND
EXCITING STARS, EXCELLED IN ALL PHASES OF
THE GAME. THIRD IN HOMERS (660), RUNS (2,062)
AND TOTAL BASES (6,066); SEVENTH IN HITS
(3,283) AND RBI'S (1,903). FIRST IN PUTOUTS
BY OUTFIELDER (7,095). FIRST TO TOP BOTH
300 HOMERS AND 300 STEALS. LED LEAGUE IN
BATTING ONCE, SLUGGING FIVE TIMES, HOME
RUNS AND STEALS FOUR SEASONS. VOTED N.L.
MVP IN 1954 AND 1965. PLAYED IN 24
ALL-STAR GAMES - A RECORD.

1979

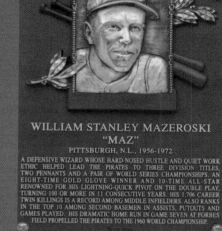

WILLIAM STANLEY MAZEROSKI
"MAZ"
PITTSBURGH, N.L., 1956-1972
A DEFENSIVE WIZARD WHOSE HARD-NOSED HUSTLE AND QUIET WORK
ETHIC HELPED LEAD THE PIRATES TO THREE DIVISION TITLES,
TWO PENNANTS AND A PAIR OF WORLD SERIES CHAMPIONSHIPS. AN
EIGHT-TIME GOLD GLOVE WINNER AND 10-TIME ALL-STAR
RENOWNED FOR HIS LIGHTNING-QUICK PIVOT ON THE DOUBLE PLAY,
TURNING 100 OR MORE IN 11 CONSECUTIVE YEARS. HIS 1,706 CAREER
TWIN KILLINGS IS A RECORD AMONG MIDDLE INFIELDERS. ALSO RANKS
IN THE TOP 10 AMONG SECOND BASEMEN IN ASSISTS, PUTOUTS AND
GAMES PLAYED. HIS DRAMATIC HOME RUN IN GAME SEVEN AT FORBES
FIELD PROPELLED THE PIRATES TO THE 1960 WORLD CHAMPIONSHIP.

2001

JOSEPH VINCENT McCARTHY
CHICAGO N.L. 1926-1930
NEW YORK A.L. 1931-1946
BOSTON A.L. 1948-1950
OUTSTANDING MANAGER WHO NEVER PLAYED
IN MAJOR LEAGUES. THE MAJOR LEAGUE
TEAMS MANAGED BY HIM DURING 24 YEARS
NEVER FINISHED OUT OF FIRST DIVISION.
WON PENNANTS CHICAGO N.L. 1929,
NEW YORK A.L. 1932-6-7-8-9-41-2-3.
WON SEVEN WORLD'S CHAMPIONSHIPS WITH
NEW YORK YANKEES-FOUR OF THEM
CONSECUTIVELY 1936-7-8-9.

1957

THOMAS F. McCARTHY
ONE OF BOSTON'S "HEAVENLY TWINS" UNDER
MANAGER FRANK SELEE. OUTSTANDING BASE
RUNNER WHO STOLE 109 BASES FOR THE
BROWNS IN 1888. PIONEER IN TRAPPING FLY
BALLS IN THE OUTFIELD. HOLDS N.L. RECORD
FOR ASSISTS IN OUTFIELD-53 WITH BOSTON IN
1893. PLAYED 1268 GAMES IN MAJOR LEAGUES

1946

WILLIE LEE McCOVEY
"STRETCH"
SAN FRANCISCO, N.L., 1959-1973, 1977-1980
SAN DIEGO, N.L., 1974-1976
OAKLAND, A.L., 1976
TOP LEFT-HANDED HOME RUN HITTER IN N.L.
HISTORY WITH 521. SECOND ONLY TO LOU GEHRIG
WITH 18 CAREER GRAND SLAMS. LED N.L. IN HOMERS
THREE TIMES AND RBI'S TWICE. N.L. ROOKIE OF
YEAR IN 1959, MVP IN 1969 AND COMEBACK PLAYER
OF THE YEAR IN '77. TEAMED WITH WILLIE MAYS
FOR AWESOME 1-2 PUNCH IN GIANTS' LINEUP.

1986

JOSEPH JEROME McGINNITY
"IRONMAN"
DISTINGUISHED AS THE PITCHER WHO HURLED
TWO GAMES ON ONE DAY THE MOST TIMES. DID
THIS ON FIVE OCCASIONS. WON BOTH GAMES
THREE TIMES. PLAYED WITH BALTIMORE,
BROOKLYN AND NEW YORK TEAMS IN N.L.
AND BALTIMORE IN A.L. GAINED MORE THAN
200 VICTORIES DURING CAREER. RECORDED
20 OR MORE VICTORIES SEVEN TIMES. IN TWO
SUCCESSIVE SEASONS WON AT LEAST 30 GAMES.

1946

WILLIAM ALOYSIUS McGOWAN
(NO. 1)
UMPIRE
AMERICAN LEAGUE 1925-1954
CAME CLOSE TO BEING EXCEPTION TO OLD
ADAGE THAT FANS DON'T PAY TO SEE THE
UMPIRE. INTRODUCED COLORFUL STYLE WITH
VIGOROUS, AGGRESSIVE GESTURES BORDERING
ON THE PUGNACIOUS. ENTHUSIASM NEVER WANED
OVER 30 MAJOR LEAGUE SEASONS WHILE
HUSTLING DEMEANOR COMMANDED PLAYERS'
RESPECT. MOST DURABLE UMPIRE IN HISTORY.
DID NOT MISS AN INNING FOR 16 YEARS
(OVER 2400 CONSECUTIVE GAMES).

1992

JOHN J. McGRAW
STAR THIRD-BASEMAN OF THE
GREAT BALTIMORE ORIOLES. NATIONAL
LEAGUE CHAMPIONS IN THE '90'S. FOR
30 YEARS MANAGER OF THE NEW YORK
GIANTS STARTING IN 1902.
UNDER HIS LEADERSHIP THE
GIANTS WON 10 PENNANTS AND 3
WORLD CHAMPIONSHIPS.

1937

WILLIAM BOYD McKECHNIE
MANAGER OF
PITTSBURGH N.L. 1922-1926
ST. LOUIS N.L. 1928-1929
BOSTON N.L. 1930-1937
CINCINNATI N.L. 1938-1946
ONLY N.L. MANAGER TO WIN PENNANTS
WITH THREE DIFFERENT CLUBS: PITTSBURGH
1925; ST. LOUIS, 1928; CINCINNATI, 1939, 1940.
WON WORLD SERIES 1925 AND 1940. NAMED
NO.1 MAJOR LEAGUE MANAGER 1937 AND
1940. ACTIVE IN BASEBALL AS MANAGER,
COACH, PLAYER, 1906 TO 1953.

1962

JOHN ALEXANDER McPHEE
"BID"
CINCINNATI, A.A., 1882-89
CINCINNATI, N.L., 1890-99
ONE OF THE 19TH CENTURY'S PREMIER SECOND BASEMEN, HE WAS A
STANDOUT FIELDER DESPITE PLAYING BAREHANDED FOR MOST OF HIS
18-YEAR CAREER. THE LAST SECOND BASEMAN TO PLAY WITHOUT A
GLOVE, HE REGULARLY LED THE LEAGUE IN DOUBLE PLAYS, FIELDING
AVERAGE, ASSISTS AND PUTOUTS. PLAYING WITH A GLOVE FOR THE
FIRST TIME IN 1896, HIS FIELDING AVERAGE WAS .982, A MARK THAT
STOOD FOR 29 YEARS. A SKILLED LEADOFF HITTER, HE COMPILED 2,250
HITS AND TOPPED THE 100-RUN MARK 10 TIMES, INCLUDING A CAREER-
BEST 139 IN 1886. KNOWN FOR HIS SOBER DISPOSITION AND
EXEMPLARY SPORTSMANSHIP.

2000

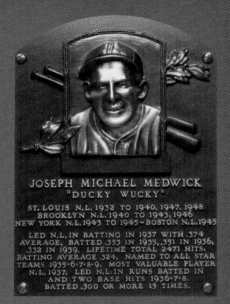

JOSEPH MICHAEL MEDWICK
"DUCKY WUCKY"
ST. LOUIS N.L. 1932 TO 1940, 1947, 1948
BROOKLYN N.L. 1940 TO 1943, 1946
NEW YORK N.L. 1943 TO 1945—BOSTON N.L. 1945
LED N.L. IN BATTING IN 1937 WITH .374
AVERAGE, BATTED .353 IN 1935, .351 IN 1936,
.332 IN 1939. LIFETIME TOTAL 2471 HITS.
BATTING AVERAGE .324. NAMED TO ALL STAR
TEAMS 1935-6-7-8-9. MOST VALUABLE PLAYER
N.L. 1937. LED N.L. IN RUNS BATTED IN
AND TWO BASE HITS 1936-7-8.
BATTED .300 OR MORE 15 TIMES.

1968

JOSÉ DE LA CARIDAD MENDÉZ BAEZ
"EL DIAMANTE NEGRO" "THE BLACK DIAMOND"
PRE-NEGRO LEAGUES, 1908-1919
NEGRO LEAGUES, 1920-1926
A SLENDER RIGHT-HANDED PITCHER WHO WAS ACKNOWLEDGED AS THE
FIRST CUBAN-BORN BASEBALL STAR IN THE PRE-NEGRO LEAGUES ERA.
UTILIZED A VAST ARRAY OF PITCHES, MAINLY RELYING ON A DECEPTIVE
FASTBALL AND SHARP-BREAKING CURVE TO DOMINATE OPPOSING
BATTERS. AS PLAYER-MANAGER, LED KANSAS CITY MONARCHS TO
THREE CONSECUTIVE NEGRO NATIONAL LEAGUE PENNANTS, 1923-1925.
CLINCHED 1924 NEGRO LEAGUES WORLD SERIES TITLE WITH THREE-HIT
SHUTOUT. HURLED 25 CONSECUTIVE SHUTOUT INNINGS AGAINST THE
CINCINNATI REDS DURING EXHIBITION COMPETITION IN 1908.

2006

JOHN ROBERT MIZE
"THE BIG CAT"
ST. LOUIS N.L., NEW YORK N.L.,
NEW YORK A.L., 1936-1953
KEEN-EYED SLUGGER SMASHED 359 HOME RUNS
AND BATTED .312 IN 15-YEAR CAREER WHILE
TOPPING .300 MARK NINE SEASONS IN A ROW.
SET MAJOR LOOP RECORDS BY HITTING THREE
HOMERS IN A GAME SIX TIMES AND TRIO IN
SUCCESSION ON FOUR OCCASIONS. WON N.L.
BATTING TITLE ONCE. LED OR SHARED LEAD
IN HOMERS AND SLUGGING PCT. FOUR TIMES.
RUNS BATTED IN AND TOTAL BASES THRICE.

1981

PAUL LEO MOLITOR
MILWAUKEE, A.L., 1978-1992
TORONTO, A.L., 1993-1995
MINNESOTA, A.L., 1996-1998
A REMARKABLY CONSISTENT CONTACT HITTER AND AGGRESSIVE BASE
RUNNER WITH EXTRAORDINARY INSTINCTS. ONE OF THREE PLAYERS WITH
MORE THAN 3,000 HITS, 600 DOUBLES AND 500 STEALS. A CAREER .306
HITTER, RANKS EIGHTH ALL-TIME WITH 3,319 HITS. HIT SAFELY IN 39
CONSECUTIVE GAMES IN 1987. A GREAT CLUTCH PERFORMER, AS
EVIDENCED BY HIS RECORD FIVE HITS IN GAME ONE OF THE 1982 WORLD
SERIES FOR THE BREWERS, AND WORLD SERIES MVP HONORS FOR THE
CHAMPION BLUE JAYS IN 1993. ELECTED TO SEVEN ALL-STAR TEAMS.

2004

JOE LEONARD MORGAN
HOUSTON, N.L. 1963-1971, 1980
CINCINNATI, N.L. 1972-1979
SAN FRANCISCO, N.L. 1981-1982
PHILADELPHIA, N.L. 1983
OAKLAND, A.L. 1984
IMPACT PLAYER WHO LIFTED CINCINNATI'S "BIG RED
MACHINE" TO HIGHER LEVEL WITH HIS MULTI-FACETED
SKILLS. TRADEMARK WAS FLAPPING LEFT ARM AS HE
AWAITED PITCH. PACKED UNUSUAL POWER INTO
EXTRAORDINARILY QUICK 150-LB. FIREPLUG FRAME. PLAYED
22 SEASONS AND ALSO HOLDS HOME RUN AND GAMES
PLAYED RECORDS FOR 2B. N.L. MVP 1975-76.

1990

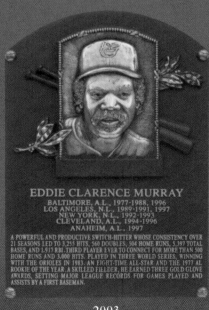

EDDIE CLARENCE MURRAY
BALTIMORE, A.L., 1977-1988, 1996
LOS ANGELES, N.L., 1989-1991, 1997
NEW YORK, N.L., 1992-1993
CLEVELAND, A.L., 1994-1996
ANAHEIM, A.L., 1997
A POWERFUL AND PRODUCTIVE SWITCH-HITTER WHOSE CONSISTENCY OVER
21 SEASONS LED TO 3,255 HITS, 560 DOUBLES, 504 HOME RUNS, 5,397 TOTAL
BASES, AND 1,917 RBI. THIRD PLAYER EVER TO CONNECT FOR MORE THAN 500
HOME RUNS AND 3,000 HITS. PLAYED IN THREE WORLD SERIES, WINNING
WITH THE ORIOLES IN 1983. AN EIGHT-TIME ALL-STAR AND THE 1977 AL
ROOKIE OF THE YEAR. A SKILLED FIELDER, HE EARNED THREE GOLD GLOVE
AWARDS, SETTING MAJOR LEAGUE RECORDS FOR GAMES PLAYED AND
ASSISTS BY A FIRST BASEMAN.

2003

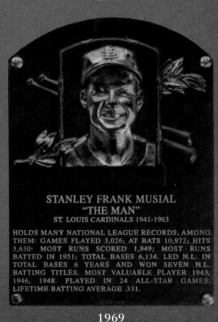

STANLEY FRANK MUSIAL
"THE MAN"
ST. LOUIS CARDINALS 1941-1963
HOLDS MANY NATIONAL LEAGUE RECORDS, AMONG
THEM: GAMES PLAYED 3,026; AT BATS 10,972; HITS
3,630; MOST RUNS SCORED 1,949; MOST RUNS
BATTED IN 1951; TOTAL BASES 6,134. LED N.L. IN
TOTAL BASES 6 YEARS AND WON SEVEN N.L.
BATTING TITLES. MOST VALUABLE PLAYER 1943,
1946, 1948. PLAYED IN 24 ALL-STAR GAMES.
LIFETIME BATTING AVERAGE .331.

1969

HAROLD NEWHOUSER
(PRINCE HAL)

DETROIT, A.L., 1939-1953
CLEVELAND, A.L., 1954-1955

ONLY PITCHER IN MAJOR LEAGUE HISTORY TO
WIN BACK-TO-BACK MVP AWARDS (1944-1945).
STRIKEOUT KING WITH BLAZING FAST BALL.
207-150 OVER 17 CAMPAIGNS. CONSECUTIVE SEASONS
OF 29-9, 25-9 and 26-9 WITH CORRESPONDING
ERA'S OF 2.22, 1.81 and 1.94 FROM 1944-1946.
HURLED PENNANT-CLINCHER IN 1945 FOLLOWED
BY 2 WORLD SERIES VICTORIES OVER CUBS.

1992

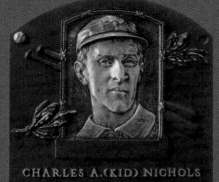

CHARLES A.(KID) NICHOLS

RIGHT HANDED PITCHER WHO WON 30 OR
MORE GAMES FOR SEVEN CONSECUTIVE
YEARS (1891-97) AND WON AT LEAST 20
GAMES FOR TEN CONSECUTIVE SEASONS
(1890-99) WITH BOSTON N.L. ALSO PITCHED
FOR ST. LOUIS AND PHILADELPHIA N.L. ONE
OF FEW PITCHERS TO WIN MORE THAN 300
GAMES, HIS MAJOR LEAGUE RECORD BEING
360 VICTORIES, 202 DEFEATS.

1949

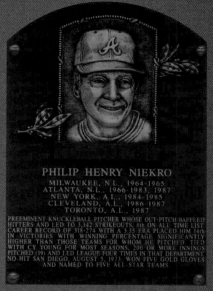

PHILIP HENRY NIEKRO

MILWAUKEE, N.L., 1964-1965
ATLANTA, N.L., 1966-1983, 1987
NEW YORK, A.L., 1984-1985
CLEVELAND, A.L., 1986-1987
TORONTO, A.L., 1987

PREEMINENT KNUCKLEBALL PITCHER WHOSE OUT-PITCH BAFFLED
HITTERS AND LED TO 3,342 STRIKEOUTS, 8th ON ALL-TIME LIST.
CAREER RECORD OF 318-274 WITH A 3.35 ERA PLACED HIM 14th
IN VICTORIES WITH WINNING PERCENTAGE SIGNIFICANTLY
HIGHER THAN THOSE TEAMS FOR WHOM HE PITCHED. TIED
WITH CY YOUNG FOR MOST SEASONS, 300 OR MORE INNINGS
PITCHED (19) AND LED LEAGUE FOUR TIMES IN THAT DEPARTMENT.
NO-HIT SAN DIEGO, AUGUST 5, 1973. WON FIVE GOLD GLOVES
AND NAMED TO FIVE ALL STAR TEAMS.

1997

WALTER O'MALLEY

BROOKLYN, N.L., 1943-1957
LOS ANGELES, N.L., 1958-1979

AN INFLUENTIAL AND VISIONARY OWNER WHO INSPIRED
BASEBALL'S MOVE WEST IN 1957. RELOCATED DODGERS FROM
BROOKLYN TO LOS ANGELES AND OPENED NEW MARKETS FOR
THE MAJOR LEAGUE GAME. SERVED AS PRESIDENT AND
PRINCIPAL OWNER WHEN HIS CLUBS WON FOUR WORLD SERIES
CHAMPIONSHIPS (1955, 1959, 1963 AND 1965) AND 11 PENNANTS.
MAINTAINED AFFORDABLE TICKET PRICES WHILE GENERATING
RECORD ATTENDANCE. DRIVING FORCE BEHIND DESIGN,
CONSTRUCTION AND FINANCING OF DODGER STADIUM, A
BENCHMARK FOR A NEW GENERATION OF MODERN BALLPARKS.

2008

JAMES H. O'ROURKE

"ORATOR JIM" PLAYED BALL UNTIL HE
WAS PAST FIFTY, INCLUDING TWENTY-ONE
MAJOR LEAGUE SEASONS. AN OUTFIELDER
AND CATCHER FOR THE BOSTON RED
STOCKINGS OF 1873, HE LATER WORE
THE UNIFORMS OF THE CHAMPIONSHIP
PROVIDENCE TEAM OF 1879, BUFFALO,
NEW YORK AND WASHINGTON.

1945

MELVIN T.(MEL) OTT
NEW YORK (N.L.) 1926-48

ONE OF FEW PLAYERS TO JUMP FROM A HIGH
SCHOOL TEAM INTO MAJORS. PLAYED OUTFIELD
AND THIRD BASE AND MANAGED CLUB FROM
DEC. 1941 THROUGH JULY 1948. HIT 511 HOME
RUNS, N.L. RECORD WHEN HE RETIRED. ALSO
LED IN MOST RUNS SCORED, MOST RUNS BATTED
IN, TOTAL BASES, BASES ON BALLS AND EXTRA
BASES ON LONG HITS. HAD A .304 LIFETIME
BATTING AVERAGE. PLAYED IN ELEVEN ALL STAR
GAMES AND IN THREE WORLD SERIES.

1951

LEROY ROBERT PAIGE
"SATCHEL"

NEGRO LEAGUES   1926-1947
CLEVELAND A.L.   1948-1949
ST. LOUIS A.L.   1951-1953
KANSAS CITY A.L.   1965

PAIGE WAS ONE OF THE GREATEST STARS
TO PLAY IN THE NEGRO BASEBALL LEAGUES.
THRILLED MILLIONS OF PEOPLE AND WON
HUNDREDS OF GAMES. STRUCK OUT 21 MAJOR
LEAGUERS IN AN EXHIBITION GAME. HELPED
PITCH CLEVELAND INDIANS TO THE 1948
PENNANT IN HIS FIRST BIG LEAGUE YEAR
AT AGE 42. HIS PITCHING WAS A LEGEND
AMONG MAJOR LEAGUE HITTERS.

1971

JAMES ALVIN PALMER
BALTIMORE, A.L. 1965-1984

HIGH-KICKING, SMOOTH-THROWING SYMBOL OF
BALTIMORE'S SIX CHAMPIONSHIP TEAMS OF 1960's,
70's AND 80's. IMPRESSIVE NUMBERS INCLUDE 268
WINS WITH .638 PCT., EIGHT 20-WIN SEASONS, 2.86
ERA AND NO GRAND SLAMS ALLOWED OVER
ENTIRE 19 YEAR CAREER. INTENSITY WAS TRADEMARK
OF 3-TIME CY YOUNG WINNER, WHO COMBINED
STRENGTH, INTELLIGENCE, COMPETITIVENESS AND
CONSISTENCY TO BECOME ORIOLES' ALL-TIME
WINNINGEST HURLER.

1990

HERBERT J.(HERB) PENNOCK

OUTSTANDING LEFT HANDED PITCHER IN
THE A.L. AND EXECUTIVE OF PHILADELPHIA
N.L. CLUB. AMONG RARE FEW WHO MADE
JUMP FROM PREP SCHOOL TO MAJORS. SAW
22 YEARS SERVICE WITH PHILADELPHIA,
BOSTON AND NEW YORK TEAMS IN A.L.
RECORDED 240 VICTORIES, 161 DEFEATS.
NEVER LOST A WORLD SERIES GAME,
WINNING FIVE. IN 1927, PITCHED 7 1/3
INNINGS WITHOUT ALLOWING HIT IN
THIRD GAME OF SERIES.

1948

ATANASIO PÉREZ RIGAL
"TONY"
CINCINNATI, N.L., 1964-1976, 1984-1986
MONTREAL, N.L., 1977-1979
BOSTON, A.L., 1980-1982
PHILADELPHIA, N.L., 1983
A CLUTCH PERFORMER THROUGHOUT AN ILLUSTRIOUS 23-YEAR
CAREER. HE TORMENTED THE OPPOSITION WITH HIS ABILITY TO
CONSISTENTLY DRIVE IN RUNS. HIS COMPOSURE UNDER PRESSURE LED
TO 379 HOME RUNS, 505 DOUBLES AND 1,652 RBI, INCLUDING SEVEN 100-
RBI SEASONS AND 954 RBI IN THE 1970s. A CATALYST OF CINCINNATI'S
TALENTED BIG RED MACHINE TEAMS DURING THE 1970s, HIS SUBTLE
LEADERSHIP AND TIMELY HITTING HELPED PACE THOSE CLUBS TO
FIVE DIVISION TITLES, FOUR PENNANTS AND TWO WORLD SERIES
CHAMPIONSHIPS.

2000

GAYLORD JACKSON PERRY
SAN FRANCISCO, N.L., 1962-1971
CLEVELAND, A.L. 1972-1975
TEXAS, A.L. 1975-1977, 1980
SAN DIEGO, N.L. 1978-1979
NEW YORK, A.L. 1980
ATLANTA, N.L. 1981
SEATTLE, A.L. 1982-1983
KANSAS CITY, A.L., 1983
ACHIEVED PITCHERS' MAGIC NUMBERS WITH 314 WINS
AND 3,534 STRIKEOUTS. PLAYING MIND GAMES WITH
HITTERS THROUGH ARRAY OF RITUALS ON MOUND WAS
PART OF HIS ARSENAL. 20-GAME WINNER 5 TIMES WITH
LIFETIME ERA OF 3.10. NO-HIT CARDS FOR GIANTS
9/17/68. OUTSTANDING COMPETITOR. ONLY CY YOUNG WINNER
IN BOTH LEAGUES.

1991

EDWARD S. PLANK
"GETTYSBURG EDDIE"
ONE OF GREATEST LEFTHANDED PITCHERS OF
MAJOR LEAGUES. NEVER PITCHED FOR A MINOR
LEAGUE TEAM, GOING FROM GETTYSBURG
COLLEGE TO THE PHILADELPHIA A.L. TEAM
WITH WHICH HE SERVED FROM 1901 THROUGH
1914. MEMBER OF ST. LOUIS F.L. IN 1915 AND
ST. LOUIS A.L. IN 1916-17. ONE OF FEW
PITCHERS TO WIN MORE THAN 300 GAMES
IN BIG LEAGUES. IN EIGHT OF 17 SEASONS
WON 20 OR MORE GAMES.

1946

ALEJANDRO POMPEZ
"ALEX"
PRE-NEGRO LEAGUES, 1916-1919
CUBAN STARS, 1920-1933
NEW YORK CUBANS, 1935-1936, 1938-1950
A FLAMBOYANT TEAM OWNER AND SHREWD TALENT EVALUATOR,
RENOWNED FOR INTRODUCING LATIN AMERICAN PLAYERS TO
THE NEGRO LEAGUES, AND EVENTUALLY, THE MAJOR LEAGUES.
HELPED CREATE AND ORGANIZE THE NEGRO LEAGUES WORLD
SERIES IN 1924. WON BY HIS NEW YORK CUBANS IN 1947. SERVED
AS VICE PRESIDENT OF NEGRO NATIONAL LEAGUE FROM 1946-
1948. CONCLUDED SEVEN-DECADE BASEBALL CAREER AS A SCOUT
FOR THE NEW YORK AND SAN FRANCISCO GIANTS.

1906

CUMBERLAND WILLIS POSEY, JR.
"CUM"
PRE-NEGRO LEAGUES, 1911-1919
HOMESTEAD GRAYS, 1920-1946
SUCCESSFUL ENTREPRENEUR OF PERENNIAL POWERHOUSE HOMESTEAD
GRAYS, WINNING NINE CONSECUTIVE NEGRO NATIONAL LEAGUE PENNANTS,
1937-1945, AND TWO NEGRO LEAGUES WORLD SERIES TITLES. BEGAN AS SEMI-
PROFESSIONAL OUTFIELDER IN 1911. BECAME BUSINESS MANAGER, THEN
MANAGER, AND FINALLY OWNER FROM 1920 TO 1946. GRAYS REIGNED AS
MOST FORMIDABLE INDEPENDENT TEAM OF 1920s, WINNING MORE THAN 80
PERCENT OF GAMES PLAYED. AN AGGRESSIVE TALENT SCOUT, SIGNED TOP
STARS, DRAWING LARGE CROWDS TO HOME GAMES AT FORBES FIELD IN
PITTSBURGH AND GRIFFITH STADIUM IN WASHINGTON, D.C.

1906

KIRBY PUCKETT
MINNESOTA, A.L., 1984-1995
A PROVEN TEAM LEADER WITH AN EVER-PRESENT SMILE AND
INFECTIOUS EXUBERANCE WHO LED THE TWINS TO WORLD SERIES
TITLES IN 1987 AND 1991. OVER 12 SEASONS HIT FOR POWER AND
AVERAGE, BATTING .318 WITH 414 DOUBLES AND 207 HOME RUNS. ALSO
A PROLIFIC RUN PRODUCER, SCORED 1,071 RUNS AND DROVE IN 1,085 IN
1,783 GAMES. A SIX-TIME GOLD GLOVE WINNER WHO PATROLLED
CENTER FIELD WITH ELEGANCE AND STYLE. ROUTINELY SCALING
OUTFIELD WALLS TO TAKE AWAY HOME RUNS. THE 10-TIME
ALL-STAR'S CAREER ENDED ABRUPTLY DUE TO IRREVERSIBLE RETINAL
DAMAGE IN HIS RIGHT EYE.

2001

CHARLIE RADBOURNE
"OLD HOSS"
PROVIDENCE, BOSTON AND CINCINNATI
NATIONAL LEAGUE 1881 TO 1891. GREATEST
OF ALL 19TH CENTURY PITCHERS. WINNING
1884 PENNANT FOR PROVIDENCE, RADBOURNE
PITCHED LAST 27 GAMES OF SEASON, WON
26. WON 3 STRAIGHT IN WORLD SERIES.

1939

HAROLD HENRY "PEE WEE" REESE
BROOKLYN N.L. 1940-1957
LOS ANGELES N.L. 1958
SHORTSTOP AND CAPTAIN OF GREAT DODGER TEAMS
OF 1940's AND 50's. INTANGIBLE QUALITIES OF SUBTLE
LEADERSHIP ON AND OFF FIELD, COMPETITIVE FIRE
AND PROFESSIONAL PRIDE COMPLEMENTED DEPENDABLE
GLOVE, RELIABLE BASE-RUNNING AND CLUTCH-HITTING
AS SIGNIFICANT FACTORS IN 7 DODGER PENNANTS.
INSTRUMENTAL IN EASING ACCEPTANCE OF JACKIE
ROBINSON AS BASEBALL'S FIRST BLACK PERFORMER.

1984

EDGAR CHARLES (SAM) RICE
WASHINGTON, A.L. 1915 TO 1933
CLEVELAND, A.L. 1934
AT BAT 600 OR MORE TIMES EIGHT
DIFFERENT SEASONS. HAD 200 OR MORE HITS
IN EACH OF SIX SEASONS. BATTED .322
FOR 20-YEAR CAREER AND HAD 2987 HITS.
SET A.L. RECORD WITH 182 SINGLES IN
1925. LED A.L. IN NUMBER OF HITS 216
IN 1924 AND 1926. LED A.L. IN PUTOUTS
FOR OUTFIELDERS WITH 454 IN 1920 AND
385 IN 1922.

1963

WESLEY BRANCH RICKEY

ST. LOUIS A.L. 1905·1906·1914
NEW YORK A.L. 1907
FOUNDER OF FARM SYSTEM WHICH HE
DEVELOPED FOR ST. LOUIS CARDINALS
AND BROOKLYN DODGERS. COPIED BY ALL
OTHER MAJOR LEAGUE TEAMS.
SERVED AS EXECUTIVE FOR BROWNS,
CARDINALS, DODGERS AND PIRATES.
BROUGHT JACKIE ROBINSON TO BROOKLYN
IN 1947.

1967

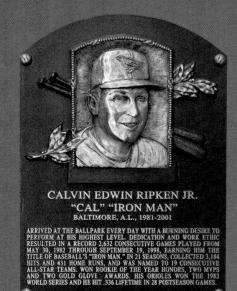

CALVIN EDWIN RIPKEN JR.
"CAL" "IRON MAN"
BALTIMORE, A.L., 1981-2001

ARRIVED AT THE BALLPARK EVERY DAY WITH A BURNING DESIRE TO
PERFORM AT HIS HIGHEST LEVEL. DEDICATION AND WORK ETHIC
RESULTED IN A RECORD 2,632 CONSECUTIVE GAMES PLAYED FROM
MAY 30, 1982 THROUGH SEPTEMBER 19, 1998, EARNING HIM THE
TITLE OF BASEBALL'S "IRON MAN." IN 21 SEASONS, COLLECTED 3,184
HITS AND 431 HOME RUNS, AND WAS NAMED TO 19 CONSECUTIVE
ALL-STAR TEAMS. WON ROOKIE OF THE YEAR HONORS, TWO MVPS
AND TWO GOLD GLOVE AWARDS. HIS ORIOLES WON THE 1983
WORLD SERIES AND HE HIT .336 LIFETIME IN 28 POSTSEASON GAMES.

2007

EPPA RIXEY

PHILADELPHIA, N.L. 1912 TO 1920
CINCINNATI, N.L. 1921 TO 1933
WON 266 LOST 251 PCT. .515 ERA 3.15
SET RECORD FOR MOST VICTORIES BY
LEFT-HANDED PITCHER. LED LEAGUE IN
VICTORIES WITH 25 IN 1922. GAVE ONLY
1082 BASE ON BALLS IN 4494 INNINGS.

1963

PHILIP FRANCIS RIZZUTO
"SCOOTER"

NEW YORK, A.L. 1941-1942, 1946-1956
OVERCAME DIMINUTIVE SIZE (5'6", 150 LBS) TO
ANCHOR SUPERB YANKEE TEAMS WHICH WON 10
PENNANTS AND 8 WORLD SERIES DURING HIS 13
MAJOR LEAGUE SEASONS. OUTSTANDING SHORTSTOP
ON FIVE CONSECUTIVE WORLD CHAMPIONSHIP
CLUBS. SKILLED BUNTER AND ENTHUSIASTIC BASE
RUNNER WITH SOLID .273 LIFETIME BATTING
AVERAGE. ALL-STAR FIVE TIMES AND A.L. MVP IN
1950 WHEN HE PEAKED AT .324 WITH 200 HITS
AND A .439 SLUGGING PCT.

1994

ROBIN EVAN ROBERTS

PHILADELPHIA N.L., BALTIMORE A.L.,
HOUSTON N.L., CHICAGO N.L.,
1948-1966
TIRELESS WORKER WHO NEVER MISSED A START
IN DECADE OF THE FIFTIES. WON 286 OVER 19
YEAR CAREER. WON 20 GAMES 6 YEARS IN A ROW
FOR PHILADELPHIA WHIZ KIDS. LED N.L. IN INNINGS
PITCHED, 1951-55 AND IN COMPLETE GAMES, 1952-56.
STARTED 5 ALL-STAR GAMES. MAJOR LEAGUE PLAYER
OF THE YEAR, 1952 AND 1955.

1976

BROOKS CALBERT ROBINSON, JR.

BALTIMORE A.L. 1955-1977
ESTABLISHED MODERN STANDARD OF EXCELLENCE
FOR THIRD BASEMEN, SETTING MAJOR LEAGUE
RECORDS AT HIS POSITION FOR SEASONS (23),
FIELDING PCT. (.971), GAMES (2,870), PUTOUTS
(2,697), ASSISTS (6,205), AND DOUBLE PLAYS (618).
HIT 268 CAREER HOME RUNS. NAMED TO 18
CONSECUTIVE ALL STAR TEAMS. MVP OF 1970
WORLD SERIES. AMERICAN LEAGUE MVP IN 1964.

1983

FRANK ROBINSON

CINCINNATI N.L., BALTIMORE A.L.,
LOS ANGELES N.L., CALIFORNIA N.L.,
CLEVELAND A.L., 1956-1976
FIRST TO BE CHOSEN MOST VALUABLE PLAYER
IN BOTH LEAGUES -- N.L. IN 1961 AND A.L.
IN 1966. SET RECORDS BY HITTING HOMERS
IN 32 DIFFERENT PARKS AND WITH PAIR OF
GRAND-SLAMMERS IN SUCCESSIVE INNINGS IN
1970. FOURTH IN HOMERS (586). FIFTH IN
EXTRA BASES ON LONG HITS (2,430), SIXTH
IN TOTAL BASES (5,373), ON RETIRING. LED
N.L. IN SLUGGING PCT. IN 1960-61-62 AND
A.L. IN BATTING, HOMERS, RUNS BATTED IN,
TOTAL BASES AND SLUGGING PCT. IN 1966.

1982

JACK ROOSEVELT ROBINSON

BROOKLYN N.L. 1947 TO 1956
LEADING N.L. BATTER IN 1949. HOLDS
FIELDING MARK FOR SECOND BASEMAN
PLAYING IN 150 OR MORE GAMES WITH .992.
LED N.L. IN STOLEN BASES IN 1947 AND
1949. MOST VALUABLE PLAYER IN 1949.
LIFETIME BATTING AVERAGE .311. JOINT
RECORD HOLDER FOR MOST DOUBLE PLAYS
BY SECOND BASEMAN, 137 IN 1951.
LED SECOND BASEMEN IN DOUBLE
PLAYS 1949-50-51-52.

1962

WILBERT ROBINSON
"UNCLE ROBBIE"

STAR CATCHER FOR THE FAMOUS
BALTIMORE ORIOLES ON PENNANT CLUBS
OF 1894, '95 AND '96. HE LATER WON FAME
AS MANAGER OF THE BROOKLYN DODGERS
FROM 1914 THROUGH 1931. SET A RECORD OF
7 HITS IN 7 TIMES AT BAT IN SINGLE GAME

1945

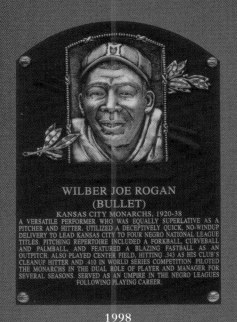

WILBER JOE ROGAN
(BULLET)
KANSAS CITY MONARCHS, 1920-38
A VERSATILE PERFORMER WHO WAS EQUALLY SUPERLATIVE AS A
PITCHER AND HITTER. UTILIZED A DECEPTIVELY QUICK, NO-WINDUP
DELIVERY TO LEAD KANSAS CITY TO FOUR NEGRO NATIONAL LEAGUE
TITLES. PITCHING REPERTOIRE INCLUDED A FORKBALL, CURVEBALL
AND PALMBALL, AND FEATURED A BLAZING FASTBALL AS AN
OUTPITCH. ALSO PLAYED CENTER FIELD, HITTING .343 AS HIS CLUB'S
CLEANUP HITTER AND .410 IN WORLD SERIES COMPETITION. PILOTED
THE MONARCHS IN THE DUAL ROLE OF PLAYER AND MANAGER FOR
SEVERAL SEASONS. SERVED AS AN UMPIRE IN THE NEGRO LEAGUES
FOLLOWING PLAYING CAREER.

1998

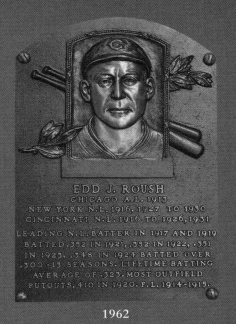

EDD J. ROUSH
CHICAGO A.L. 1913
NEW YORK N.L. 1916, 1927 TO 1930
CINCINNATI N.L. 1916 TO 1926, 1931

LEADING N.L. BATTER IN 1917 AND 1919
BATTED .352 IN 1921, .352 IN 1922, .351
IN 1923, .348 IN 1924 BATTED OVER
.300 -13 SEASONS. LIFETIME BATTING
AVERAGE OF .323. MOST OUTFIELD
PUTOUTS, 410 IN 1920. F.L. 1914-1915.

1962

CHARLES HERBERT RUFFING
"RED"
BOSTON, A.L. 1924-1930
NEW YORK, A.L. 1930-1946
CHICAGO, A.L., 1947
WINNER OF 273 GAMES.
WON 20 OR MORE GAMES IN EACH OF FOUR
CONSECUTIVE SEASONS. LED IN COMPLETE
GAMES 1928. TIED IN SHUTOUTS 1938-1939.
WON 7 OUT OF 9 WORLD SERIES DECISIONS.
SELECTED FOR ALL STAR TEAMS
1937 -1938 -1939

1967

AMOS WILSON RUSIE
"THE HOOSIER THUNDERBOLT"
INDIANAPOLIS N.L. NEW YORK N.L.
CINCINNATI N.L., 1889-1895
1897-1898 AND 1901
GENERALLY CONSIDERED FIREBALL KING OF
NINETEENTH-CENTURY MOUNDSMEN. NOTCHED
BETTER THAN 240 VICTORIES IN TEN-YEAR
CAREER. ACHIEVED 30-VICTORY MARK FOUR
YEARS IN ROW AND WON 20 OR MORE GAMES
EIGHT SUCCESSIVE TIMES. LED LEAGUE IN
STRIKEOUTS FIVE YEARS AND LED OR TIED
FOR MOST SHUTOUTS FIVE TIMES.

1977

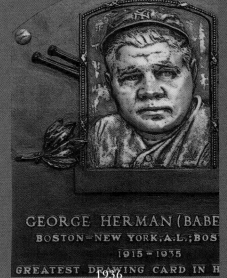

GEORGE HERMAN (BABE
BOSTON—NEW YORK, A.L.; BOS
1915 – 1935
GREATEST DRAWING CARD IN H

1936

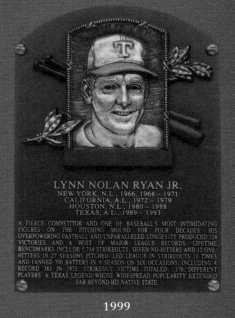

LYNN NOLAN RYAN JR.
NEW YORK, N.L., 1966, 1968 – 1971
CALIFORNIA, A.L., 1972 – 1979
HOUSTON, N.L., 1980 – 1988
TEXAS, A.L., 1989 – 1993
A FIERCE COMPETITOR AND ONE OF BASEBALL'S MOST INTIMIDATING
FIGURES ON THE PITCHING MOUND FOR FOUR DECADES. HIS
OVERPOWERING FASTBALL AND UNPARALLELED LONGEVITY PRODUCED 324
VICTORIES AND A HOST OF MAJOR LEAGUE RECORDS. LIFETIME
BENCHMARKS INCLUDE 5,714 STRIKEOUTS, SEVEN NO-HITTERS AND 12 ONE-
HITTERS IN 27 SEASONS. PITCHED. LED LEAGUE IN STRIKEOUTS 11 TIMES
AND FANNED 300 BATTERS IN A SEASON ON SIX OCCASIONS, INCLUDING A
RECORD 383 IN 1973. STRIKEOUT VICTIMS TOTALED 1,176 DIFFERENT
PLAYERS. A TEXAS LEGEND WHOSE WIDESPREAD POPULARITY EXTENDED
FAR BEYOND HIS NATIVE STATE.

1999

RYNE DEE SANDBERG
"RYNO"
PHILADELPHIA, N.L., 1981
CHICAGO, N.L., 1982-1994, 1996-1997
A SURE-HANDED SECOND BASEMAN WITH POWER AND SPEED WHO
DIGNIFIED THE GAME WITH HIS PROFESSIONALISM, QUIET LEADERSHIP
AND TIRELESS PREPARATION. SET CAREER RECORDS AMONG SECOND
BASEMEN FOR HOME RUNS (277 OF 282 OVERALL), FIELDING
PERCENTAGE (.989), CONSECUTIVE ERRORLESS GAMES IN A SEASON (90),
AND OVER TWO SEASONS (123). EARNED NINE GOLD GLOVES, LED
LEAGUE IN RUNS SCORED THREE TIMES. ELECTED TO 10 ALL-STAR
TEAMS, AND NAMED NATIONAL LEAGUE MVP IN 1984. HELPED THE CUBS
TO TWO DIVISION TITLES, HITTING .385 IN 10 POST-SEASON GAMES.

2005

LOUIS SANTOP
"TOP"
PRE-NEGRO LEAGUES, 1909-1919
NEGRO LEAGUES, 1920-1926
A DURABLE BACKSTOP WITH AN EXCEPTIONALLY STRONG
ARM, AND ONE OF BLACK BASEBALL'S MOST POWERFUL
BATTERS DURING THE FIRST QUARTER OF THE TWENTIETH
CENTURY. HIT FOR AVERAGE AND ALSO CELEBRATED FOR THE
DISTANCE HE COULD DRIVE A BASEBALL. A TOP DRAWING
CARD DURING HIS PRIME, CAUGHT FOR SOME OF THE BEST
TEAMS OF HIS ERA, INCLUDING THE NEW YORK LINCOLN
GIANTS, BROOKLYN ROYAL GIANTS, AND HILLDALE DAISIES.
FORMED FAMOUS BATTERY WITH SMOKEY JOE WILLIAMS.

2006

RAYMOND WILLIAM SCHALK
CHICAGO A.L. 1912 TO 1928
NEW YORK N.L. 1929
HOLDER OF MAJOR LEAGUE RECORD FOR
MOST YEARS LEADING CATCHER IN FIELDING
EIGHT YEARS; MOST PUTOUTS, NINE YEARS;
MOST ASSISTS IN ONE MAJOR LEAGUE (1810)
MOST CHANCES ACCEPTED (8965). CAUGHT
FOUR NO-HIT GAMES INCLUDING PERFECT
GAME IN 1922.

1955

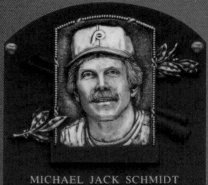

MICHAEL JACK SCHMIDT

PHILADELPHIA, N.L. 1972-1989

UNPRECEDENTED COMBINATION OF POWER AND DEFENSE WITH UNUSUAL MIXTURE OF STRENGTH, COORDINATION AND SPEED MADE HIM ONE OF THE GAME'S GREATEST THIRD BASEMEN. 7TH ON ALL-TIME LIST WITH 548 HOMERS. HIS 8 HOMERUN TITLES (1 TIE) BETTERED ONLY BY BABE RUTH. BELTED 40 OR MORE ON 3 OCCASIONS AND TOPPED 30 TEN OTHER TIMES. 48 HOMERUNS IN 1980 MOST EVER BY THIRD BASEMAN. HIT 4 IN ONE GAME IN 1976. 3-TIME MVP WITH 10 GOLD GLOVES FOR FIELDING EXCELLENCE.

1995

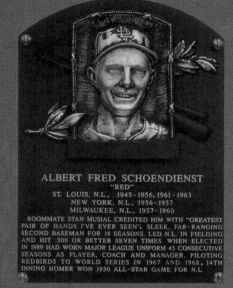

ALBERT FRED SCHOENDIENST
"RED"

ST. LOUIS, N.L., 1945-1956, 1961-1963
NEW YORK, N.L. 1956-1957
MILWAUKEE, N.L. 1957-1960

ROOMMATE STAN MUSIAL CREDITED HIM WITH "GREATEST PAIR OF HANDS I'VE EVER SEEN". SLEEK, FAR-RANGING SECOND BASEMAN FOR 18 SEASONS. LED N.L. IN FIELDING AND HIT .300 OR BETTER SEVEN TIMES. WHEN ELECTED IN 1989 HAD WORN MAJOR LEAGUE UNIFORM 45 CONSECUTIVE SEASONS AS PLAYER, COACH AND MANAGER. PILOTING REDBIRDS TO WORLD SERIES IN 1967 AND 1968. 14TH INNING HOMER WON 1950 ALL-STAR GAME FOR N.L.

1989

GEORGE THOMAS SEAVER

NEW YORK, N.L., 1967-1977, 1983
CINCINNATI, N.L., 1977-1982
CHICAGO, A.L., 1984-1986
BOSTON, A.L., 1986

FRANCHISE POWER PITCHER WHO TRANSFORMED METS FROM LOVABLE LOSERS INTO FORMIDABLE FOES. WON 311 GAMES OVER 20 SEASONS. SET N.L. CAREER RECORD FOR STRIKEOUTS BY RHP (3,272) AND MODERN RECORD FOR LOWEST ERA (2.73). WHIFFED 200 OR MORE N.L. RECORD 10 TIMES (19 IN A SINGLE GAME). N.L. ROOKIE OF YEAR, 1967 AND 3-TIME CY YOUNG AWARDEE. NO-HIT CARDS IN 1978.

1992

FRANK GIBSON SELEE

BOSTON, N.L., 1890-1901
CHICAGO, N.L., 1902-1905

A MASTER STRATEGIST AND AN IMPECCABLE JUDGE OF TALENT WHO BECAME ONE OF THE GAME'S MOST SUCCESSFUL FIELD MANAGERS. GUIDED THE NATIONAL LEAGUE'S BOSTON BEANEATERS AND CHICAGO CUBS, COMPILING 1284 VICTORIES OVER 16 SEASONS. HIS EXCEPTIONAL WINNING PERCENTAGE OF .598 IS FOURTH HIGHEST ALL-TIME. ASSEMBLED CHICAGO'S RENOWNED DOUBLE PLAY COMBINATION OF TINKER, EVERS AND CHANCE, AND LAID THE FOUNDATION FOR THE CUBS' THREE SUCCESSIVE PENNANTS FROM 1906 - 1908. A COURTEOUS AND MILD-MANNERED LEADER, HE CAPTURED FIVE PENNANTS AND MANAGED 12 FUTURE HALL OF FAMERS.

1999

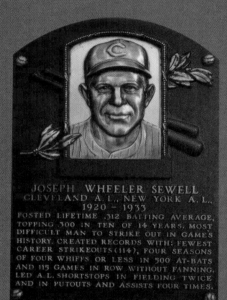

JOSEPH WHEELER SEWELL

CLEVELAND A.L., NEW YORK A.L.,
1920 - 1933

POSTED LIFETIME .312 BATTING AVERAGE, TOPPING .300 IN TEN OF 14 YEARS. MOST DIFFICULT MAN TO STRIKE OUT IN GAMES HISTORY. CREATED RECORDS WITH: FEWEST CAREER STRIKEOUTS (114), FOUR SEASONS OF FOUR WHIFFS OR LESS IN 500 AT-BATS AND 115 GAMES IN ROW WITHOUT FANNING. LED A.L. SHORTSTOPS IN FIELDING TWICE AND IN PUTOUTS AND ASSISTS FOUR TIMES.

1977

ALOYSIUS HARRY SIMMONS

PLAYED WITH 7 MAJOR LEAGUE CLUBS 1924-1944. STAR WITH PHILA. (A.L.). BATTED .308 TO .392 FROM 1924 TO 1934. LEADING BATTER .381 IN 1930, .390 IN 1931. MOST HITS BY A.L. RIGHT-HANDED BATTER WITH 2851. LED LEAGUE RUNS BATTED IN, RUNS SCORED, HITS AND TOTAL BASES SEVERAL SEASONS. HIT 3 HOME RUNS, JULY 15, 1932. LIFETIME BATTING AVERAGE .334.

1953

GEORGE HAROLD SISLER

ST. LOUIS-WASHINGTON A.L.
BOSTON, N.L.-1915-1930

HOLDS TWO AMERICAN LEAGUE RECORDS, MAKING 257 HITS IN 1920 AND BATTING .41979 IN 1922. RETIRED WITH MAJOR LEAGUE AVERAGE OF .341. CREDITED WITH BEING ONE OF BEST TWO FIELDING FIRST BASEMEN IN HISTORY OF GAME.

1939

ENOS BRADSHER SLAUGHTER
"COUNTRY"

ST. LOUIS N.L. 1938-1953
NEW YORK A.L. 1954-1955, 1956-1959
KANSAS CITY A.L. 1955-1956 MILWAUKEE N.L. 1959
HARD-NOSED, HUSTLING PERFORMER WHO PLAYED THE GAME WITH INTENSITY AND DETERMINATION. FLAT, LEVEL SWING MADE HIM A LIFETIME .300 HITTER WHO INVARIABLY CAME THROUGH IN CLUTCH SITUATIONS. EXCELLENT OUTFIELDER WITH STRONG ARM. DARING BASERUNNER FAMOUS FOR HIS MAD DASH HOME TO WIN 1946 WORLD SERIES FOR CARDINALS. BATTED .291 IN 5 WORLD SERIES.

1985

HILTON LEE SMITH

NEGRO LEAGUES, 1932-1948

A QUIET BUT CONFIDENT RIGHTHANDER WHOSE DEVASTATING FASTBALL COMPLEMENTED WHAT MANY REGARD AS THE BEST SWEEPING CURVEBALL IN NEGRO LEAGUES HISTORY. AFTER BEGINNING HIS CAREER WITH THE MONROE MONARCHS, WAS CREDITED WITH 20 OR MORE WINS IN EACH OF 12 SEASONS WITH THE KANSAS CITY MONARCHS, INCLUDING A DOMINATING RECORD OF 93-11 FROM 1939 TO 1942. THE SIX-TIME ALL-STAR PITCHED A NO-HITTER VERSUS THE POWERFUL CHICAGO AMERICAN GIANTS IN 1937 AND POSTED A NEAR-PERFECT 25-1 MARK IN 1941. PLAYED ON SEVEN PENNANT WINNERS AND ONE WORLD SERIES CHAMPIONSHIP TEAM.

2001

OSBORNE EARL SMITH
"Ozzie" "The Wizard"
SAN DIEGO, N.L., 1978-1981
ST. LOUIS, N.L., 1982-1996
REVOLUTIONIZED DEFENSIVE PLAY AT SHORTSTOP WITH HIS ACROBATIC
FIELDING AND ARTISTIC TURNING OF DOUBLE PLAYS. THE 13-TIME GOLD
GLOVE WINNER SET SIX MAJOR LEAGUE FIELDING RECORDS AMONG
SHORTSTOPS, INCLUDING MOST ASSISTS, DOUBLE PLAYS AND CHANCES
ACCEPTED. AN EFFECTIVE OFFENSIVE PLAYER, HE ACCUMULATED 2,460
HITS AND STOLE 580 BASES. NAMED TO 15 ALL-STAR TEAMS. HIS
RELENTLESS PURSUIT OF PERFECTION HELPED LEAD THE CARDINALS TO
THREE WORLD SERIES, INCLUDING A 1982 CHAMPIONSHIP. HIS
CONGENIAL PERSONALITY, CONSUMMATE PROFESSIONALISM AND
TRADEMARK BACK FLIP MADE "THE WIZARD" A FAN FAVORITE.

2002

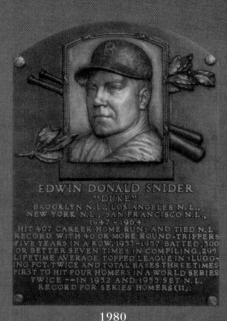

EDWIN DONALD SNIDER
"DUKE"
BROOKLYN N.L., LOS ANGELES N.L.,
NEW YORK N.L., SAN FRANCISCO N.L.,
1947-1964
HIT 407 CAREER HOME RUNS AND TIED N.L.
RECORD WITH 40 OR MORE ROUND-TRIPPERS
FIVE YEARS IN A ROW, 1953-1957. BATTED .300
OR BETTER SEVEN TIMES IN COMPILING .295
LIFETIME AVERAGE. TOPPED LEAGUE IN SLUGG-
ING PCT. TWICE AND TOTAL BASES THREE TIMES.
FIRST TO HIT FOUR HOMERS IN A WORLD SERIES
TWICE -- IN 1952 AND 1955. SET N.L.
RECORD FOR SERIES HOMERS (11).

1980

WILLIAM HAROLD SOUTHWORTH
"BILLY"
ST. LOUIS, N.L., 1929, 1940-1945
BOSTON, N.L., 1946-1951
A SHARP, SERIOUS AND SUCCESSFUL MANAGER WITH A RELENTLESS
DESIRE FOR VICTORY ADMIRED BY HIS PLAYERS, GUIDED HIS TEAMS
TO 90 OR MORE WINS SIX TIMES IN 13 SEASONS. WON THREE
STRAIGHT N.L. PENNANTS WITH 100-WIN CAMPAIGNS FROM 1942-
1944, INCLUDING WORLD TITLES IN 1942 AND 1944. REBUILT AND
SKIPPERED BOSTON BRAVES, GUIDING CLUB TO 1948 N.L. PENNANT.
HIS .597 WINNING PERCENTAGE RANKS FIFTH BEST ALL-TIME.
MANAGING TEAMS TO A 1,044-704 MARK. IN NINE FULL SEASONS, HIS
TEAMS NEVER POSTED A LOSING RECORD.

2008

WARREN EDWARD SPAHN
BOSTON N.L., MILWAUKEE N.L.,
NEW YORK N.L., SAN FRANCISCO N.L.,
1942-1965
BECAME FIFTH BIGGEST WINNER IN MAJORS'
HISTORY WITH 363 VICTORIES. MOST
VICTORIES FOR A LEFT-HANDER. WON 20
OR MORE GAMES 13 SEASONS, SIX IN A ROW.
SET ALL-TIME RECORDS FOR YEARS LEADING
LEAGUE IN VICTORIES (8) AND COMPLETE
GAMES (9). ALSO N.L. CAREER HIGHS WITH
665 GAMES STARTED; 5,264 INNINGS;
2,583 STRIKEOUTS. PITCHED NO-HITTER
IN 1960, ANOTHER IN 1961.

1973

ALBERT GOODWILL SPALDING
ORGANIZATIONAL GENIUS OF BASEBALL'S
PIONEER DAYS. STAR PITCHER OF FOREST
CITY CLUB IN LATE 1860'S, 4-YEAR
CHAMPION BOSTONS 1871-1875 AND
MANAGER-PITCHER OF CHAMPION
CHICAGOS IN NATIONAL LEAGUE'S FIRST
YEAR. CHICAGO PRESIDENT FOR 10
YEARS. ORGANIZER OF BASEBALL'S FIRST
ROUND-THE-WORLD TOUR IN 1888.

1939

TRISTRAM E. (TRIS) SPEAKER
BOSTON (A) 1909-15
CLEVELAND (A) 1916-26
WASHINGTON (A) 1927
PHILADELPHIA (A) 1928
GREATEST CENTREFIELDER OF HIS
DAY. LIFETIME MAJOR LEAGUE BATTING
AVERAGE OF .344. MANAGER IN 1920
WHEN CLEVELAND WON ITS FIRST
PENNANT AND WORLD CHAMPIONSHIP.

1937

WILVER DORNEL STARGELL
"WILLIE"
PITTSBURGH, N.L., 1962-1982
INTIMIDATING PRESENCE BETWEEN THE LINES
AND CHARISMATIC PATRIARCH IN CLUBHOUSE
AND DUGOUT. CRUSHED 475 HOMERS, MANY
OF TAPE-MEASURE VARIETY AND HIT MOST
BY ANY PLAYER DURING 1970'S. LIKE HIS
ROUND-TRIPPERS, HIS 1,540 RBI'S ALSO MOST
EVER BY A PIRATE. BATTED .282 OVER 21
SEASONS, ALL WITH PITTSBURGH. SHARED N.L.
MVP HONORS IN 1979, AND NAMED MVP IN '79
N.L. CHAMPIONSHIP SERIES AND WORLD SERIES.

1988

NORMAN THOMAS STEARNES
"TURKEY"
NEGRO LEAGUES 1923-1941
ONE OF THE NEGRO LEAGUES' MOST FEARED HITTERS, HE HIT BETTER
THAN .300 IN 14 OF 19 SEASONS, COLLECTED SIX HOME RUN TITLES AND
LED THE LEAGUE IN TRIPLES FOUR TIMES. A GRACEFUL CENTER
FIELDER AS WELL, HE PLAYED IN FOUR EAST-WEST ALL STAR GAMES.
PLAYED 11 SEASONS FOR THE DETROIT STARS, ALSO EXCELLING WITH
THE NEW YORK LINCOLN GIANTS, KANSAS CITY MONARCHS, CHICAGO
AMERICAN GIANTS AND PHILADELPHIA STARS.

2000

CHARLES DILLON STENGEL
"CASEY"
MANAGED NEW YORK YANKEES 1949-1960.
WON 10 PENNANTS AND 7 WORLD SERIES WITH
NEW YORK YANKEES. ONLY MANAGER TO WIN
5 CONSECUTIVE WORLD SERIES 1949-1953.
PLAYED OUTFIELD 1912-1925 WITH BROOKLYN,
PITTSBURGH, PHILADELPHIA, NEW YORK AND
BOSTON N.L. TEAMS. MANAGED BROOKLYN
1934-1936, BOSTON BRAVES 1938-1943,
NEW YORK METS 1962-1965.

1966

HOWARD BRUCE SUTTER
CHICAGO, N.L., 1976-1980
ST. LOUIS, N.L., 1981-1984
ATLANTA, N.L., 1985-1988

A DOMINANT CLOSER WHO REVOLUTIONIZED THE SPLIT-FINGERED FASTBALL, WHICH CONFOUNDED BATTERS. EARNED 300 SAVES AND POSTED A 2.83 ERA WHILE OFTEN PITCHING TWO OR MORE INNINGS. A SIX-TIME ALL-STAR SELECTION. RANKED AMONG THE TOP TEN IN NATIONAL LEAGUE MVP AND CY YOUNG VOTING FIVE TIMES EACH AND LEAD THE LEAGUE IN SAVES FIVE TIMES. WON 1979 N.L. CY YOUNG, POSTING 37 SAVES WHILE STRIKING OUT 110, ALLOWING 67 HITS IN 101.1 INNINGS. SAVED TWO GAMES AND RECORDED THE FINAL SIX OUTS FOR THE 1982 WORLD SERIES CHAMPION CARDINALS.

2006

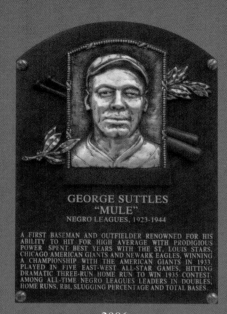

GEORGE SUTTLES
"MULE"
NEGRO LEAGUES, 1923-1944

A FIRST BASEMAN AND OUTFIELDER RENOWNED FOR HIS ABILITY TO HIT FOR HIGH AVERAGE WITH PRODIGIOUS POWER. SPENT BEST YEARS WITH THE ST. LOUIS STARS, CHICAGO AMERICAN GIANTS AND NEWARK EAGLES, WINNING A CHAMPIONSHIP WITH THE AMERICAN GIANTS IN 1933. PLAYED IN FIVE EAST-WEST ALL-STAR GAMES, HITTING DRAMATIC THREE-RUN HOME RUN TO WIN 1935 CONTEST. AMONG ALL-TIME NEGRO LEAGUES LEADERS IN DOUBLES, HOME RUNS, RBI, SLUGGING PERCENTAGE AND TOTAL BASES.

2006

DONALD HOWARD SUTTON
LOS ANGELES, N.L., 1966-80, 1988
HOUSTON, N.L., 1981-82
MILWAUKEE, A.L., 1982-84
OAKLAND, A.L., 1985
CALIFORNIA, A.L., 1985-1987

A STALWART ON THE MOUND FOR 23 MAJOR LEAGUE SEASONS, HIS IMPRESSIVE PITCHING RECORD INCLUDES 324 VICTORIES, 3,574 STRIKEOUTS AND A 3.26 ERA. STRIKEOUT TOTAL IS FIFTH BEST ALL-TIME, WHILE WIN TOTAL RANKS TIED FOR 12TH. DID NOT MISS A TURN IN THE STARTING ROTATION DUE TO INJURY OR ILLNESS. CONSISTENCY AND MODEL-CONTROL LED TO 15 OR MORE WINS IN 12 SEASONS AND 100 OR MORE STRIKEOUTS 21 TIMES. THE RIGHT-HANDER PITCHED IN FOUR WORLD SERIES AND WAS NAMED TO FOUR ALL-STAR TEAMS.

1998

BENJAMIN HARRISON TAYLOR
"BEN" "OLD RELIABLE"
PRE-NEGRO LEAGUES, 1908-1919
NEGRO LEAGUES, 1920-1929

A SOFT-SPOKEN AND MODEST TEAM LEADER WHO TRANSITIONED FROM SUCCESSFUL PITCHER TO TOP-FLIGHT DEFENSIVE FIRST BASEMAN AND CLUTCH HITTER. PRODUCTIVE LINE-DRIVE HITTER WHO BATTED OVER .300 WITH REGULARITY, EXCELLING FOR NINE SEASONS WITH INDIANAPOLIS ABCs. COMBINATION OF VAST KNOWLEDGE OF THE GAME, STRONG LEADERSHIP SKILLS AND TEACHING ABILITIES LED TO MANAGING POSITIONS WITH A NUMBER OF NEGRO LEAGUES TEAMS. THE YOUNGEST OF FOUR PROFESSIONAL BASEBALL-PLAYING BROTHERS.

2006

WILLIAM HAROLD TERRY
NEW YORK N.L. 1923 to 1941

BATTED .401 AND TIED N.L. RECORD FOR BASE HITS WITH 254 IN 1930. MADE 200 OR MORE HITS IN SIX SEASONS. RETIRED WITH LIFETIME BATTING AVERAGE OF .341. A MODERN N.L. RECORD FOR LEFT-HANDED BATTERS. MOST VALUABLE PLAYER IN 1930. SUCCEEDED JOHN McGRAW AS MANAGER IN 1932 AND WON PENNANTS IN 1933-36-37.

1954

SAMUEL LUTHER THOMPSON
DETROIT N.L., PHILADELPHIA N.L.
1885-1898; DETROIT A.L. 1906

ONE OF THE FOREMOST SLUGGERS OF HIS DAY. LIFETIME BATTING AVERAGE .336. BATTED BETTER THAN .400 TWICE. GREAT CLUTCH HITTER. COLLECTED 200 OR MORE HITS IN A SEASON THREE TIMES. TOPPED N.L. IN HOME RUNS AND RUNS BATTED IN TWICE.

1974

JOSEPH B. TINKER
FAMOUS AS A MEMBER OF ONE OF BASEBALL'S GREATEST DOUBLE PLAY COMBINATIONS—FROM TINKER TO EVERS TO CHANCE. A BIG LEAGUER FROM 1902 THROUGH 1916 WITH THE CHICAGO CUBS AND CINCINNATI REDS AND THE CHICAGO FEDS. MANAGER CINCINNATI 1913 AND CHICAGO N.L. 1916. SHORTSTOP ON CUBS' TEAM THAT WON PENNANTS IN 1906, '07 '08 AND 1910.

1946

CRISTÓBAL TORRIENTE
"CARLOS"
PRE-NEGRO LEAGUES, 1913-1919
NEGRO LEAGUES, 1920-1928, 1932

A COMPACT AND POWERFUL FIVE-TOOL PLAYER WITH TREMENDOUS EXTRA-BASE POWER TO ALL FIELDS. PLAYED 17 SEASONS OVERALL AND RANKS AMONG ALL-TIME NEGRO LEAGUES LEADERS IN DOUBLES, TRIPLES, SLUGGING PERCENTAGE, TOTAL BASES AND RBI. LED CHICAGO AMERICAN GIANTS TO THREE SUCCESSIVE NEGRO NATIONAL LEAGUE TITLES, 1920-1922. EXCEPTIONAL SPEED AND RANGE ALLOWED HIM TO COVER CENTER FIELD WITH GREAT EASE. PRIOR TO THE FORMATION OF THE NEGRO LEAGUES, STARRED IN HIS NATIVE CUBA. FAMED FOR OUTPLAYING BABE RUTH DURING A NINE-GAME BARNSTORMING SERIES IN 1920.

2006

HAROLD J. (PIE) TRAYNOR
RATED AMONG THE GREAT THIRD BASEMEN OF ALL TIME, BECAME A REGULAR WITH THE PITTSBURGH N.L. TEAM IN 1922 AND CONTINUED AS A PLAYER UNTIL CONCLUSION OF 1937 SEASON. MANAGED THE PIRATES FROM JUNE, 1934, THROUGH SEPT. 1939. HOLDS SEVERAL FIELDING RECORDS AND COMPILED A LIFETIME BATTING MARK OF .320. ONE OF FEW PLAYERS EVER TO MAKE 200 OR MORE HITS DURING A SEASON, COLLECTING 208 IN 1923.

1948

ARTHUR CHARLES (DAZZY) VANCE
BROOKLYN N.L. 1922 TO 1932, 1935
PITTSBURGH N.L. – NEW YORK A.L.
ST. LOUIS N.L. – CINCINNATI N.L.
FIRST PITCHER IN N.L. TO LEAD IN
STRIKEOUTS FOR 7 STRAIGHT YEARS, 1922 TO
1928. LED LEAGUE WITH 28 VICTORIES IN
1924; 22 IN 1925. WON 15 STRAIGHT IN 1924.
PITCHED NO-HIT GAME AGAINST PHILLIES
1925. MOST VALUABLE PLAYER N.L. 1924.

1955

JOSEPH FLOYD VAUGHAN
"ARKY"
PITTSBURGH N.L. 1932-1941
BROOKLYN N.L. 1942-1948
AMONG HALL OF FAME SHORTSTOPS, HIS .318
LIFETIME BATTING AVERAGE IS SECOND ONLY TO
HONUS WAGNER'S .329. LED LEAGUE WITH .385 IN
1935. HOMERED TWICE IN 1941 ALL-STAR GAME.
FANNED ONLY 276 TIMES IN 6622 CAREER AT-BATS.
POLISHED FIELDER AND ACCOMPLISHED BASE
RUNNER, LEADING N.L. WITH 20 STOLEN BASES IN
1943.

1985

BILL VEECK
OWNER OF INDIANS, BROWNS AND WHITE SOX,
CREATED HEIGHTENED FAN INTEREST AT EVERY STOP
WITH INGENIOUS PROMOTIONAL SCHEMES, FAN
PARTICIPATION, EXPLODING SCOREBOARD, OUTRAGEOUS
DOOR PRIZES, NAMES ON UNIFORMS. SET M.L.
ATTENDANCE RECORD WITH PENNANT-WINNER AT
CLEVELAND IN 1948; WON AGAIN WITH 'GO-GO'
SOX IN 1959. SIGNED A.L.'S FIRST BLACK PLAYER,
LARRY DOBY IN 1947 AND OLDEST ROOKIE, 42 YEAR
OLD SATCHEL PAIGE IN 1948.
A CHAMPION OF THE LITTLE GUY.

1991

GEORGE EDWARD WADDELL
"RUBE"
COLORFUL LEFTHANDED PITCHER WHO WAS
IN BOTH LEAGUES, BUT WHO GAINED FAME
AS A MEMBER OF THE PHILADELPHIA A.L.
TEAM. WON MORE THAN 20 GAMES IN FIRST
FOUR SEASONS WITH THAT CLUB AND
COMPILED MORE THAN 200 VICTORIES
DURING MAJOR LEAGUE CAREER. WAS
NOTED FOR HIS STRIKEOUT ACHIEVEMENTS

1946

HONUS WAGNER
LOUISVILLE, N.L., 1897-1899.
PITTSBURGH, N.L., 1900-1917.
THE GREATEST SHORTSTOP IN BASEBALL
HISTORY. BORN CARNEGIE, PA., FEB. 24, 1874
KNOWN TO FAME AS "HONUS," "HANS" AND
"THE FLYING DUTCHMAN." RETIRED IN 1917,
HAVING SCORED MORE RUNS, MADE MORE
HITS AND STOLEN MORE BASES THAN
ANY OTHER PLAYER IN THE HISTORY
OF HIS LEAGUE

1936

RODERICK J. WALLACE
CLEVELAND-ST. LOUIS-CINCINNATI N.L.
ST. LOUIS A.L. – 1894 TO 1918
ONE OF LONGEST CAREERS IN MAJOR
LEAGUES. OVER 60 YEARS AS PITCHER,
THIRD-BASEMAN, SHORTSTOP, MANAGER,
UMPIRE AND SCOUT. ACTIVE AS PLAYER
FOR 25 YEARS. SET A.L. RECORD FOR
CHANCES IN ONE GAME AT SHORTSTOP, 17,
JUNE 10, 1902. RECOGNIZED AS ONE OF
GREATEST SHORTSTOPS. PITCHED FOR
CLEVELAND IN 1896 TEMPLE CUP SERIES.

1953

EDWARD ARTHUR WALSH
"BIG ED"
OUTSTANDING RIGHTHANDED PITCHER OF
CHICAGO A.L. FROM 1904 THROUGH 1916.
WON 40 GAMES IN 1908 AND WON TWO
GAMES IN THE 1906 WORLD SERIES. TWICE
PITCHED AND WON TWO GAMES IN ONE
DAY, ALLOWING ONLY ONE RUN IN
DOUBLEHEADER AGAINST BOSTON ON
SEPT. 29, 1908. FINISHED BIG LEAGUE PITCHING
CAREER WITH BOSTON N.L. IN 1917.

1946

LLOYD JAMES WANER
"LITTLE POISON"
PITTSBURGH N.L., BOSTON N.L.,
CINCINNATI N.L., PHILADELPHIA N.L.,
BROOKLYN N.L. 1927-1945
MADE 223 HITS IN 1927 FIRST YEAR
WITH PITTSBURGH INCLUDING 198 SINGLES,
A MODERN MAJOR LEAGUE RECORD.
LED N.L. IN MOST SINGLES 1927-1928-1929-1931.
LIFE TOTAL 2459 HITS. BATTING AVERAGE .316.
WITH BROTHER PAUL, "BIG POISON"
STARRED IN PITTSBURGH OUTFIELD
1927-1940

1967

PAUL GLEE WANER
(BIG POISON)
PITTSBURGH-BROOKLYN-BOSTON, N.L.
NEW YORK, A.L.
1926-1945
LEFT HANDED HITTING OUTFIELDER BATTED
.300 OR BETTER 14 TIMES IN NATIONAL
LEAGUE. ONE OF SEVEN PLAYERS EVER TO
COMPILE 3,000 OR MORE HITS. SET MODERN
N.L. RECORD BY COLLECTING 200 OR MORE
HITS EIGHT SEASONS. MOST VALUABLE PLAYER
IN 1927 AND FOUR TIMES SELECTED FOR
ALL STAR GAME.

1952

JOHN MONTGOMERY WARD
1878 - 1894
PITCHING PIONEER WHO WON 158,
LOST 102 GAMES IN SEVEN YEARS.
PITCHED PERFECT GAME FOR PROVIDENCE
OF N.L. IN 1880.
TURNED TO SHORTSTOP AND MADE 2,151 HITS.
MANAGED NEW YORK AND BROOKLYN IN N.L.
PRESIDENT OF BOSTON, N.L. 1911-1912.
PLAYED IMPORTANT PART IN ESTABLISHING
MODERN ORGANIZED BASEBALL.

1964

EARL SIDNEY WEAVER
BALTIMORE, A.L. 1968-1982, 1985-1986
MANAGED ORIOLES WITH INTENSITY, FLAIR AND
ACERBIC WIT FOR 17 SEASONS. .583 WINNING
PERCENTAGE (1480-1060) RANKS FIFTH ALL-TIME
AMONG 20TH CENTURY MANAGERS WITH 10 OR MORE
YEARS SERVICE. 94.3 WINS PER SEASON RANKS FIRST.
FIVE 100-WIN SEASONS SECOND ON ALL-TIME LIST.
WON SIX A.L. EAST TITLES, FOUR PENNANTS AND 1970
WORLD SERIES

1996

GEORGE MARTIN WEISS
MASTER BUILDER OF CHAMPIONSHIP TEAMS.
WAS CLUB EXECUTIVE IN MINORS AND
MAJORS FROM 1919 TO 1966.
DEVELOPED BEST MINOR LEAGUE CHAIN
IN GAME AS NEW YORK YANKEE FARM
MANAGER, 1932-1947. GENERAL MANAGER
OF THE YANKEES FROM 1947-1960 WHICH
WON 10 PENNANTS AND 7 WORLD SERIES
DURING THIS PERIOD.
PRESIDENT OF THE NEW YORK METS
1961-1966.

1971

MICHAEL FRANCIS WELCH
"SMILING MICKEY"
TROY N.L. 1880-1882
NEW YORK N.L. 1883-1892
CREDITED WITH MORE THAN 300 VICTORIES
DURING 13 SEASONS IN MAJORS. WON 17
GAMES IN A ROW IN 1885 WHILE COMPILING
44-11 RECORD FOR LEAGUE-LEADING .800
WINNING PERCENTAGE. TOPPED 30-VICTORY
TOTAL IN FOUR YEARS.

1973

WILLIE JAMES WELLS
NEGRO LEAGUES 1924-1948
COMBINED SUPERIOR BATTING SKILLS, SLICK FIELDING
AND SPEED ON THE BASES TO BECOME AN EIGHT-TIME
ALL STAR IN THE NEGRO LEAGUES. A POWER-HITTING
SHORTSTOP WITH GREAT HANDS, RANKS AMONG THE
ALL-TIME NEGRO LEAGUE LEADERS IN DOUBLES, TRIPLES,
HOME RUNS AND STOLEN BASES. PLAYED ON THREE
PENNANT-WINNING TEAMS WITH THE ST. LOUIS STARS,
ONE WITH THE CHICAGO AMERICAN GIANTS AND ONE
WITH THE NEWARK EAGLES. OVERALL HE PLAYED FOR
MANY NEGRO LEAGUE CLUBS WITH STINTS IN THE CANADIAN,
MEXICAN AND CUBAN LEAGUES. PLAYER-MANAGER
IN THE NEGRO LEAGUES AS WELL.

1997

ZACHARIAH (ZACK) DAVIS WHEAT
BROOKLYN N.L. 1909-1926
PHILADELPHIA A.L. 1927
BROOKLYN OUTFIELDER FOR 18 YEARS.
HOLDS BROOKLYN RECORDS FOR-GAMES
PLAYED 2,318, AT BAT 8,859, HITS 2,804,
SINGLES 2,038, DOUBLES 464, TRIPLES 171,
TOTAL BASES 4,003, EXTRA BASE HITS 766.
BATTED .375 (1923) .375 (1924) .359 (1925)
LEAGUE BATTING LEADER .335 (1918)
LIFETIME BATTING AVERAGE .317 WITH
2,884 HITS. PLAYED 2,406 GAMES.

1959

KING SOLOMON WHITE
"SOL"
PRE-NEGRO LEAGUES, 1887-1912
NEGRO LEAGUES, 1920-1926
AN OUTSTANDING PLAYER AND MANAGER WHO STARRED FOR FIVE
SEASONS AS AN INFIELDER IN INTEGRATED MINOR LEAGUES, BEFORE
EXCELLING WITH SEVERAL PROMINENT INDEPENDENT TEAMS. HELPED
CREATE DOMINANT PHILADELPHIA GIANTS IN 1902, PLAYING FOR AND
MANAGING THEM THROUGH 1909. BEFORE WORKING WITH PRE-NEGRO
LEAGUES TEAMS IN BROOKLYN AND NEW YORK, AND NEGRO LEAGUES
TEAMS IN COLUMBUS, CLEVELAND AND NEWARK. AUTHORED "SOL
WHITE'S OFFICIAL BASE BALL GUIDE" OF EARLY BLACK BASEBALL
TEAMS, PLAYERS, AND PLAYING CONDITIONS.

2006

JAMES HOYT WILHELM
NEW YORK N.L. 1952-1956   ST. LOUIS N.L. 1957
CLEVELAND A.L. 1957-1958 BALTIMORE A.L. 1958-1962
CHICAGO A.L. 1963-1968   CALIFORNIA A.L. 1969
ATLANTA N.L. 1969-1970, 1971 CHICAGO N.L. 1970
LOS ANGELES N.L. 1971-1972
BASEBALL'S PREMIER RELIEF PITCHER. USED KNUCKLE
BALL TO WIN 143 GAMES (A RECORD 124 IN RELIEF)
AND AMASSED 227 SAVES OVER 21-YEAR CAREER.
NO-HIT YANKEES ON SEPT. 20, 1958 IN INFREQUENT
START FOR ORIOLES. PITCHED IN RECORD 1070
GAMES WITH LIFETIME ERA OF 2.52.

1985

J. LESLIE WILKINSON
"J. L." "WILKIE"
KANSAS CITY MONARCHS, 1920-1948
AN INNOVATIVE AND GENEROUS OWNER WHO FOUNDED AND OPERATED THE KANSAS
CITY MONARCHS FROM 1920-1948. RESPECTED FOR HONESTY AND FAIRNESS WITH HIS
PLAYERS, PLUS TWO NEGRO LEAGUES WORLD SERIES CHAMPIONSHIPS. CREATED MULTI-
RACIAL ALL-NATIONS BARNSTORMING TEAM THAT FLOURISHED FROM 1912-1918,
THEN HELPED FOUND NEGRO NATIONAL LEAGUE IN 1920. DEVISED PORTABLE
LIGHTING SYSTEM WHICH ALLOWED TEAMS TO PLAY NIGHT GAMES AND HELP
SURVIVE THE GREAT DEPRESSION. SENT MORE PLAYERS, INCLUDING JACKIE
ROBINSON, TO MAJOR LEAGUES THAN ANY OTHER NEGRO LEAGUES OWNER.

2006

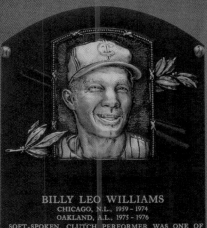

BILLY LEO WILLIAMS
CHICAGO, N.L., 1959 – 1974
OAKLAND, A.L., 1975 – 1976
SOFT-SPOKEN, CLUTCH PERFORMER WAS ONE OF
MOST RESPECTED HITTERS OF HIS DAY. BATTED SOLID
.290 OVER 18 SEASONS SOCKING 426 HOME RUNS. HIT 20
OR MORE HOMERS 13 STRAIGHT SEASONS. 1961 N.L.
ROOKIE OF YEAR. 1972 N.L. BATTING CHAMPION WITH
.333. HELD N.L. RECORD FOR CONSECUTIVE GAMES
PLAYED WITH 1117.

1987

JOSEPH WILLIAMS
"SMOKEY" "CYCLONE"
NEGRO LEAGUES, 1910 – 1932
A STAR PITCHER IN THE EARLY DAYS OF THE NEGRO LEAGUES.
THE LANKY RIGHT-HANDER WITH THE SMOOTH, OVERHAND
DELIVERY, WAS DESTINED FOR GREATNESS WITH HIS PINPOINT
CONTROL, EFFECTIVE CHANGE OF PACE PITCH AND FASTBALL THAT
TRAVELED WITH EXCEPTIONAL VELOCITY. PLAYING FOR SEVERAL
TEAMS, THE NEW YORK LINCOLN GIANTS (1911-23) AND THE
HOMESTEAD GRAYS (1925-32) WERE THE PRIMARY BENEFICIARIES OF
HIS ACCOMPLISHMENTS. THE EASY-GOING TEXAN ROUTINELY
REACHED DOUBLE-DIGITS IN STRIKEOUTS IN A GAME AND ON
AUGUST 7, 1930, HE STRUCK OUT 27 MONARCHS IN A 12-INNING
CONTEST. VOTED THE TOP PITCHER IN NEGRO LEAGUES HISTORY IN A
1952 POLL CONDUCTED BY THE PITTSBURGH COURIER.

1999

RICHARD HIRSCHFELD WILLIAMS
"DICK"
BOSTON, A.L., 1967-1969, OAKLAND, A.L., 1971-1973
CALIFORNIA, A.L., 1974-1976, MONTREAL, N.L., 1977-1981
SAN DIEGO, N.L., 1982-1985, SEATTLE, A.L., 1986-1988
AN INTENSE COMPETITOR AND FIERY LEADER NOTED FOR TURNING
UNDERPERFORMING TEAMS INTO WINNERS. LED HIS CLUBS TO 90 OR MORE
WINS SEVEN TIMES. CAPTURED CONSECUTIVE WORLD SERIES
CHAMPIONSHIPS WITH OAKLAND IN 1972-1973. SECOND MANAGER IN
HISTORY TO LEAD THREE DIFFERENT CLUBS TO THE WORLD SERIES,
WINNING FOUR PENNANTS OVERALL. GAINED EARLY FAME FOR
TRANSFORMING NINTH-PLACE RED SOX INTO 'IMPOSSIBLE DREAM' 1967
AMERICAN LEAGUE CHAMPIONS. PILOTED PADRES TO FIRST WORLD SERIES
IN 1984. CAREER 1,571-1,451 RECORD IN 21 MANAGERIAL SEASONS.

2008

THEODORE SAMUEL WILLIAMS
"TED"
BOSTON RED SOX A.L. 1939 – 1960
BATTED .406 IN 1941. LED A.L. IN BATTING
6 TIMES; SLUGGING PERCENTAGE 9 TIMES;
TOTAL BASES 6 TIMES; RUNS SCORED 6 TIMES;
BASES ON BALLS 8 TIMES. TOTAL HITS 2654
INCLUDED 521 HOME RUNS. LIFETIME BATTING
AVERAGE .344; LIFETIME SLUGGING AVERAGE
.634. MOST VALUABLE A.L. PLAYER 1946 & 1949.
PLAYED IN 18 ALL STAR GAMES. NAMED PLAYER
OF THE DECADE 1951 - 1960.

1966

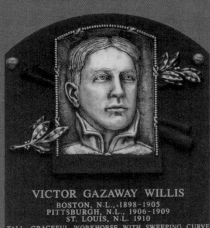

VICTOR GAZAWAY WILLIS
BOSTON, N.L., 1898-1905
PITTSBURGH, N.L., 1906-1909
ST. LOUIS, N.L. 1910
TALL, GRACEFUL WORKHORSE WITH SWEEPING CURVE
THAT MADE HIM A STRIKEOUT ARTIST WHILE
COMPILING 249 - 205 RECORD. POSTED 50
SHUTOUTS AND 2.63 ERA AND COMPLETED 388 OF 471
STARTS. 45 COMPLETE GAMES IN 1902 ARE MOST IN
N.L. IN 20TH CENTURY. MAINSTAY OF BOSTON
BEANEATERS' STAFF BEFORE TRADE TO PITTSBURGH,
WHERE HE AVERAGED 22 WINS A SEASON.

1995

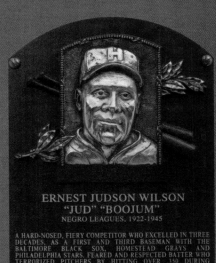

ERNEST JUDSON WILSON
"JUD" "BOOJUM"
NEGRO LEAGUES, 1922-1945
A HARD-NOSED, FIERY COMPETITOR WHO EXCELLED IN THREE
DECADES, AS A FIRST AND THIRD BASEMAN WITH THE
BALTIMORE BLACK SOX, HOMESTEAD GRAYS AND
PHILADELPHIA STARS. FEARED AND RESPECTED BATTER WHO
TERRORIZED PITCHERS BY HITTING OVER .350 DURING
CAREER, INCLUDING SEVERAL SEASONS OVER .400. CAPTAINED
RENOWNED 1931 HOMESTEAD GRAYS AND PLAYED ON FOUR
CHAMPIONSHIP TEAMS. NAMED TO THREE EAST-WEST ALL-
STAR TEAMS AND STARRED IN THE CUBAN WINTER LEAGUE.

2006

LEWIS ROBERT WILSON
"HACK"
NEW YORK N.L., CHICAGO N.L.,
BROOKLYN N.L., PHILADELPHIA N.L.,
1923 – 1934
ESTABLISHED MAJOR LEAGUE RECORD OF 190
RUNS BATTED IN AND NATIONAL LEAGUE HIGH
OF 56 HOMERS IN 1930. LED OR TIED FOR N.L.
HOMER TITLE FOUR TIMES. COMPILED LIFETIME
.307 BATTING AVERAGE AND DROVE IN 100 OR
MORE RUNS SIX YEARS. HIT TWO HOMERS IN
INNING IN 1925 AND THREE IN GAME IN 1930.

1979

DAVID MARK WINFIELD
SAN DIEGO, N.L., 1973-1980, NEW YORK, A.L., 1981-1990
CALIFORNIA, A.L., 1990-1991, TORONTO, A.L., 1992
MINNESOTA, A.L., 1993-1994, CLEVELAND, A.L., 1995
A COMPLETE PLAYER WHO INTIMIDATED THE OPPOSITION WITH HIS
IMMENSE STATURE, POWER, AGGRESSIVE BASERUNNING AND DOMINANT
DEFENSE. ADVANCED DIRECTLY FROM COLLEGE TO THE MAJOR LEAGUES. THE
12-TIME ALL-STAR COMPILED 3,110 HITS, 465 HOME RUNS, 1,833 RBI AND A
.283 CAREER AVERAGE. THE MULTITALENTED OUTFIELDER, RENOWNED FOR
LONG STRIDES AND A ROCKET ARM, EARNED SEVEN GOLD GLOVE AWARDS.
AMONG ALL-TIME LEADERS IN HITS, RBI, GAMES, DOUBLES, EXTRA BASE HITS,
TOTAL BASES AND PUTOUTS. HIS 11TH INNING, TWO-OUT DOUBLE IN GAME SIX
CLINCHED TORONTO'S 1992 WORLD SERIES TITLE.

2001

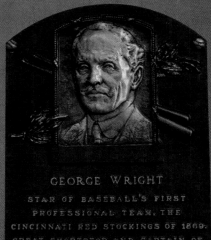

GEORGE WRIGHT
STAR OF BASEBALL'S FIRST
PROFESSIONAL TEAM, THE
CINCINNATI RED STOCKINGS OF 1869.
GREAT SHORTSTOP AND CAPTAIN OF
CHAMPION BOSTONS IN NATIONAL
LEAGUE'S PIONEER YEARS.

1937

HARRY WRIGHT

MANAGER AND CENTERFIELDER OF FAMOUS CINCINNATI RED STOCKINGS, UNDEFEATED IN 69 GAMES IN 1869-1870. FIRST MANAGER TO WIN FOUR STRAIGHT PENNANTS WITH BOSTON NATIONAL ASSOCIATION 1872-73-74 75. BROTHER OF GEORGE WRIGHT ALSO IN HALL OF FAME. SPONSORED FIRST BASEBALL TOUR TO ENGLAND IN 1876. INTRODUCED KNICKER UNIFORMS. HIT 7 HOME RUNS IN GAME AT NEWPORT, KY. IN 1867.

1953

EARLY WYNN
"GUS"
WASHINGTON A.L., CLEVELAND A.L., CHICAGO A.L. 1939-1963
WINNER OF 300 MAJOR LEAGUE GAMES. SET RECORD BY PITCHING 23 YEARS IN MAJORS. GAINED 20 OR MORE VICTORIES FIVE TIMES AND LED A.L. IN EARNED-RUN AVERAGE IN 1950. LEADER IN INNINGS PITCHED THREE SEASONS AND IN STRIKEOUTS TWICE. TIED FOR MOST VICTORIES WITH 23 IN 1954 AND LED LEAGUE WITH 22 WINS AT AGE 39 IN 1959 TO EARN CY YOUNG AWARD.

1972

CARL MICHAEL YASTRZEMSKI
"YAZ"
BOSTON, A.L., 1961-1983
SUCCEEDED TED WILLIAMS IN FENWAY'S LEFT FIELD IN 1961 AND RETIRED 23 YEARS LATER AS ALL-TIME RED SOX LEADER IN 8 CATEGORIES. PLAYED WITH GRACEFUL INTENSITY IN RECORD 3,308 A.L. GAMES. ONLY A.L. PLAYER WITH 3,000 HITS AND 400 HOMERS. 3-TIME BATTING CHAMPION. WON MVP AND TRIPLE CROWN IN 1967 AS HE LED RED SOX TO "IMPOSSIBLE DREAM" PENNANT.

1989

THOMAS AUSTIN YAWKEY

GAVE BASEBALL MORE THAN FOUR DECADES OF DEDICATED SERVICE AS OWNER-PRESIDENT OF BOSTON RED SOX FROM 1933 TO 1976. RATED ONE OF SPORT'S FINEST BENEFACTORS. SET PRECEDENT FOR A.L. IN 1936 AS FIRST TO HAVE TEAM TRAVEL BY PLANE. HIS CLUB WON PENNANTS IN 1946, 1967 AND 1975 -- AND NARROWLY MISSED IN 1948, 1949 AND 1972. VICE-PRESIDENT OF A.L. FROM 1956 TO 1973.

1980

DENTON T. (CY) YOUNG
CLEVELAND (N) 1890-98
ST. LOUIS (N) 1899-1900
BOSTON (A) 1901-08
CLEVELAND (A) 1909-11
BOSTON (N) 1911
ONLY PITCHER IN FIRST HUNDRED YEARS OF BASEBALL TO WIN 500 GAMES. AMONG HIS 511 VICTORIES WERE 3 NO-HIT SHUTOUTS. PITCHED PERFECT GAME MAY 5, 1904, NO OPPOSING BATSMAN REACHING FIRST BASE.

1937

ROSS MIDDLEBROOK YOUNGS
"PEP"
NEW YORK N.L. 1917-1926
STAR RIGHT FIELDER OF CHAMPION GIANTS OF 1921-22-23-24 WHEN HE BATTED .327,.331, .336, AND .356. COMPILED LIFETIME AVERAGE OF .322, TOPPING .300 IN NINE OF TEN YEARS. TWICE MADE 200 OR MORE HITS IN A SEASON. LED LEAGUE IN DOUBLES IN 1919 AND RUNS SCORED IN 1923. LED N.L. OUTFIELDERS IN ASSISTS TWICE AND TIED ONCE.

1972

ROBIN R. YOUNT
MILWAUKEE, A.L., 1974-1993
A PROLIFIC HITTER WITH A STOIC DEMEANOR WHO WAS EQUALLY GRACEFUL AT SHORTSTOP AND IN CENTER FIELD. ONE OF THREE PLAYERS TO EARN MVP HONORS AT TWO POSITIONS. PRODUCED 3,142 HITS, 7TH MOST IN AMERICAN LEAGUE HISTORY. HIT .300 SIX TIMES, 40 DOUBLES FOUR TIMES, 20 HR FOUR TIMES AND SCORED 100 RUNS FIVE TIMES. EXCEPTIONAL CONDITIONING AND EXTRAORDINARY WORK ETHIC MADE HIM A BASTION OF CONSISTENCY AND DURABILITY FOR 20 SEASONS AN EVERY DAY MAJOR LEAGUER AT AGE 18.

1999

PHOTO CREDITS AND PERMISSIONS

All photos by Bruce Curtis unless otherwise noted.

Copyrighted

©**AP Images:** pp 65, 184, 187.

©**Bettmann/Corbis**: pp 75, 128 bottom, 154-155.

©**David Leeds/Allsport/Getty Images:** p 137.

©**Herb Scharfman/Time & Life Pictures/Getty Images:** p 119.

©**James Drake/Sports Illustrated/Getty Images:** p 129.

©**Jerry Cooke/Sports Illustrated/Getty Images:** p 100.

©**Joshua McDonnell:** pp 7, 68, 79, 140, 156, 178, 182, 190, 208, 212, 224 upper-right and lower left, 225 upper-right, 226-227, 272.

©**Mark Rucker/Transcendental Graphics/Getty Images:** p 83.

©**National Baseball Hall of Fame Library:** pp 14, 16, 17, 22, 34, 52, 57, 71, 74, 77, 80, 88, 93, 110, 112, 115, 116, 120, 123, 124, 127, 135, 138, 153, 164, 198-199, 200, 203, 206.

©**NBHOF/Milo Stewart:** pp 8, 10, 11, 133, 139.

©**Photo File/MLB Photos via Getty Images:** pp 108, 113

©**Sporting News/Reprinted with Permission:** p 87.

**Courtesy of the National Baseball Hall of Fame Library,
Cooperstown, New York**

pp 4, 25, 26, 30, 38, 41, 44, 47, 48, 50, 55, 58, 61, 62, 64, 66, 67, 69, 70, 83, 92, 96, 102, 107, 142, 144, 147, 150, 152, 154, 170, 188.

INDEX

1936: The First Class

CHRISTY MATHEWSON
NEW YORK, N.L., 1900-1916.
CINCINNATI, N.L., 1916.
BORN FACTORYVILLE, PA., AUGUST 12, 1880.
GREATEST OF ALL THE GREAT PITCHERS
IN THE 20TH CENTURY'S FIRST QUARTER.
PITCHED 3 SHUTOUTS IN 1905 WORLD SERIES.
FIRST PITCHER OF THE CENTURY EVER TO
WIN 30 GAMES IN 3 SUCCESSIVE YEARS.
WON 37 GAMES IN 1908
"MATTY WAS MASTER OF THEM ALL"

TYRUS RAYMOND COBB
DETROIT-PHILADELPHIA, A.L. - 1905-1928
LED AMERICAN LEAGUE IN BATTING
TWELVE TIMES AND CREATED OR
EQUALLED MORE MAJOR LEAGUE
RECORDS THAN ANY OTHER PLAYER.
RETIRED WITH 4191 MAJOR LEAGUE HITS.

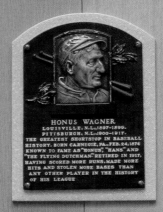

HONUS WAGNER
LOUISVILLE, N.L., 1897-1899.
PITTSBURGH, N.L., 1900-1917.
THE GREATEST SHORTSTOP IN BASEBALL
HISTORY. BORN CARNEGIE, PA., FEB. 24, 1874
KNOWN TO FAME AS "HONUS", "HANS" AND
"THE FLYING DUTCHMAN" RETIRED IN 1917,
HAVING SCORED MORE RUNS, MADE MORE
HITS AND STOLEN MORE BASES THAN
ANY OTHER PLAYER IN THE HISTORY
OF HIS LEAGUE

GEORGE HERMAN (BABE) RUTH
BOSTON-NEW YORK, A.L.; BOSTON, N.L.
1914-1935
GREATEST DRAWING CARD IN HISTORY OF
BASEBALL. HOLDER OF MANY HOME RUN
AND OTHER BATTING RECORDS. GATHERED
714 HOME RUNS IN ADDITION TO FIFTEEN
IN WORLD SERIES.

WALTER PERRY JOHNSON
WASHINGTON-1907-1927
CONCEDED TO BE FASTEST BALL PITCHER
IN HISTORY OF GAME. WON 414 GAMES
WITH LOSING TEAM BEHIND HIM MANY YEARS.
HOLDER OF STRIKE OUT AND SHUT OUT RECORDS